PRESCHOOL SCREENING

PRESCHOOL SCREENING

The Measurement and Prediction
of Children At-Risk

By

KEITH E. BARNES, Ph.D.

Psychologist/Director
Kelowna Mental Health Centre
Kelowna, British Columbia
Canada

CHARLES C THOMAS • PUBLISHER
Springfield • Illinois • U.S.A.

Published and Distributed Throughout the World by

CHARLES C THOMAS · PUBLISHER
2600 South First Street
Springfield, Illinois 62717 U.S.A.

© 1982 *by* CHARLES C THOMAS · PUBLISHER

ISBN 0-398-04668-9

Library of Congress Catalog Card Number: 81-21344

With THOMAS BOOKS careful attention is given to all details of manufacturing and design. It is the Publisher's desire to present books that are satisfactory as to their physical qualities and artistic possibilities and appropriate for their particular use. THOMAS BOOKS will be true to those laws of quality that assure a good name and good will.

Printed in the United States of America

Library of Congress Cataloging in Publication Data

Barnes, Keith E.
    Preschool screening.

    Bibliography: p.
    Includes indexes.
    1. Prediction of scholastic success--Examinations,
questions, etc. I. Title.
LB1131.B3219   372.12'64
ISBN 0-398-04668-9   81-21344
                                                AACR2

DEDICATION

To Stella and Graham, with love and appreciation

PREFACE

THE PURPOSE OF THIS BOOK is to provide, on a selective basis, what the author considers to be the essential elements of preschool screening as we enter the decade of the '80s. The book is selective in the sense that it is not a comprehensive handbook or directory on developmental testing or measurement but rather its focus is on those objective screening measures which appear to have the greatest potential for preschool assessment on a low-cost large-scale screening basis, administered by trained volunteers, health technicians and other paraprofessionals in the fields of public health, mental health, day care and preschool education.

The book has been divided up into three parts; the first is a general introduction and overview of the developmental screening field and may be read by anyone who wishes to have some general understanding concerning what preschool predictive screening is all about. The second and third parts are somewhat more technical in that they focus on the essential requirements for the development and construction of good predictive screening instruments (Section II) and what appears to be the most promising and the most carefully constructed screening measures currently available (Section III).

The book specifically does not cover preschool diagnostic tests, or those developmental, pediatric or other medical screening measures that require professional administration, scoring or interpretation simply because they do not fit the framework of low-cost large-scale screening procedures. Essentially, this book is aimed at those professionals in the fields of public health, mental health, day care and preschool education who may, in a variety of ways, be responsible for the planning or the implementation of preschool screening at the community level. It may be used as a general introductory text on screening and measurement for students enrolled in nursing, preschool or early education, psychology, sociology and social work programs, as well as for students in health and social-service technician programs. The book may also provide helpful information to the many nonprofessional but caring people who carry out preschool screening on a voluntary basis in their respective communities.

This book was written while the author was a visiting scholar in the Department of Psychology at Stanford University. The task of writing a book is never accomplished without the assistance of other people and the author wishes to express his appreciation to Drs. Albert Bandura and Lee Cronbach of Stanford University for their overall assistance and many helpful comments during the preparation of the manuscript. Special thanks go to my wife, Stella, for her editorial expertise and her ability to translate psychological terminology into readable and understandable English; to my secretary, Brenda Schnell, for her enthusiasm, organizational skills and precision in the typing of the various pre-publication drafts and the final manuscript; and, finally to the British Columbia Health Research Foundation for its generous financial support, which, in the final analysis, made the writing of this book possible.

Keith E. Barnes, Ph.D.   Kelowna, British Columbia

CONTENTS

PRESCHOOL SCREENING

Section I
Overview and Current Status

Chapter 1

AN INTRODUCTION TO THE FIELD OF PRESCHOOL PREDICTIVE SCREENING

HISTORICAL OVERVIEW AND CURRENT STATUS

THE HISTORY OF PRESCHOOL SCREENING for developmental disabilities has its roots in both the fields of medicine and psychology. One of the earliest recorder of infant development was Charles Darwin, who in the late nineteenth century produced one of the first biographical reports on infant behavior (Darwin, 1877). At about the same time Frances Galton was involved in the pioneering work of measuring sensorimotor functioning together with the development of the first sensorimotor tests (Anastasi, 1954).

The development of the first objective screening tests came during the period of World War I when it became necessary to screen inductees into the armed forces for personal suitability. Woodworth's Personal Data Sheet (Anastasi, 1954) was extensively used as a screening measure for such purposes. However, it was not until the development of child guidance clinics (in the late 1930s) that interest became focussed on screening measures for preschool children. The pioneer in this area was, of course, Arnold Gesell who created and ultimately published the Gesell Developmental Schedules (Gesell, 1940; Gesell & Amatruda, 1941).

From these early pioneering works has come a plethora of screening measures, many of which are directed towards the early detection of highly specific disabilities rather than a more general measurement of preschool development. For example, today we have screening measures for anemia, phenylketonuria, congenital heart disease, sex chromosome abnormalities as well as the more

5

well-known measures for vision, hearing, language and school readiness. The thrust for more and more detailed screening measures and for more comprehensive screening programs has come from a variety of sources, including demands of professionals in the fields of health and social welfare and government legislation. The first piece of this type of legislation in the United States was passed in 1967 and was in the form of an amendment to the Social Security Act which required that all children from birth to twenty--one years of age whose families were in receipt of Social Welfare must be subjected to health screening. The second piece of legislation, which perhaps has had the most profound effect on the entire screening movement, is Public Law 94-142; the *Education For All Handicapped Children Act,* which was passed in November of 1975. This piece of legislation was designed to ensure that all handicapped children would be educated at a level commensurate with their individual needs and in the least restrictive setting available. The major consequence of this Act has been a demand on the part of both state government officials and educators for earlier and earlier recognition or detection of handicapping conditions prior to entry into grade one.

The proliferation of screening measures in the last five years to try and meet this demand has been enormous. Unfortunately, as we shall see in later discussions, the quality of many of these measures leaves much to be desired, and in some cases there is little or no evidence on their effectiveness. Despite this qualifying statement, the field of preschool screening has much to offer not only on the humanistic grounds of detecting disorders at an earlier presymptomatic state, but also because the field demands that we learn more about what constitutes the range of normal development in preschool children. One of the positive side-effects of this demand has been on the one hand to get health and other social service personnel to look more carefully and objectively at individual development, while on the other hand it has directed researchers in child development and psychological measurement to assess more closely what aspects of preschool behavior and development can actually be measured with a reasonable degree of accuracy.

THE PURPOSE AND PROCESS OF PRESCHOOL SCREENING

Let us begin this section with an attempt to define what screening is all about. The Britannica World Language Edition of Funk and Wagnall's *Standard Dictionary* (Volume Two) gives the following definition of the word "screen," a transitive verb used in psychology:

> To separate from a group those individuals showing indications of, or tendencies toward, mental or physical incapacity for specified activities.

(Funk and Wagnall, 1965).

In 1951, the United States Commission on Chronic Illness defined screening in the following way:

> The presumptive identification of unrecognized disease or defects by the application of tests, examinations or other procedures which can be applied rapidly. Screening tests sort out apparently well persons who probably do not have a disease from those who probably do have the disease.

In summary, preschool screening may be defined as a process of early detection for all those preschool children, who, for a variety of reasons (social, emotional, intellectual, biological, physical, linguistic, environmental or any combination of such), will be unable to attain optimum growth and/or normal development.

Before looking at the screening process itself and its accompanying measures, some reference should be made about related identification procedures such as case-finding, early diagnosis and assessment for treatment and follow-up.

Case-Finding

Although case-finding is related to screening in the sense that the more thorough and complete the case-finding procedures are in a community, the greater the number of children made available for mass screening, it is not, by any means, an identical procedure. In fact, case-finding is a series of procedures (Cross, 1977), which, unless a community's screening program includes everyone from a given population, usually precedes the screening process. The procedures employed in case-finding may include: *public awareness programs* about a community's forthcoming screening and diagnostic programs; *agency contact programs* to alert professional service workers to be on the lookout for certain types of cases; and *community canvas programs* where a door-to-door census may be taken for a particular target population.

In essence, case-finding is a systematic process for helping to locate, in a given community, at-risk or potentially at-risk children who could benefit from early intervention programs. The actual procedures used will depend, to a considerable extent, on the goals and objectives of a particular community or community agency. The process may involve not only searching for and locating children for specific screening programs, but also referring children who are at high risk to specific diagnostic services. Furthermore, it may include such activities as defining target populations for further study, encouraging referrals to other agencies, surveying the community for children in need of services, or simply increasing public awareness of currently available community services.

In general, then, case-finding aids community screening by helping to seek out those children from a particular target population that should be screened; however, this type of helping relationship does not occur when case-finding procedures are used to locate obviously identifiable high-risk children. In these types of situations, comprehensive case-finding activities will actually reduce the number of children available for mass screening, as the case-finders will immediately refer such children directly to diagnostic programs.

Diagnosis

When one moves from case-finding to diagnostic and treatment programs, one invariably enters service programs that call upon highly trained professional personnel. In most situations, diagnosis is a set of clinical procedures which may include interviews as well as the use of both subjective and objective measures. Interpretations of the information collected are rarely, if ever, made on a pass/fail basis and part or all of the diagnostic procedures may be repeated as frequently as required. In essence, diagnosis involves an in-depth look at the referred child and his environment partly to determine the *presence* or *absence* of an actual handicapping condition or a significant developmental delay; partly to differentiate, if possible, the *causes* of the identified handicap or delay.

For example, if a preschool child does not identify objects appropriately or consistently, is this because of a physiological impairment in visual acuity, a perceptual learning problem, a specific cognitive deficit, inadequate visual stimulation in his home environment or simply an inability to attend to visual stimulation? If a handicapping condition is confirmed, an appropriate treatment program can then be developed for the child or he can be referred to the best available resource.

Depending on the nature of the potential problem, the diagnostic work-up may involve one or two professionally trained clinicians or a multidisciplinary team of developmental specialists, each of which makes a particular contribution to the overall picture of the child's handicapping condition(s). On the basis of the diagnostic findings, the child will either be considered nonhandicapped or referred to a treatment/education facility for follow-up. The particular program the child then receives may be formulated and implemented by one or more of the specialists involved in the diagnostic evaluation or by another group of trained professionals.

Follow-up Assessment

Once a child has been identified and diagnosed as having a handicap or significant developmental delay, he is then referred for treatment and/or special educational services.

In certain handicapping conditions the treatment may consist of drugs, the wearing of special equipment (eye glasses, hearing aids, etc.), or special forms of therapy (speech, psychiatric or physical). However, many forms of treatment may be mainly in the form of special educational programs. In situations which call for this type of treatment, other types of assessment procedures are required to determine the specific content of the required treatment program. In other words, now that the child's handicapping condition has been verified, a treatment program has to be designed which will be individually tailored to meet his specific needs. Although, as was mentioned earlier, a diagnostic specialist may also be involved in the child's treatment program, frequently this is not the case. For example, a child may be diagnosed by a psychiatrist as having a severe behavioral disturbance, but the treatment program may be designed and implemented by a psychologist, psychiatric social worker or mental health nurse. Similarly, a psychologist may diagnose a child as having a severe reading disorder, but the treatment program will invariably be formulated and carried out by a reading or language specialist.

The assessment procedures employed here may vary according to the disorder; however, they almost always will employ a careful analysis of the child's strengths and weaknesses, the situation in which the disorder is most debilitating and an assessment of base-line functioning level from which the treatment program can be evaluated. For example, if we take the case of a child with a reading disorder, treatment assessment may reveal specific problems in certain language areas and not in others, substantial discomfort when the child is required to read orally in front of the class and a base-line reading level of three years below chronological age.

THE SCREENING PROCESS

At the very outset of our discussion it should be pointed out that mass or selective preschool screening is only *one* component of a community's early detection/early intervention system. Other essential components, such as case-finding, diagnosis and follow-up assessment, have been briefly distinguished; however, the major focus of this book is on preschool screening as a *separate,* but *integral* part of the whole early identification process.

Traditionally, preschool or developmental screening has stemmed from the fields of public health nursing and pediatrics; it is only in more recent years that specialists from other fields (psychology, audiology, ophthalmology, and education) have become actively involved in the screening process. Initially, the preschool child was either seen in well-baby clinics or in the pediatrician's office and was carefully weighed, measured, interviewed and otherwise observed in what was usually a fairly subjective evaluation. The objective was, of course, to record basic developmental growth and development and to look for possible signs of disability or abnormality.

Before looking at the objective and subjective components of screening in detail, we must first determine what the actual screening process is all about. Figure 1 describes pictorially the way the screening process works in most communities or regions in North America.

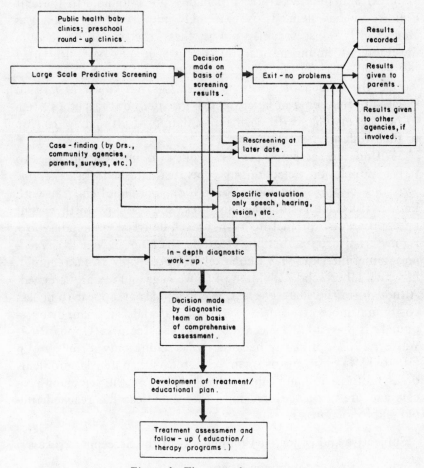

Figure 1. The screening process.

Preschool screening itself may be defined as the application of a series of observation and measurement procedures used to identify those children in the general population who may be at-risk for a specific disability or who may otherwise need special services or programs in order to develop to their maximum potential. The procedures themselves should be fast and simple to administer, capable of pass, fail, or questionable scoring, inexpensive, able to identify at-risk children with predictive accuracy, easily administered by trained nonprofessional personnel, possess high utility value (cost efficient and useful when compared to other procedures) and noninvasive or not highly objectionable to the children receiving them. It is extremely important to realize, as Rogers (1971) has so aptly put it, that "the search for delay in development among normal children is seen as a part of a larger 'well-child' orientation to community child health." In other words, the preschool screening process is not a *witch hunt* to single out children and label them as *diseased,* but rather a system of health surveillance to enable all children to ultimately develop to their fullest potential.

Within the screening process itself, two major approaches to target population selection may be distinguished: (a) *selective screening* or the screening of only those preschool children with known risk factors in their histories, such as low birth weight (⟨ 2500 grams), premature birth, breech delivery, prenatal hypoxia, maternal drug addiction, etc., and (b) *large scale-mass screening* (sometimes known as comprehensive or universal screening), in which all preschool children of a given age and sex are screened. Although on the surface selective screening may appear to be less costly and more efficient, in terms of materials and manpower required. It has in fact been less than satisfactory (Oppe, 1967, Walker, 1967), primarily because by screening only a small group (10 to 15%) of all births, many children with potential problems or asymptomatic handicaps are excluded from the screening process and are not discovered until their handicap has reached full-blown proportions.

Subjective and Objective Components of the Screening Process

Both these components are essential ingredients in any screening procedure. The subjective aspects are best described as those procedures that do not involve objective evaluation through the use of standardized measures of performance. The best example of subjective evaluation is the taking and recording of the child's developmental history together with informal observations of the child's behavior, the mother's behavior and the interaction between the two of them. Most professional health workers generally agree that it is important to take a child's developmental history as early as possible and that such a procedure should be carried out by a trained professional, i.e. pediatrician, family physician or public health nurse. It is believed, further, that both mother and child should be seen together so that the examiner can compare what the mother says the child can do and what the examiner actually sees the child do. Taking a history of the child's development also provides the examiner with the opportunity to observe not only the mother and child interacting with each other, but also the mother's ability to recall and describe her child's performance, her level of affect, her mood states and whatever doubts and anxieties she may have as a mother.

As we shall discuss in more detail later, it is generally well recognized that the physical, psychological and social environment of the child may significantly influence his development and so every effort should also be made to assess the child's home environment not only to validate the significance of the above developmental observations, but also because physical, social and psychological factors may strongly influence how well the child may perform on actual standardized screening measures.

Egan, Illingworth and MacKeith (1969) have discussed in some detail those developmental ages which they believe are the optimal times for screening to occur and in what areas. They put forward the thesis that the following transitional stages of development provide the richest opportunities for early child and mother-child observations.

Six Weeks

At this stage one should observe the emergence of smiling, visual fixation and vocalization in normal infants.

Six Months

At this stage one should see social responsiveness to strangers, the ability to roll over in both directions, the transfer of objects from hand-to-hand, palmar grasping, the chewing of solid food and the emergence of modeling behavior.

Ten Months

At this stage one should see the emergence of crawling, the ability of the infant to pull himself up to a standing position, initial attempts to walk holding on to furniture or other objects, ability to feed himself cookies, and the ability to play simple games (like clap hands). Other transitional periods considered to be of significant importance in later development include: eighteen months (independent walking and single or double word production); two years (emerging self-care feeding, toileting, dressing); three years (language production, sentences and grammar); and four and a half years (fine motor control, peer relationships-social skills and emotional development). It is at these later transitional stages that Egan et al. (1969) believe more objective measures should be employed in conjunction with subjective evaluation, particularly in such areas as gross motor, fine motor, vision, hearing, language and social-emotional reactions.

These authors strongly urge as do others (Rogers, 1971; Capute and Biehl, 1973 and Frankenburg, 1975) that preschool screening should never consist of a one-shot, single-time evaluation, but rather that infants and preschoolers should have a series of developmental screening examinations, if for no other reason than to determine whether they have developed appropriate new skills commensurate with their respective chronological ages. This is an important point when one takes into account the fact that there are often wide individual differences found in development in any one age-group at any given time.

The objective components of the screening process primarily refer to the administration, scoring and interpretation of standardized screening measures. The word standardized is used here to mean that the measures themselves have been administered to specific sample populations or sub-populations of normal children and that the system of presenting the tasks and scoring them has been worked out in a detailed and replicable manner, and that these testing procedures have been published and are readily available in an examiner's manual. The screening measures themselves are simply tools that have been developed to assist the examiner in quickly and economically evaluating large groups of preschool children, some of whom may be harboring an asymptomatic disorder in one or more areas of development, including vision and hearing as well as speech, language, preschool readiness and social-emotional skills.

Frankenburg (1970), has eloquently stated the following:

> Screening tests are not intended to make diagnoses nor are they
> intended as substitutes for complete health appraisals; instead

they are intended as a method of surveying a large population of asymptomatic individuals in order to identify those individuals who have high probability of harboring the particular disease under study.

There are many aspects of these *objective* measures that will be discussed in detail in later sections of this book; however, two comments should be made at this point in the discussion; one is that, whenever possible, the measures used in the screening process should be considered *appropriate* and *acceptable* to those professionals in the community who will be responsible for diagnostic follow-up and/or treatment/educational programs. The second point to be made is that the measures should be used in conjunction with the child's developmental history and any observations made of the child's behavior while performing the screening tasks themselves. In this way, the screening process ultimately ensures a blending or synthesis of both subjective and objective components so as to provide as total a picture of the child's development as time allows. Although the subjective component, as was mentioned earlier, is usually conducted by a trained professional and therefore does not lend itself to the central focus of this book, the point being made here is that subjective and objective data on the child should be integrated in the overall screening process and not kept in isolation from each other or from the people ultimately responsible for the screening program. It also goes without saying that any competent screening examiner, regardless of his level of training, is likely to incorporate *subjective* factors (feelings, intuitions, observations) into his final appraisal of the child's performance.

At this point, one may well ask the question: what really differentiates the *objective* measures from the *subjective* measures in the screening process? At this stage in the development of the screening measurement movement one can only say that good *objective* screening tests are norm-referenced which is to say that they compare a child's performance in a particular developmental area with the performances of other children who are of the same chronological age, sex, socioeconomic status and who come from the same geographic region of the country. Hence, if these measures also possess high reliability (consistency) and validity (predictive power) they are the measures of choice in many ways because they not only compare the scores of the child being screened against the scores of those children who are his direct and most relevant peers, but also they do not rely to any real extent on personal opinion or subjective clinical impressions, i.e. they are more actuarial than clinical in nature.

Norm-referenced measures must not be confused with *criterion-referenced* measures (Harbin, 1977; Shaycoft, 1979), which are designed and used to determine the *actual level* at which the child is functioning; these latter measures are designed not for screening-purposes, but rather to facilitate daily programming of task assignments for the child in remedial programs and to evaluate treatment effectiveness.

Screening Personnel: Who Should Screen?

The Case for Paraprofessionals, Volunteers and Even Parents

One of the major financial costs in any screening program is the one related to manpower. In an average community of 80,000 persons, between 6,000 and 8,000, or approximately 8 to 10 percent, will be of preschool age. The task of screening such a large number of preschoolers is usually well beyond the means of health and social service professionals in most communities.

If one really wishes to achieve low-cost mass screening one may well ask, why don't we simply use parental reports on their child's development? The choice of parents as screening personnel seems an obvious one; since they observe their children in many situations over substantial periods of time, why not have them simply report on their child's performance or progress in specific areas of development? However, there are several problems with such an approach. One of the biggest problems is related to the fact that parents have their own set of individual standards for what constitutes normal developmental progress. What may be considered normal progress by one parent may be thought of as *delayed* by another and perhaps even *accelerated* by a third. Another difficulty with using parents to screen their own children is that some parents may be oversensitive to their child's development and report minutiae, while others may be so insensitive to their child's developmental progress that they report a delay only when it is of monumental proportions. A third problem is that

parents are emotionally involved in their child and his development, and although many parents may be quick to point out when
their child's progress is exceptionally good, many are not as willing
or eager to face the possibility that their child may have some
form of developmental delay. A final problem has to do with the
whole issue of studying individuals retrospectively. For decades
professional health workers and researchers in the behavioral and
social sciences have attempted to determine the antecedents (fore-
runners) of handicapping conditions or even the development of
normality on the basis of the retrospective recall of parents and
other family members. The twin problems here are the accuracy
with which actual behavioral events are observed and the accuracy
with which such observations are recalled and reported on. These
two factors are, of course, ones that plague the professional
health worker when recording a child's developmental history;
however, the worker can at least partially correct for potential
bias by comparing the parent's report with his or her own observations.

At the present time, however, it is probably safe to say that
not all the evidence is in as to the use of parents as screening examiners for their own children. The major concern about parental
reports on methods of developmental screening is that the various
biases discussed above will either create excessively large numbers
of referrals for diagnostic work-ups which are not warranted, i.e.
because the parent reports the child is significantly *delayed*
when he is not (false-positive error), or the child is not referred
because the parent reports *no* developmental *delay* when, in fact,
the child's performance is significantly below normal (false-negative error).

There is now some evidence to suggest, however, that parental
reports of their child's progress may be used for certain screening
purposes. Capute and Biehl (1973) report that parents may be
exceptionally good observers of their child's behaviors and have
little difficulty in reporting their observations accurately providing
that the questions they are asked to respond to deal directly with
their child's usual daily activities. The reliability of parental reports goes down, on the other hand, when parents are asked to
respond to questions that call for interpretation of observations

or deal with activities not usually experienced in daily living. Similarly, Colligan (1976) reports that in a study on the prediction of reading success in preschool children, the Minnesota Child Development Inventory (MCDI), which is a parent observation scale for the assessment of preschool child development, was very successful in predicting reading achievement by the end of the kindergarten year. These very promising results must, however, be supported in the future by follow-up studies in the primary grades and by good cross-validational studies. Finally, Knobloch, Stevens, Malone, Ellison and Risembert (1979) report on a study that used the Developmental Questionnaire (DQ), which is a parental questionnaire based on selected behavioral items from the Gesell Developmental Schedules. Parental responses to the DQ when their respective children were twenty-eight weeks of age were compared with a full Gesell Developmental and Neurological Examination when the children were forty weeks of age. The false-positive error rate was 6 percent and the false-negative error rate was 12.6 percent, results which indicate a remarkably good level of accuracy on the part of the parents' observations.

The use of paraprofessionals (health technicians, health unit aides) and volunteers in preschool screening programs has increased since more and more objective measures have been made available. In many ways the scoring methods of these measures (pass, fail, questionable) lend themselves to use by nonprofessionally trained people as does the fact that these measures do not call for clinical interpretations or diagnostic classification. Another significant reason for the ever-increasing use of paraprofessionals and volunteers in the screening process is the increasing shortage of professionally trained health workers coupled with the rapidly escalating cost of all forms of health care.

The question that is frequently raised is whether paraprofessional and volunteer health workers can function as proficient screening examiners. Although this is a question that has not been studied extensively, personal reports from many professionals in the health field would indicate that paraprofessionals, if adequately trained, make excellent screening examiners. In the last few years, this type of personal opinion has been bolstered by a certain amount of research on the topic (Frankenburg, Goldstein,

Chabot, Camp and Fitch, 1970; Furuno and Connor, 1970; Frankenburg, Goldstein and Camp, 1971; Goldstein and Camp, 1971; and Thorpe and Werner, 1974). In essence, what these studies show is that the more careful the training and retraining these nonprofessionals receive, the more proficient and *expert* they become as screening examiners. Such findings are indeed gratifying, for nonprofessional health workers constitute one of the community's most valuable resources.

THE PLANNING AND IMPLEMENTATION
OF COMMUNITY SCREENING PROGRAMS

The practical and ethical issues involved in the creation and planning of a large-scale screening program are not always given the consideration they require by government or municipal administrators. In fact, even within the health and social service fields themselves, many program directors or administrative heads do not always consider some of the more basic issues involved when a large-scale screening program is undertaken in a particular community or geographic region. Fortunately, several excellent articles in this area have recently been published exploring the different types of criteria that should be considered before embarking on any mass-screening endeavour (Frankenburg, 1975; Colligan, 1976; and Lillie, 1977). The author considers these articles to be so important that they will be briefly summarized below.

Frankenburg (1975) lists ten basic criteria which he believes are crucial to the selection of a particular disorder for large-scale screening. (1) The disorder or condition to be screened for should be serious or potentially serious; i.e. if the underlying condition is not discovered early, it will permanently or seriously handicap a child throughout the rest of his life. (2) The diagnostic procedures available are capable of clearly and accurately differentiating the presence of the disorder from a borderline condition or its complete absence. (3) The prognosis for treatment of the disorder should be improved if the disorder is identified and treated earlier than the usual time of diagnosis. (4) Early screening will improve the amount of lead time for diagnosis; i.e. the diagnosis of a particular disorder is moved up in time as a result of screening. (5) The disorder should be amenable to current treatment programs or at least capable of being controlled. (6) The disorder being screened for should have a relatively high prevalence rate in a given population, since the rarer the disorder, the greater the costs of detecting a particular number of asymptomatic children. (7) The screening procedures to be used should in no way be harmful or seriously discomforting to the child being screened. (8) If a child is found to be at-risk on a screening test, facilities should be available locally to provide diagnostic work-ups and treatment programs, if required. (9) The costs of early screening, diagnosis and treatment must be compared with the costs (humanistic as well as financial) of when the disorder is finally discovered and treated after the appearance of various symptoms. (10) The large scale screening for a particular disorder or condition must be acceptable to the general public.

Colligan (1976) raises some very basic questions concerning the issues of ethics and practice in large-scale screening programs. For example from an ethical viewpoint, are the measures selected sufficiently reliable, valid and adequately standardized to justify their use in the screening program under consideration? What are the short-term and long-term pay-offs of the program as compared to its costs? In R. S. Illingworth's terms, "What good will it do? What harm will it do? What harm is there in not doing it?" (Quoted in Frankenburg, 1978).

Is the screening program being initiated without due regard for diagnostic referral services and the availability of early intervention-treatment programs? What are the potential harmful effects to the participants in the program, i.e. the problems of *labelling, negative self-fulfilling prophecy, truly informed consent?* What guidelines have been prepared for ensuring the confidentiality of an individual child's scores on the screening measures used? What are the consequences of the false-positive and false-negative error rates for the measures being used and how will these be interpreted?

In discussing practice, he asks what are the specific goals of the organization responsible for the screening program? Are the results to be used for applied research, epidemiology, early intervention, future evaluation or early school tracking? Who is to implement the screening program? Should it be the community mental health center, the public health unit, public day-care centers, public school or private practitioners? Who will be responsible for the actual screening examinations, professionally trained health workers, health technicians, health aides or trained volunteers? Which persons and organizations will be responsible for the interpretation of the child's performance and any follow-up that may be required? What age-groups of children should be screened, why, and at whose request? What kinds of disorders or conditions are to be screened for, vision, hearing, behavioral or cognitive? How much time and money is to be allocated to the program and who should pay the costs, the state, the municipality, the individual client (fee-for-service)? What are the major demographic features of the population to be screened? How are they related (or not related) to the screening measures to be used? For example, if the measures have been standardized on only white, middle class, culturally advantaged children and they are to be used on a target population that is low SES, black and culturally disadvantaged, then, at the most minimal level of acceptability, local norms of performance on such a target group will have to be collected before the screening program can be implemented.

Finally, Lillie (1977) presents six guidelines that should be used whenever a decision is required concerning a particular screening program. Basically, these six guidelines are a synopsis of the various issues and criteria discussed by Frankenburg (1975) and Colligan (1976). He not only reiterates the importance of such factors as the availability of diagnostic and treatment resources and the efficacy of such services; but he also adds that the measures used must be inexpensive, readily available and predictively accurate. On the issue of prevalence of the disorder to be screened for, he reports that the incidence rate, in the general population, of the handicap sought should be relatively high unless the consequences of failing to detect the disorder early are extremely severe.

AT-RISK AND OTHER DEFINITIONS
OF ASYMPTOMATIC CONDITIONS

The definition of at-risk and the detection of children who fall into such a classification is not as simple a task as many people may believe. For example, as Garmezy (1976) has so clearly pointed out, a child may be considered at-risk for a particular disorder if actuarial data exists which indicates that certain children with a cluster of specific attributes (which our sample child shares) are known to be much more likely to develop the disorder at a later date than a randomly selected group of children of the same age, sex, SES and geographic region. The problem here is two-fold; first there is often very little, if any, actuarial data available on many potentially disabling conditions.

Secondly, the specific attributes which make up the cluster may be either poorly defined or related to the later-developing disorder in very uncertain ways. If, on the other hand, the etiology of a particular disorder is clearly defined and well known, then the task of detecting at-risk children is relatively simple and consists of merely screening all those individuals that possess the etiological components of the disorder; i.e. the at-risk group. However, in reality, few disorders, except certain physiological ones such as phenylketonuria (PKU) amblyopia and diabetes have such clearly defined etiological components, which makes the screening of at-risk populations that much more difficult and problematical. These problems are often magnified in preschool developmental screening because so many of the later-developing handicapping conditions, like reading disabilities, language disorders, drug and alcohol dependency, affective disorders and schizophrenia, have very few, if any, well-known clearly defined etiological components.

What, then, does at-risk screening mean? Usually, it refers to the *presymptomatic* detection of a particular disorder which could seriously interfere with a child's normal development, if left undetected. Obviously a child can be at-risk in a variety of developmental areas including vision, hearing, speech, language, sensorimotor, cognition and personal-social, to name just a few. The child could, of course, be at-risk for certain physiological conditions as well, such as anemia, congenital heart disease, or a peptic ulcer. The important point to recognize in any preschool screening program is that even when a child is classified as being at-risk, it does *not mean,* necessarily, that the child *actually has a particular disorder* or, in fact, will develop one at a later date. Such a classification as at-risk acts as an early-warning signal that says, in effect, check this child out more thoroughly, preferably by referral to a diagnostic team of developmental specialists.

As Rogers (1971) has previously pointed out so well in regards to the classification of the child at-risk . . .

> some children are considered to be at increased risk of sub-sequent handicap because of genetic endowment or adverse environmental influences during fetal, prenatal, neonatal or post-natal development.

Other children, however, may be considered at-risk without any prior evidence for genetic factors or adverse environmental influences. Furthermore, it is important to distinguish between children who may be detected as being at-risk and those children who actually have clearly recognizable or diagnostically identified handicapping conditions. This latter group is clearly handicapped or disabled in some way and should be enrolled in treatment or rehabilitation programs.

In the same article Rogers (1971) has also indicated the importance of recognizing a third group of children whom he has classified as children at *High Risk*. He states the following:

> There is a small group (5 - 10%) of infants (who) are at considerably increased risk because of "high risk" factors such as maternal rubella in pregnancy, low birth weight (short gestation and/or retarded intrauterine growth), severe prenatal hypoxia or birth injury, and neonatal hyperbilirubinaemia.

Since 1971 another *High Risk* factor that might be added to this list is maternal smoking and drug addiction (Norman-Taylor and Dickinson, 1972; Harlap and Davies, 1974; and Tager, Weiss, Rosner and Speizer, 1979).

EVALUATION OF SCREENING PROGRAMS
AND THE MEASURES USED

A sound large-scale screening program should provide health and social service personnel with sufficient information for them to decide whether, at the time of screening, the child has no indications of developmental delay or asymptomatic handicap; whether his performance on the measures used was *questionable* (border-line) and he should be seen again for reappraisal at a later date; or whether the child displayed definite signs of developmental delay or handicap and should be referred for a thorough professional diagnostic work-up. Whether, in fact, the program actually achieves these outcomes and does it efficiently and at the lowest level of cost (both human and financial) can only be determined through evaluation.

Program evaluation procedures may, of course, be applied to all of the components of a community's early detection — early intervention system; i.e. case-finding, screening, diagnosis and follow-up treatment. For our purposes, however, the focus of the discussion will be on the screening component.

The evaluation of a large-scale screening program should provide information to a variety of groups who may be involved directly or indirectly in providing services to children. These groups may include the staff members of the agency actually involved in the screening process itself; i.e. health technicians, trained paraprofessionals and volunteers as well as professionally trained health workers. The evaluation results should indicate to these people how comprehensive their screening program is, its cost efficiency, the referral rates to other professionals (audiologists, speech therapists, psychologists, ophthalmologists and pediatricians) for diagnostic work-ups and what percentage of the referrals made were confirmed as having a specific handicapping condition. Professionally trained people involved in the diagnostic, treatment and follow-up services, who, by comparing the number of valid referrals they receive from other sources with the actual number of valid referrals from the screening program, can evaluate the comprehensiveness of the program itself as well as the number of invalid (false-positive) referrals received. Evaluation reports should also go to the program directors or administrators, who require evaluative information whenever they must consider the overall priorities of their respective service programs. Program evaluation data is also very important when decisions must be made as to which screening programs should be expanded, curtailed, abolished or maintained at their current levels. The funding agency (state government, private foundation, board of management) has a right to know how well its investment has paid-off in terms of developing human potential or reducing severely handicapping disorders and human misery. The general public also have a right to know how their tax money is being spent and whether the program is significantly benefitting certain groups of children in their community.

Moore (1977) has distinguished two types of evaluation for screening programs. The first he calls *Formative Evaluation,* which refers to the assessment of a screening program over a short time-span, with the major objective of providing feedback to screening staff members as to whether their program is running according to plan or whether it requires modification in order to stay on course.

The second type he calls *Summative Evaluation,* which refers to the assessment of a screening program over a fairly substantial period of time (one to three years) and has as the major objective an overall evaluation of the program in terms of cost/benefit ratios, the efficient and productive use of manpower, success rates and consumer satisfaction. It should probably be added here that both of these types of evaluations should be *planned for* and *built-in prior* to the implementation of any new screening program.

The essence, then, of program evaluation is to provide detailed information and empirical data on the merits of a given screening program; it should tell us specifically whether the benefits, both financial and humanistic, outweigh the costs (also financial and humanistic) of not carrying out the program. Indirectly, it should also provide us with considerable information on the screening measures themselves.

Evaluation of Screening Measures

The effectiveness of screening measures may be evaluated in two main ways. One is in terms of how well they have been constructed and standardized, and their levels of consistency over time, which is the subject of discussion in Chapters 2 and 3. The second way is in terms of how accurately their scores predict to certain outcome measures, which is the topic of discussion in Chapter 4.

Because of the nature of the job it is required to do, the results obtained on a screening test should correlate highly with such outcome measures as professional diagnosis and/or the results found on specific diagnostic laboratory tests. One of the keys to a screening measure's effectiveness is the number of false-positive and false-negative predictions it makes as well as the actual number of valid-positive and valid-negative predictions. Valid-positive predictions refer to the number of children who scored as at-risk on the screening test and were diagnosed as having a handicapping condition, while valid-negatives refer to the number of children who scored as normal or better on the screening measure and were diagnosed as having no handicapping condition. The false-positives are all those children designated as at-risk on the screening test but found *not to have* the disorder on diagnostic work-up. The false-negatives are all those children who were classified as normal on the screening measure, but who at a later date were found to have the handicapping condition. Table I illustrates, in two-by-two matrix form, these four different predictive categories.

Table I

CLASSIFICATION OF PREDICTIVE CATEGORIES

PREDICTIVE SCREENING MEASURE

Outcome Measure (Diagnosis)	Negative (Normal)	Positive (At-Risk)
Negative (No Handicap)	All children falling in this category are "valid negatives."	All children falling in this category are "false positives."
Positive (Handicap Present)	All children falling in this category are "false negatives."	All children falling in this category are "valid positives."

A detailed discussion of this table and the calculations necessary for computing a screening measure's predictive effectiveness is provided in Chapter 5. Suffice it to say here that the lower the number of false-positives and false-negatives, the higher the screening test's predictive accuracy for detection of asymptomatic conditions and the more cost effective it is, both in financial and human terms.

In addition to this kind of numerical predictiveness, a screening measure must possess high acceptability to the professionals in the community providing the diagnostic follow-ups (otherwise they may refuse the children referred for diagnosis or may even attempt to discredit the entire screening program), and it must be acceptable to the children taking it. If the screening test is embarrassing or painful, then the children may refuse to take it or behave in a very noncooperative manner. Finally, the screening test should be simple in design. To be maximally effective for large-scale screening programs, it should require little or no equipment, be simple to administer and score, be of relatively short duration in time and capable of being given in a wide variety of settings.

One of the great difficulties of evaluating a screening measure's effectiveness has to do with our lack of knowledge on prevalence or base-rates for many of the disorders being screened for, and our lack of local or regional norms. This lack of base-rate data comes about because of the paucity of both normative and long-term epidemiological research on disorders of childhood. In most communities and even large geographic regions of North America, we just do not have normative data on most of the screening measures currently being used. This is very unfortunate, to say the least, because without local norms on the test being used, we have no way of knowing whether the number of children detected is abnormally high or extraordinarily low; in other words, we have no standard with which to compare the screening measure's accuracy or consistency over time, and no way of comparing the children being screened with their peers from the same community. To add to this dilemma, we do not even have up-to-date norms on general preschool development; the data collected by Gesell (1940) on what constituted normal development during the first five years of life is now over *forty years old.*

The actual prevalence or base-rate of a particular disorder is of critical importance in the evaluation of a screening measure's effectiveness because the magnitude of the prevalence of a given disorder in the general population will affect the probability values of the test; the lower the prevalence, the higher will be the number of false-positives (Fleeson and Wenk, 1970). For an in-depth discussion of this problem, see Chapter 5.

Prevalence rates only come from the carrying out of extensive, frequently costly epidemiological studies, where the actual incidence rate of a specific disorder is determined by tabulating the actual number of people in the general population who have been diagnosed as having the condition. Unfortunately, as mentioned before, we do not have accurate national base-rates for reading disorder, cognitive defects, speech defects, or significant developmental delay, to name just a few areas. What tends to be used in place of epidemiological base-rates are estimates or probably more accurately, guesstimates, although the recent study by Werner and Smith (1977) on children on the Island of Kauai is the exception to this rule.

One way of rectifying this general problem would be through the carrying out of careful follow-up studies on screening programs, which would constitute an extension of summative evaluation as previously discussed by Moore (1977). Such follow-up evaluation would provide a much broader range of information than we currently have now. For example, long-term follow-up studies would tell us how predictively accurate the screening measures were over time as well as whether false-positive and false-negative rates were subject to change. By following all the children screened over several years, we would not only have information on the number and type of specific disorders identified, but also would have evaluation data on the efficiency of the follow-up referral services of the screening agencies themselves and the quality or effectiveness of follow-up treatment services for those children identified as being handicapped. In essence, this type of follow-up evaluation is the only method currently available to accurately determine the efficacy of the effects of early treatment and to assess the impact of early screening programs on maintaining the overall health of children. In fact, the author believes that this type of long-term follow-up evaluation should be built into all preschool screening programs, not only as a check on the program's overall effectiveness and the accuracy of the measures used, but also as a way of building a data-bank to provide much needed information on regional and local norms and base-rates for specific handicapping conditions.

PROGRESS AND PROBLEMS IN THE FIELD
OF PRESCHOOL SCREENING

Despite considerable progress in certain areas, the field of preschool screening still has a long way to go before fulfilling its promise as a method of preventing or alleviating handicapping conditions in children. No one seems to disagree with the fact that we need a comprehensive program for the early detection of at-risk children, nor to deny the humanistic and financial advantages of early intervention. However, despite this general consensus of professional opinion, there are certain problems related to such an approach many of which have to do with our current lack of knowledge and understanding in the field of human development and others to do with problems of the measures themselves. As Satz, Taylor, Friel and Fletcher (1979) have previously noted, the predictive value of a preschool screening program is directly related to the predictive error rates of the measures employed; i.e. the higher the error rates, the lower the utility value of the program because of the large number of children screened who are misclassified.

Another very serious problem in the screening field is the obvious lack of an adequate theoretical framework for conceptualizing the nature of the handicapping conditions and the precipitating factors that lead up to them. For example, what are the antecedent conditions for developmental delay, cognitive deficit or reading disability? As Satz et al. (1979) point out "Without a testable theory one lacks guidelines for the selection of a test battery which purports to identify the potentially high-risk child." It is only through the development of theoretical constructs and their empirical validation that we can ever hope to understand the etiology of so many of the handicapping conditions of childhood.

Although this lack of a theoretical framework presents a serious challenge to researchers in the developmental screening field, most of the problems otherwise are associated with the measures themselves. To begin with, there are no mandatory minimum standards for the development and construction of screening tests, and although the American Psychological Association's *Standards for Educational and Psychological Tests* (APA, 1974) are excellent and extremely applicable to the construction of screening measures, they do not have to be adhered to legally by any test publisher. One of the consequences of such a condition has been a proliferation over the past decade of various screening measures that do not come close to meeting APA standards.

Then, there are the problems associated with the actual construction and validation of the measures themselves. For example, most of the screening measures constructed in the last few years have employed items selected from other tests of development such as Gesell Scales, the Yale Developmental Inventory and the Bayley Scales of Infant Development. Although there is nothing intrinsically wrong in using such a procedure, most of these measures were not constructed for screening purposes and it is not always clear as to their relevance in the detection of an underlying handicapping condition. A second problem here has to do with the short-term and long-term prediction of a later developing disorder. First, there are the difficulties associated with selecting an appropriate criterion measure, particularly if that measure is another objective test. In this situation we have the problems of correlating our screening measure with a criterion (outcome) measure which itself may be poorly constructed, inadequately standardized or have dubious levels of reliability and validity. Secondly, we have the problems of predictive validation associated with the passage of time. What may constitute excellent criterion measures at age six may be totally inappropriate by age ten. For instance, in the short-term prediction of reading disability it would appear that the most appropriate outcome measures of screening at grade one would be of sensorimotor-perceptual factors; however, by grade four the best criterion tests would appear to be measures of conceptual-linguistic skills, or cognitive processing (Satz et al., 1979). The problem is complicated further by the fact that increases in failure rates on the outcome measures may occur from grade to grade not because the children themselves perform at a lower level, but because the difficulty level of a particular outcome measure at grade five may have significantly higher (more difficult) ceiling levels than a similar measure at grade two. Similarly, an outcome measure used at grade five may be tapping different constructs than the one used at grade two; for example, at grade five a reading test may be tapping cognitive processing and speed of decoding while at grade two a reading measure may be tapping visual sequencing and word recognition.

Another problem with determining the long-term predictive utility of a screening test has to do with the actual significant changes that may occur over time in an individual child's life, especially in such areas as developmental growth, human learning and experiential factors. For a complete appraisal of the problems associated with preschool screening measures, see Gallagher and Bradley (1972) and Satz and Fletcher (1979).

The predictive accuracy of a screening measure may also be strongly influenced by a whole host of other factors which may have nothing to do with the test itself. For example, there is now considerable evidence (Alberman, 1973; Werner and Smith, 1977; Spreen, 1979) to suggest that successful achievement in school, in reading, in cognitive development and in mental health is strongly influenced not only by general physical development, specific abilities and acquired skills, but also by such background variables as the socioeconomic level of the child's family, his level of stimulation and achievement in the home, the extent of his mother's education, personal-motivational factors, and the cultural values of his parents as well as teacher and peer variables in his school setting.

Adelman and Feshbach (1971) and Feshbach et al. (1977) have proposed, in the area of screening for academic readiness, that the failure in predictive accuracy of so many screening measures may be due not only to the fact that they have generally ignored the importance of socioeconomic, emotional and environmental factors, but also that many of them are administered to preschoolers on an individual basis. This situational factor, they claim, differs so markedly from the performance conditions found in the typical classroom that it alone could account for the high false-negative predictive error rates found in so many of the studies evaluating predictive effectiveness.

Finally, when looking at the problems related to predictive screening, we must also consider the possible reasons why a particular child may fail to pass a given screening test. First, and most obvious, the child may fail because he is truly an at-risk child; i.e. asymptomatic of a handicapping condition. The child may fail, however, for a wide variety of other reasons; for example, he may be afraid or apprehensive of the testing situation; he may dislike or be afraid of the screening examiner, or for whatever reason he may not be motivated to be cooperative on the day he is to be screened. It is important for those involved in

the screening process to remember, as Flavell (1977) has previously pointed out, that "All tasks demand more from the child
than the target . . . entity the examiner is interested in assessing."

Together with those problem factors associated with the child
himself, we must also consider problems related to the screening
examiner. Thorpe and Werner (1974) have argued that some of
the factors that may influence a child's success on a screening
test include: the sensitivity of the examiner to the behavior of
the young child; the examiner's appreciation of the importance of
nonverbal clues, from facial expressions to eye movements and
gestures; the degree of rapport established between examiner and
child as well as his personal style of dealing with young children.
Related to their concern with the influential effects of examiner
variables, the authors also point out some of the shortcomings
associated with the programs used for the training of screening
examiners; these include few, if any, standards, very little opportunity for practical experiences with preschool children together
with low levels of supervision by highly trained and experienced
examiners both during training and afterwards while on the job.

Some of the problems related to screening programs and the
measures used in them will probably never be resolved. It is
doubtful, for example, whether we will ever be able to control
adequately for certain person variables; such factors as the child's
personality, the personality of the examiner and their respective
levels of motivation for cooperativeness, friendliness and emotional stability will always exist as error variance. However, some
of the other problems are capable of resolution; for instance, examiners can be trained to be more sensitive to behavioral clues
and to establish good rapport before testing; they can also be
given more opportunities for practical experiences, receive more
supervision and be trained to meet certain essential standards of
competence. Similarly, with adequate preparation and parent
education, preschool children can be helped to overcome their
fears of testing and/or the screening examiner.

The problem of adequate outcome studies can be resolved,
at least partially, by selecting well-constructed, highly valid and
reliable criterion measures; ones that have preferably been used

on large homogeneous groups of children, in order to cut down on predictive errors that may be associated with sex, race, socio-economic levels or cultural variables.

Finally, many poor or inadequately constructed screening tests would be eliminated by adopting such minimum requirements as those classified as *essential* in the APA *Standards for Educational and Psychological Tests*. The problem of the actual changes that occur in a child's life over time and which invariably affect the predictiveness of any screening measure may be partially eliminated by the administration of a series of overlapping screening tests during the first five years of the child's life.

After reading through what must appear to be an almost endless array of problems, one might well ask what progress, if any, has been made in the field of preschool screening in the last decade?

First, let us try and put things in perspective; traditionally, as has been pointed out in detail elsewhere (Garmezy, 1976) professionals and nonprofessionals alike have for decades attempted to determine the nature of normal development or the etiology of handicapping conditions on the basis of retrospective studies. In part, we may construe screening programs as an attempt to study children prospectively and to try and get around the incredible unreliability (Yarrow, Campbell and Burton, 1970) of so many of these retrospective studies on children.

Secondly, screening for certain handicapping conditions has been remarkably successful. The early detection of PKU, Amblyopia and serious vision and hearing deficits are the consequences of screening programs we can be proud of, for they have, indeed, prevented the development of very severe functional handicaps later in the child's life.

A third potential advantage of early screening for those children who may be at-risk is that it can get them into the diagnostic referral stream much earlier, which may be of considerable significance given the frequent long delay between initial referral and active professional attention. It also, of course, provides for earlier treatment if on diagnostic work-up they are found to have a significant underlying delay or disorder.

Finally, what valid screening measures can also do is pick out at-risk children well before they enter the school system (which is when most of them used to be discovered). This procedure has, according to Satz, Taylor, Friel and Fletcher (1979), two very distinct advantages; it identifies the child when his central nervous system may be more plastic (malleable) and thus more responsive to change, and it reaches the child at an age when he has not yet been subjected to the damaging consequences of repeated academic and/or social failure.

As we reach the end of this overview of the field of preschool screening, what can be said about the *state of the art?*

First, such screening is based on the assumption that the child at-risk for a later handicapping condition can be detected early and in a reliable and predictively valid manner. It assumes further that once the underlying condition is detected, there exist comprehensive diagnostic procedures for identifying what it is and how it might best be treated. A third assumption made is that the earlier in a child's development a potential disability is detected, the more effective and beneficial the necessary treatment program will be.

Secondly, many developmental disorders may be due not only to organic (physiological) factors, but also to home environment, culture and socioeconomic variables, either separately or in a variety of combinations. In fact, in a study on children in Kauai by Werner, Bierman and French (1971), the authors reported that significant handicapping conditions were associated ten times more frequently with poor early environment than they were with organic etiology.

Thirdly, although a considerable amount of valuable information on a child's development in a variety of areas can be gained from specific screening measures, they nearly all suffer from the lack of precision necessary for diagnosis, and it would be unethical for them to be used under any circumstances to label children. However, screening measures are not designed to be that precise or specific; rather they are designed to be administered singly or together in a battery with this single objective of detecting children at-risk. One of the greatest difficulties associated with preschool screening is that many aspects of human development are subject to considerable variation in time and also across individuals; furthermore, certain developmental delays also seem capable of spontaneous self-correction. Thus, when a child is found to be at-risk on a screening examination, there may be several different consequences. For example, on diagnostic evaluation, the child may or may not be found to have a handicapping condition. If the child is considered not at-risk by the diagnostic team, but clearly in the at-risk group on the screening measures, such a discrepancy may come about for a variety of reasons, including the belief on the part of the diagnostic team that the child is normal but is one who passes through certain developmental sequences at a slower rate (temperamental characteristic) than other children; that the child's performance, although lower than average, falls within diagnostic *normal* limits for human development; or, finally, that despite *positive* findings, the handicapping condition will spontaneously correct itself over time.

Finally, it should be abundantly clear by now that preschool screening for at-risk children is not a precise or exact science and it is highly likely that, as Spreen (1979) has recently reported, a 75 percent accuracy of prediction rate for screening measures is as high as we will ever achieve when basing prediction on screening measure scores alone. However, after reviewing the work of so many authors and research workers in the field of screening, one cannot help but be impressed with the seemingly universal sequencing of human development. One sees so many examples of the gradual unfolding of skills and abilities that one cannot help but believe in the logical progression of developmental events. Whether the area of development is gross or fine motor control, language ability, visual processing or social skills, each step in the developmental sequence seems to build on some other step. Although the appearance and completion of these developmental steps may vary, sometimes considerably, from child to child, they seem to be an invariable component of human development.

If this sequential process should hold true for all individuals, and if the acquisition of certain skills or the completion of certain steps, is essential at certain critical stages of maturation in order for the child to progress at an optimum level, then one of the greatest services that preschool screening can offer is the early detection of *delayed* children. Such detection would enable the child to receive individual training or other special educational programs, either through parents and other family members, or on a group basis through such community service agencies as child day care or public health.

Section II
Essential Requirements for the
Development of Screening
Instruments

Chapter 2

TEST CONSTRUCTION, STANDARDIZATION, NORMS, AND ADMINISTRATION

The Development and Construction of Preschool Screening Measures

T HE EFFECTIVENESS OF ANY PSYCHOLOGICAL measure depends upon a variety of different characteristics. These characteristics will include not only the selection of test items, the make-up of the sample population that is drawn upon and the collection of normative data, but also the reliability, validity and utility characteristics of the measure after the items have been put together in test form. It must be emphasized from the very outset that the development and construction of any screening measure involves a whole series of interrelated tasks and is not something that can be done in a short time.

Before the time-consuming procedure of actually constructing a new screening measure is undertaken, a considerable degree of time and effort should be spent on reviewing the need for a new instrument of detection. Such a review should include whether currently available measures could be revised to meet such a need (if it has been clearly established) and whether it is feasible to actually construct a new test which will adequately meet this need. Other factors which also should be reviewed are the relative costs of test construction, the extent of the population the new measure will be used on, and its predictive utility over whatever methods of early detection are currently being used. If, after such an extensive evaluation, it is clear that the test will produce early detection at relatively low financial cost plus major benefits to those children detected as at-risk, then obviously the development and construction of a new screening measure should be implemented without delay.

Although the above procedure may appear to be self-evident, it is sometimes surprising to learn the number of times such a preliminary evaluation is not undertaken.

ITEM SELECTION AND ITEM ANALYSIS

Item Selection

The selection of items for any given measure is a task that requires a great deal of time and careful thought. The actual items selected will depend in part on the content specifications established in the process of planning the test and, in part, on the particular statistical characteristics of each item. The method by which items may be selected will depend on the particular bent of the individual constructor; one common method is to draw items from other measures which have already been used to assess similar target areas or populations. Another method is to use some items from already existing tests and to write up or collect new items as required. Finally, in those areas where no measures have previously existed, the test constructor is required to write up or otherwise acquire a total pool of new items. This last method is by far the most time-consuming and requires the test constructor to have some very clearly defined objectives as to what he is proposing to measure.

The method of acquiring new items may best be illustrated by way of an example. Let us say that our test constructor is about to develop the first measure ever devised on reading ability. His first task in planning such a measure will be to determine what the essential components of reading actually are. If he decides, through an extensive review of the research on reading, that it consists of a visual component, a perceptual organization component, sub-vocal cognition and decoding and visual memory, then he will look for a wide variety of items that will measure accurately and precisely those particular areas. On obtaining several hundred or perhaps a thousand of such items, his task now is to select those that appear to be the best predictors of actual reading ability. To aid him in this initial task, he may turn to a group of reading experts or other specialists to sort through the many items he has collected and select out those that, in their professional opinion, have the greatest discriminating power for differentiating poor readers from proficient readers. At this point our test constructor may put these items together in a *rough draft* or *experimental edition* of his proposed measure and administer them to a representative sample of appropriately aged people in order to check for such factors as ceiling effects (everybody passes all of the items), skewness of fit (90% of the sample pass most of the items while the rest of the items are passed by only 10% of the sample) and item ambiguity (some people in the sample interpret the item in one way while others interpret it differently). The representativeness of this initial sample of people should be as similar as possible to the future standardization sample, so that items included will all be valid for the larger group.

The information on individual items gleaned from this initial procedure places the test constructor in a position to revise the experimental or rough draft of his measure so that it can now be administered to a wider range and larger sample of the general population (standardization group). However, one cannot stress enough the tremendous importance of this initial procedure together with the fact that the test itself must have a sufficiently high number of items for each subtest area; otherwise, the sampling of actual reading performance will be so limited that the actual discrimination of poor readers from proficient ones may be almost impossible to achieve.

Item Analysis

A test constructor can greatly aid a test user if he states somewhere in the test manual the criteria and principles under which he either wrote the test items or selected them from other measures. The major goal of item analysis is to evaluate each test item in regards to fairness, appropriateness, freedom from ambiguity and cultural/response bias and whether it is too easy (everyone passes it) or too difficult (no one passes it). This last factor (difficulty level) is very important because it relates to the ability of a test item to discriminate across individuals. For example, if everyone passes or everyone fails a particular item, then that item would have zero discrimination power because it could not differentiate across individuals and would, therefore, be unable to tell the test constructor anything of significance about a specific individual's performance relative to the performance of anyone else who took that item. Hence, what is usually required in a well-constructed test is a large variety of items that are capable of discriminating across individuals at various difficulty levels; for example, at one end of the continuum we require items that are relatively easy, say, passed by 90 percent of the prestandardization sample, while at the other end of the continuum we require items that are relatively difficult (passed by only 10 percent of the sample.). Ideally, the largest number of items should discriminate at the level of 0.5; i.e. approximately 50 percent of the sample pass the item and 50 percent do not. It is the items that discriminate at the 0.5 level that the test constructor is most interested in because, as has been reported elsewhere (Thorndike, 1967), a highly reliable test is one where the *average* difficulty level of the items is 50 percent, i.e. approximately 50 percent of the sample group passed each item. The actual distribution of items according to their difficulty levels will depend on the way each item relates to all the other items in the measure. If, for example, there is a high inter-item correlation, i.e. each item correlates highly with each other item, then the test should have a wide scatter of item difficulties around the main level of 50 percent difficulty; however, if the inter-item correlation is low, the corresponding scatter of item difficulties may also be low.

An example of a test with high item inter-correlation would be one which has been developed for the purpose of measuring a narrow and specific segment of ability, say fine motor coordination. In such a measure, items would be selected to aid in our assessment of a person's fine motor coordination and the higher the number of items passed, the higher the person's total score on fine motor coordination (and hopefully, of course, the higher his actual level of fine motor coordination). In this case, we are not really interested in each item's correlation with an external criterion; we are, however, most concerned with each item's correlalation with the test's total score. This form of item analysis, i.e. correlating each test item with the total test score, is called *internal consistency analysis.* Another form of item analysis is required, however, when one is concerned with measuring a very broad level of ability, say managerial competence. In the measurement of this type of ability, one frequently has a great many items of the wide range variety, many of which may have no basic relationship (correlation) with each other. In this case, the items selected must be subjected to individual scrutiny because there is no reason for us to believe that they represent some unified aspect of the person's personal competence. What the test constructor is required to do here is to evaluate the effectiveness of each item against some outside criterion such as (in this example) managerial success on the job. Hence, the validity of an item response will be determined by the relationship it held with success or frequency of success in business management. Thus, if those individuals who respond to an item in a particular way are found to be highly successful in their work situations, then that item would have high validity. This kind of analysis, correlating each item's response to some external criterion, is known as *item validation.*

Item analysis through the use of extreme groups can be a very useful procedure when there exists a high positive relationship (correlation) between success on an item and total test score; i.e. a high linear relationship. Through the use of the extreme groups method of analysis, a test constructor can obtain the most accurate arrangement of items on a continuum from least discriminating to most discriminating; in other words, he will be able to rank order the items on the basis of their ability to discriminate. The problem with employing a method which splits a sample population into high and low scores is that substantial quantities of information may be lost by excluding a large number of individuals who score in the middle range. Fortunately, this problem was very nicely resolved, statistically, by T. L. Kelley many years ago, (Kelley, 1939) when he demonstrated that the most accurate way to arrange items in their best order of discriminating power occurred when the item analysis was performed using the scores from the top 27 percent and the bottom 27 percent of the population tested.

Before leaving this section on item selection and analysis, some mention should be made about the adequacy of item sampling. Although there are no set rules as to how many items should be selected for a given measure, it is important to consider the fact that a test with an inadequate number of items in it invariably does not discriminate very well across individuals. The major reason for this is usually that a test with too few items does not adequately sample individual behavior or actual task performance and hence individual scores may cluster together; with a greater sampling of responses, individual performance can be more clearly differentiated.

The Standardization Process

When we talk about the standardization process of test construction, we are really talking about two interrelated types of standardization. One type has to do with the standardization of procedures and materials such as uniform item administration, response recording and item sampling, together with uniform materials and environmental test conditions; the other type has to do with the selection of sample populations both nationally and on a regional basis, the collection of normative data, plus reliability and validity studies and the publication of a test manual.

Obviously the major task in constructing any type of screening measure is to put together a variety of items that can be administered and scored in a standardized way so that the same items may be applicable to all subjects of a given age, sex, ethnic origin and socioeconomic status; these items should accurately and efficiently discriminate between those children or adults who may possess a particular ability or condition from those who do not. On the surface, this may seem to be a relatively simple task; however, in the instance of screening such is frequently not the case. For example, in the area of screening for speech and language disability, the individual variability of language development for children under three years of age is very substantial; hence, not only must the measure have a good cross-section of speech and language items of varying difficulty levels, but also the test must try and control for the influences of the level of language sophistication in the child's home environment; for example, the differ--

ing opportunities the child is given for language usage; the amount of time his parents and siblings actually spend talking with him as well as whether the child may come from a bilingual home. Many or all of these influential factors may affect the child's speech and language development and actual ability. Selecting a truly representative sample in the standardization process together with the adequate collection of normative data will aid greatly in achieving an accurate screening measure.

Another crucial aspect of the standardization process is that the screening test be administered and scored in a uniform and consistent manner. This means that all the children assessed must receive the same set of directions, the same presentation of items, the same time limits (if the items are timed) and, whenever possible, take the test under the same kind of environmental conditions; i.e. appropriate lighting, heating, ventilation, sound control and freedom from interruption. A third condition of critical importance in the standardization process is that all the items must be scored according to some clearly defined set of criteria; this condition is of particular significance if some of the items are of a behavioral type, i.e. talks in sentences; is not shy with strangers. If all of the items are of a behavioral type, then not only must there be clearly defined scoring criteria, but also all the examiners using the screening test must be trained to achieve some appropriate inter-rater criterion level (usually an agreement ratio of .90 to .95) before being allowed to administer the measure.

After the details of scoring and test administraton are finalized, the next step is the selection of an appropriate standardization sample and the collection of normative data. This step is followed by checking the test's reliability and validity and finally the publication of an examiner's manual. Sampling procedures, the collection of norms and the publication of the test manual are topics that will be discussed below; however, both the reliability and validity aspects of test construction will be covered in considerable detail in Chapters 3 and 4. At this stage in our discussion, it is sufficient to state that any newly constructed screening measure must be reliable; i.e. measure the same thing accurately over time using different examiners in different test situations and it must be valid; i.e. predict or screen-out those individuals with a given disability or the potential for developing it.

Sampling and Sampling Adequacy

We now come to the question of the selection of a sample population for the standardization procedure. The crucial question here is what should the sample population consist of? The answer to such a question depends on what kinds of groups the measure has been constructed for and the overall purpose of the test. If the measure has been designed to screen preschool children across the country, then the population selected must adequately sample all preschool age-groups of both sexes across at least racial, ethnic and socioeconomic lines. If the measure, however, is designed for more specific groups, say white middle class three- and four-year-olds living in the Pacific Northwest, then the sample of children selected must truly represent the population of that region of North America. A second question related to adequate sampling has to do with the actual size of the sample selected. In general, relatively large stratified random samples offer the greatest number of advantages, although the cost of administering the test to such a sample can be substantial. Nevertheless, as both Bentzen (1963) and Satz (1975) have previously pointed out, samples based on large populations offer protection against potential attrition rates if follow-up studies are to be carried out on the original sample, a greater opportunity to provide more reliable base rate or prevalence rate estimates for a given disorder, and, in the identification of a disorder itself, a greater opportunity to reduce the potential confounding effects of sex, race, socioeconomic status and various cultural factors.

Although there are no legal or mandatory requirements that the test constructor has to meet before publishing a particular measure, the American Psychological Association has published an excellent book entitled *Standards for Educational and Psychological Tests* (1974), which clearly illustrates the *essential, very desirable,* and *desirable* elements in any published test. Unfortunately, for the field of measurement in general, and screening in particular, these standards are rarely, if ever, met. Probably the major reason is cost, followed closely by the reasons of time and personnel factors. The irony of this situation is frequently illustrated by the harsh criticism levelled at many measures and their constructors because the tests themselves do not do the job they are supposed to do, which, of course, is invariably related to the fact that the measure frequently does not meet even the minimum of the A.P.A. standards. Despite this rather common state of affairs, and in fairness to some test constructors, there are some tests published that do meet the high A.P.A. standards and do actually measure at a high level of accuracy.

Reference Groups in the Collection of Normative Data

In most test construction situations, the sample selected for the standardization of the measure will also be the standard by which all future test scores will be based. In other words, the average performance of the subjects in the standardization sample becomes the basic *reference performance* or *norm* against which future individual scores or performance will be compared. Because of the importance of this original sample of individuals in the future use of the test, it is not surprising that the individuals selected for this original sample must be truly representative. For if they do not adequately represent the future populations to be assessed, then the use of their test scores for normative purposes would be grossly inappropriate. Thus it is worth reiterating here that if a measure is to be used on a nation-wide basis, then the individuals selected for the standardization sample must reflect the population of the nation who will be assessed in the future. If, on the other hand, the measure is designed to be used on simply a regional or local basis, then the representativeness of the original sample should simply reflect the make-up of that particular region or locality. Although these latter two groups do not pose the same kinds of selection requirements or problems as a nation-wide sample would, they still require to be selected with the same kind of precision, with careful attention to such factors as socioeconomic status, urban/rural/suburban location, sex, occupation, education, race, ethnic origin and public, private or parochial school instruction (Angoff and Anderson, 1967).

Before leaving this section on standardization and norms, some brief mention should be made of criterion-referenced measures. As stated earlier, a person's score on an appropriately constructed and standardized test is interpreted in terms of its relationship to the distribution of scores of the original standardization sample. Therefore, the major characteristic of what is quite frequently referred to as a norm-referenced measure is that scores are interpreted on the basis of where the individual stands with respect to some appropriate larger population. Unlike norm-referenced tests, scores on criterion-referenced measures are interpreted as possessing some sort of absolute meaning in themselves regardless of the scores made by the normative group. In other words, the score an individual obtains is indicative of a specific level of performance or specific degree of mastery.

Criterion-referenced measures fall into two basic categories; domain-referenced and objective-referenced. A domain-referenced test is one in which the individual's overall score has absolute meaning; i.e. the score indicates what proportion of a specific domain (subject area) the individual has mastered. For example, one might wish to determine a child's overall ability to spell; a domain-referenced test to measure this ability might consist of a list of the 200 most commonly printed words in the English language (as defined by the Thorndike-Lorge List of Word Frequencies; Thorndike and Lorge (1944). The child's score on such a measure would indicate his specific level of performance in the area of spelling. On the other hand, an objective-referenced test refers to a specific objective that is to be achieved by the individual. Such a test usually consists of a relatively small number of items which have been drawn from a larger set of possible items. Frequently the objective of such a measure is mastery of a particular skill or the acquisition of a specific piece of information, and, logically, we might expect that mastery be defined by a perfect score. However, in real life situations, most test constructors and field practitioners find it extremely difficult to get all individuals to perform in such a perfect way and so they usually settle for something a little less than perfect, such as 90 percent correct. This is, of course, an example of using normative data as the basis of establishing the standard of performance (the criterion score). This kind of criterion score can be found in such a screening test as the Denver Developmental Screening Test, where the criterion of a *pass* on a given item for a given age-group is defined as one that was *passed* by 90 percent of the normative group (standardization sample).

Because both norm-referenced and criterion-referenced measures are constructed according to the same basic psychological measurement principles, a short general discussion of some of their different characteristics may be of benefit. First, it is important to realize that some measures may be both norm-referenced and criterion-referenced; in other words, norm-referenced and criterion-referenced measures are not mutually exclusive. In fact, in many situations, it is essential that a criterion-referenced test have appropriate norms, otherwise the user of the measure will have no idea of what level of performance it is reasonable to expect. For example, in determining the level of vocabulary mastery of a three-year-old, what is a reasonable expectation of word acquisition, 500 words, 10,000, 25,000? Normative data from an appropriate sample of three-year-olds will tell us what is reasonable. Furthermore, norms for criterion-referenced tests are collected in the same way as we have previously discussed for norm-referenced measures. The norms themselves may be used in a very similar way, to evaluate the performance of an individual in relation to some standard group; for objective criterion-referenced tests the norms provide the standard by which an individual may be considered as having *passed* or *failed* a particular objective (skill). Hence, in many ways, criterion-referenced measures are simply a special category of norm-referenced tests, frequently used for different purposes, i.e. achievement, course or subject evaluation, absolute level of learning, but they are definitely not a separate species.

There are, of course, some basic differences between norm-referenced and criterion-referenced measures. For example, one basic difference has been beautifully explained by Popham and Husek (1969) as follows:

> The issue of variability is at the core of the difference between norm-referenced and criterion-referenced tests. Since the meaningfulness of a norm-referenced score is basically dependent on the relative position of the score in comparison with other scores, the more variability in the scores the better. With a norm-referenced test, we want to be able to tell Jamie from Joey from Frank, and we feel more secure about telling them apart if their scores are very different.
>
> With criterion-referenced tests, variability is irrelevant. The meaning of the score is not dependent on comparison with other

scores; it flows directly from the connection between the items and the criterion. It is, of course, true that one almost always gets variance scores on any psychological test; but the variability is not a necessary condition for a good criterion-referenced test.

In other words, what these authors seem to be saying is that one can have a worthwhile and useful criterion-referenced test with low variability of scores; i.e. individuals either master a particular task or objective or they don't.

Another basic difference between the two is in the area of prediction. By and large, the major purpose of many measures is to predict something in the future, such as (1) success in school, business or college, or (2) mastering the content of a course, a book, or (3) the absence or presence (actual or potential) of a particular condition or disorder. In essence, criterion-referenced measures have as their basic purpose evaluative measurement, not predictions; they generally provide a direct measure of whether a particular and specific criterion has been achieved. Thus, in a sense, predictive validity has very little meaning when applied to criterion-referenced measures, because their major purpose is to describe what the individual is capable of doing right now (when compared to a specific criterion) and not what he may be capable of achieving (or not achieving) in the future. Of course, it is possible that the score on a criterion-referenced test may be correlated to some future event or circumstance, and in that sense predicted; however, such a prediction is coincidental to the major purpose of the measure. In other words, the *criterion* of a criterion-referenced test is always in the here and now; it is what the test measures and has nothing to do with predicting future performance. In this case, unlike with a predictive measure, we are primarily concerned with what the test actually measures rather than what it predicts and how well. For example, a good predictive measure of success in architecture may be high scores on a visual and spatial memory test; in that case we are not directly interested in how well the test measures visual and spatial memory, only that scores on this particular test highly predict success in architecture. For a very comprehensive and much more detailed discussion of criterion-referenced testing, see Shaycoft (1979).

Test Manuals and Their Construction

When the test construction process, including, of course, both reliability and validity studies, is done, the final phase of the standardization procedure can be completed. This final phase consists of a rather detailed write-up of a test manual. The manual should clearly and concisely provide the test user with such information as the basic purpose or objectives of the screening measure, the population(s) for which it has been devised and its recommended uses. Other information which should be provided includes: details (composition, etc.) of the standardization sample, the actual norms of performance by age, sex, geographic region (if a nation-wide measure) and any other significant variables the test constructor may have collected data on; item selection, item difficulty levels, item discrimination, item and subtest intercorrelations and which items, if any, are timed; the measure's reliability coefficients, the types of coefficients computed and the standard error of measurement; the validity coefficients, types of validity assessed and the criteria used and, specifically, if a screening measure, the predictive hit rates achieved together with the test's degree of sensitivity and specificity; the measure's relationships with other tests (if computed) and an evaluation of the test's particular strengths and limitations, both for the purposes for which it was designed and in regards to other uses it might be considered appropriate for; and, finally, detailed instructions for item administration, scoring and interpretation.

Administration, Scoring, Interpretation and the Reporting of Test Findings

No matter how well a test constructor may have done his job, his measure is simply a tool to be used by test examiners. Consequently, the success of the measure for the purposes for which it has been designed will be directly related to how well it is administered and the accuracy with which it is scored and interpreted. Even in the case of large-scale screening tests, which normally do not require administration by professionally trained personnel, the importance of trained paraprofessional or volunteer examiners cannot be emphasized enough, as Thorpe and Werner (1974) have previously pointed out so well. Related to the issue

of the adequate training of screening examiners is the demonstrated necessity (Frankenburg, Goldstein and Camp, 1971; Reid,
1970) for random but periodic reliability checks on examiner
accuracy in both test administration and scoring. Obviously, one
of the aims of any mass screening program is the administration
of the measure in as uniform a manner as possible, so that regardless of who the examiner is, each child is given the test in exactly
the same way. As mentioned earlier, this uniformity is of critical
importance when the items are concerned with specific behaviors
which have to meet a certain criterion level of performance.

There is less issue concerning the interpretation of the results
of a screening measure than there is for a diagnostic measure, for
example, which usually calls for a clinical judgment of some kind;
however, when the screening examiner is in doubt as to whether
a child passed or failed the screening test, consultation with an
experienced health professional is highly desirable. The actual
reporting of the results of an individual's performance on the
screening measure is one that is usually best left to the health
professional who is responsible for the primary care of the child;
however, whoever reports the results to the parents and other
involved health personnel should do so promptly and with considerable care and sensitivity.

Chapter 3

RELIABILITY

THIS CHAPTER is not meant to be a definitive discussion on the concept of reliability in psychological measurement, but rather it is intended as a general introduction to a vast and complex topic.

In this book we are primarily concerned with preschool screening measures and their relative merits and potential deficiencies. As is well known in the psychological measurement field, all measures are subject to error and screening tests are no exception. In the selection of a particular screening measure, we not only want to know how well it has been constructed but also whether it is a reliable and valid instrument. We will discuss the validity issue in the next chapter, but here we will try and grapple with the issue of test reliability.

First, it is a fact of life that whenever anything is measured, whether it be a physical, biological or psychological characteristic or attribute, that measurement will contain a certain amount of chance error. As a consequence of this error, when we measure a particular attribute a second time, we are not likely to obtain exactly the same score as we did the first time. This inconsistency in test scores from one administration to another may vary from minimal to substantial, but in either case will constitute the measure's level of unreliability. On the other hand, however, repeated measures of a particular characteristic nearly always show some degree of consistency (due to an individual's stable and persistent characteristics in responding) and it is this tendency towards consistency from one test administration to another that we call reliability. Hence, in any measure we may consider, screening

53

or otherwise, we will find some degree of reliability and unreliability with one becoming greater as the other becomes less; i.e. if a measure has very high consistency from one administration to another, then the amount of inconsistency will be correspondingly low and we will have found a measure with high reliability.

To illustrate more fully this point, suppose we were to subject a particular substance to a series of measures; for example, 100 repeated chemical analyses to determine the percentage of strontium 90 in a single batch of milk. What we would obtain is 100 *estimates* of the *true* percentage of strontium 90 in the batch of milk. These one hundred estimates would have a frequency distribution of a certain range, which would constitute the variance of the distribution and would tell us the variability and, hence, the size or magnitude of the errors of measurement of our particular chemical analysis. We would expect, in the above example, that this error variance, as it is more commonly called, would be relatively small, providing, of course, that the personnel, the equipment and purity of the chemicals used in the analysis were kept constant. Were we, however, to use a variety of different personnel, equipment and batches of chemicals in our 100 estimates, we might expect the variability (range) across estimates to be somewhat wider with a corresponding increase in the size of our errors of measurement. (Due in part to differences in the judgements of personnel involved, variations and accuracy of the equipment used and the differences in the purity of the chemical used in the analysis.)

One might well ask why the particular example above was used and not one that involved repeated measurements on human subjects, as this is supposed to be a book on the screening of human behavior. In theory it is possible to carry out repeated measures on specific human behaviors and/or attributes; however, in practice it is rarely if ever done because over the course of a long series of independent repeated measures, the individual does not remain exactly the same, he gets tired, remembers items from previous administrations, corrects items he thought he got wrong before, improves his performance with practice and so on. As a result of such individual effects, the test variance and errors of measurement on tests of human behavior are usually estimated indirectly.

Obviously the degree of reliability of a particular measure or set of measurements is of critical importance in the consideration and selection of any given test. This is true not only in research situations but also in practical situations where the measure is going to be used on a day-to-day basis. In fact, this latter situation probably requires the most serious consideration of a measure's reliability because, on the basis of its results, some very significant decisions may be made about an individual's future; for example, referral or nonreferral, on the part of a screening examiner, to a diagnostic or other specialist centre, or selection for a particular job, career or training program on the part of a psychologist in industry, personnel work or education.

Accuracy of a particular measure, then, is of prime importance to the screening examiner and other things being equal, i.e. the test is valid, he will always be looking for the most reliable test available; in other words, he will want to select that measure which will provide the most precise estimate of the characteristic (attribute) being studied. Thus, any degree of unreliability in a particular test is, in a sense, undesirable and distressing because it means that a judgement made by the screening examiner must be to a certain extent tentative. Of course, it goes without saying that the lower the reliability of the measure, the more tentative the examiner's judgement or decision will be until at the extreme case, i.e. zero reliability, the individual's score on the test provides *no basis* for any kind of decision or judgement.

Given that the reliability of a measure is directly affected by errors of measurement, of one kind or another, the following section will look at the various sources of variation in test scores. Although we will try to document all the possible sources of variance, the major focus of the discussion will be on those sources of variation that affect the reliability of screening measures in particular. Table II, which is reproduced from Stanley (1971), provides an overview of the possible sources of variance of scores on a particular test.

Table II

POSSIBLE SOURCES OF VARIANCE OF SCORES
ON A PARTICULAR TEST

I. Lasting and general characteristics of the individual
   A. Level of ability on one or more general traits, which operate in a number of tests
   B. General skills and techniques of taking tests ("test wiseness" or "test naiveté")
   C. General ability to comprehend instructions

II. Lasting but specific characteristics of the individual
   A. Specific to the test as a whole (and to parallel forms of it)
      1. Individual level of ability on traits required in this test but not in others
      2. Knowledge and skills specific to particular forms of test items
      3. Stable response sets, e.g. to mark A options more frequently than other options of multiple-choice items, to mark true-false items "true" when undecided, or to choose socially desirable options.
   B. Specific to particular test items
      1. The "chance" element determining whether the individual does or does not know a particular fact (sampling variance in a finite number of items, not the probability of his guessing the answer)
      2. Item types, such as the data-sufficiency items of the Scholastic Aptitude Test, with which various examinees are unequally familiar (c.f. II. A. 2)

III. Temporary but general characteristics of the individual
   (Factors affecting performance on many or all tests at a particular time)
   A. Health
   B. Fatigue
   C. Motivation
   D. Emotional strain
   E. Test-wiseness (partly lasting; cf. I. B)
   F. Understanding of mechanics of testing
   G. External conditions of heat, light, ventilation, etc.

IV. Temporary and specific characteristics of the individual
   A. Specific to a test as a whole
      1. Comprehension of the specific test task (insofar as this is distinct from I. B)
      2. Specific tricks or techniques of dealing with the particular test materials (insofar as distinct from II. A. 2)
      3. Level of practice on the specific skills involved (especially in psychomotor tests)
      4. Momentary "set" for a particular test
   B. Specific to particular test items
      1. Fluctuations and idiosyncrasies of human memory
      2. Unpredictable fluctuations in attention or accuracy, superimposed upon the general level of performance characteristic of the individual

V. Systematic or chance factors affecting the administration of the test or the appraisal of test performance
   A. Conditions of testing — adherence to time limits, freedom from distractions, clarity of instructions, etc.
   B. Interaction of personality, sex, or race of examiner with that of examinee to facilitate or inhibit performance
   C. Unreliability or bias in grading or rating performance

VI. Variance not otherwise accounted for (chance)
   A. Luck in selection of answers by sheer guessing
   B. Momentary distraction

From Julian C. Stanley, Reliability, in R. L. Thorndike (Ed.), *Educational Measurement*, second edition. Washington, American Council on Education, 1971. Reprinted by permission.

As will be noted in the discussion that follows, there are two basic sources of variation, one we may call *systematic variance* which may be defined as a *persistent lasting characteristic of each individual, causing stable individual differences in test performance.* For example, a person's general level of reading ability or his ability to comprehend verbal instructions are both general personal characteristics that each and every one of us possesses and which will in a general way influence the way we perform in a test situation; they become a source of variance, however, because each person has them in different degrees and so they will affect the way each of us performs, although they will do so in a systematic way. The other source of variation is due to what we may call nonsystematic or *error variance* and may be defined as unpredictable and short-term unstable characteristics of our performance; they constitute such things as how we feel at the time of testing (tired, keyed up, emotionally upset), freedom from distractions in the test situation, the kind of examiner we get and so on. These factors do not systematically affect the way we perform because they may vary from day to day or hour to hour or may be present in varying degrees at one test time and completely absent at another.

As one can observe from Table II, the possible sources of variation are substantial and the task of the test constructor to control all of these sources of variance is almost an impossible one; however, the more sources he is successful in controlling for, the higher the probability that he will end up with a reliable measure. There are, however, two types of persistent general factors that are almost impossible for a test constructor to completely control for; one of these is the individual's general ability to comprehend instructions; the other is the individual's *test wiseness,* i.e. his degree of wisdom in testing and test situations, his shrewdness in knowing when to guess, his perceptiveness in picking up cues from either the examiner or the format of the test itself and his general freedom from anxiety and emotional tension). Unless we are actually testing for these two factors, it is imperative that their effects be kept to a minimum because the more they influence test performance, the less the test is actually measuring what it is designed to measure.

Lasting, but specific characteristics of the individual refer basically to persistent characteristics of a person's performance, but ones which only apply in certain areas, say spelling or arithmetic and not in other tests of performance; for example, a person may always be inconsistent in his ability to spell words or compute arithmetically, but his ability in areas such as language comprehension or concept formation may be extremely consistent. Similarly, on a spelling test the format of the test itself may affect the way that the specific individual characteristics operate; i.e. one individual may perform very effectively on a spelling test if the words are presented orally and he writes them down, while another individual may be more efficient if the words are presented visually and then he has to recognize which words are spelled incorrectly. Another factor, which is often of concern in screening measures, (although frequently ignored by many constructors of screening tests) has to do with the stability of response sets. Many screening measures are of the multiple choice, true-false or yes-no type and there is now a substantial amount of evidence to suggest that individuals frequently perform on these types of measures in a very consistent way; i.e. they may more frequently respond *yes* than *no* or *true* than *false* or choose wherever possible the most socially desirable response. (See Couch and Keniston, 1960; Edwards, 1957; 1959; and Orne, 1962, for more detailed discussions on these issues.)

Temporary but general characteristics of the individual are factors which are particularly germane to measures of screening because so many of those screened are young children. Factors such as health, fatigue, level of motivation, emotional upset and certain extraneous conditions such as heat, light and ventilation can substantially affect a young child's test performance. However, these factors probably become progressively less and less significant in screening as the individual moves from infancy and preschool age to adolescence and adulthood, although the degree of their significance would partly depend on whether we were testing for general vocabulary or emotional characteristics such as mood or feeling tone.

Temporary and specific characteristics of the individual will include such factors as the individual's general level of practice at the time of testing (particularly significant if the test is measuring complex coordination or specific motor skills), his mental set (for example, the individual's emphasis on speed or accuracy on a timed test), his ability to get the hang of certain techniques required for optimal test performance and his level of understanding or his personal ideas about how the test scores may be used (very important if the measures taken are assessing personality, personal and social interests and attitudes).

Systematic or chance factors affecting the administration of the test or the appraisal of test performance are also of particular importance in the development of screening measures. Nearly all screening tests, and particularly those used for children, involve the administration of test items by one or more examiners. These measures are frequently administered in health centers, doctors' offices and educational or pre-educational settings. Hence, such factors as variations in noise levels, degree of distraction and privacy of the testing area commonly affect the results of developmental screening in such settings and can bring about considerable variability in test performance. Similarly, the experience and rapport-building qualities of the examiners, their ability to follow test directions in both administration and scoring and their ability to make nonbiased judgements when appraising individual behavior are all factors that must be identified and controlled for as much as possible in order to reduce the error variance of the measure used.

Finally, in all tests and measures so far devised, there is always some amount of variance that cannot be identified precisely; this variance is usually designated as resulting from pure chance; i.e. such things as guessing at answers or momentary distractions of the individual through time.

As all the above factors may, in one way or another, affect the consistency of any given measure (screening tests included), we are faced with the problem of determining the type of consistency which, to us, seems the most significant to evaluate. Essentially, we have to answer two basic questions: do we wish to know how consistent our test is in measuring individual performance at a particular moment in time, and do we wish to know how consistent individual performance is over time, i.e. from day to day or week to week? For some people, consistency at a particular moment in time will be of the greatest importance; however, for the purposes of screening, we wish to use our test results to predict something about the individual in the future; hence, we require a measure that is reliable (consistent) over a period of time.

The final section of this chapter will be devoted to a discussion of the various procedures for estimating reliability. Some of these procedures are more commonly used for estimating reliability for screening measures than others and these will be given more detailed coverage; however, all the procedures are relevant and may be used, depending, of course, on how the test has been constructed, i.e. one form or two.

Before these major procedures are discussed, one or two more general comments should be made. First, in the evaluation of the reliability of any given measure, we are attempting to determine its *consistency* preferably through repeated measurements of the same objects or items or groups of items; however, as discussed earlier, in tests of human behavior, this is not really feasible because the individual is likely to be changed from one administration to the next; hence, it is necessary to limit the number of times a single person is measured. The usual practice for obtaining reliability estimates on measures of human behavior is to get *two* measurements for each individual in a representative group. The stability of the results is acheived not, then, by increasing the number of measurements on each individual, but by increasing the number of individuals receiving the test. It may be of additional interest for the reader to know that in a similar way the reliability of a measure may be increased by increasing the number of its items. (See Sax, 1974, for a more detailed discussion.) In most cases, these measurements yield two sets of scores (one for each test administration) and it is these two sets of scores that are used for the analysis of the reliability coefficient. This analysis usually consists of computing the coefficient of correlation between the two sets of scores, which provides an *estimate* of the average consistency of the test for the group taking it. The closer the correlation coefficient (subscript r) approaches 1.00, the lower the errors of measurement; so, a test with perfect reliability would have an r of 1.00 and there would be *no* errors of measurement. A reliability coefficient of .90 would mean that 90 percent of the variance of obtained scores on a given measure was due to true score variation, while 10 percent of the variance of the obtained scores was due to errors of measurement. One point that should be noted here is that the score that an individual makes on any given measure is not his *true* score but is his *obtained* score, i.e. it is the score he obtained from one administration of the test. To find out what an individual's true score is on any given test would require numerous (say 500) administrations and then the computing of the mean (average) of those 500 scores. As this procedure is neither necessary nor feasible (because of potential changes to the individual over time), we estimate a person's *true* score from his *obtained* score plus the *error variance* score for the test given. Frequently, this error variance score is referred to as the *standard error of measurement,* which is simply the square root of the test's error variance.

In any discussion of procedures for estimating reliability, it is usual to include considerable detailed analysis of the various testing and statistical procedures proposed for determining the necessary coefficient of correlation. However, the purpose of this book is not statistical in nature, but rather is to provide a more general overview of the concepts and measurement procedures behind screening measures. Therefore, instead of detailed analyses of statistical formulae, etc., the procedures will be discussed in general terms and a specific formula for computing a particular coefficient will be referred to by name and an appropriate reference given should the reader wish to pursue the matter in greater depth.

Procedure I: Administration of two equivalent tests and correlation of the resulting scores.* This procedure is often referred to as the parallel forms technique and consists of correlating the scores of each individual on two parallel forms of the same measurement; the Pearson *product moment correlation coefficient* is usually computed and the resulting *r* provides an estimate of the degree of equivalence between the two forms. The resulting

---

*The descriptive headings for the basic procedures on estimating the test reliability are taken from Thorndike (1967).

correlation coefficient *(r)* may yield two basic pieces of information depending on whether both forms were administered on the same day or whether they were given several days or a couple of weeks apart. If both forms were given on the same day, we will essentially obtain an *estimate of equivalence* or the degree to which each form is measuring the same thing (characteristic, attribute, etc.). Whatever unreliability exists (1.00 - *r*) we can assume stems from differences in *item sampling* (within the two forms) and not from changes in the individuals themselves. If, however, the two forms are given several weeks apart, the corresponding correlation coefficient will provide us with not only an estimate of equivalence but also an *estimate of stability*. In other words, this second correlation coefficient includes not only those errors of measurement related to item sampling, but also errors related to temporal changes and individual changes in performance. The idea behind having two parallel forms of the same measure is that one form may be substituted for another (a particularly useful option if the examiner wishes to determine the effects of a particular treatment, or other intervention procedure, given between the administration of the two different forms).

The task of designing two equivalent forms for a particular measure is not necessarily a difficult one, although it may be more time-consuming because one requires a substantially larger number of items in the sample pool than for a test that will only consist of one form. The only time the task of constructing two parallel forms may become truly difficult is when either the test itself is a truly unique one, i.e. a one-of-a-kind problem-solving task, or when exposure to the test the first time is such a learning experience for the individual that he is quite *changed* by the time of the second administration because the experience of being tested the first time increased his knowledge or practice significantly.

At the present time, the author knows of only one screening measure that is currently available in equivalent or parallel forms, the Peabody Picture Vocabulary Test, but should anyone consider designing such a screening device in the future, certain detailed specifications should be drawn up in advance of any actual test construction. Such specifications should include the types of items required, the difficulty levels, the procedures and standards by which the items are to be judged and the distribution of items in regards to the content to be covered. Each equivalent form should then be built according to the specifications made and within these specifications each test should be made up of a random sampling of items. Usually, the most practical way of constructing parallel forms is to put together the two forms from a single (large) pool of items which have already been tried out for suitability, etc. Within the total test, items from the sample pool should be assigned to the two forms so that each form has the same distribution of item difficulties and the same distribution of item - test correlations, i.e. the degree to which each item correlates with the total test score.

Procedure II: Repeated administration of the same test form or testing procedure and correlation of the resulting scores. The procedure to be discussed here is more commonly called the test-retest technique and consists of two administrations of the same test to the same individuals, but separated by some period of time (in days or weeks or sometimes months). These two sets of scores are then computed, again using the Pearson *product moment correlation coefficient,* to provide an estimate of the test's stability over time. This procedure is the one most commonly used in determining the reliability coefficients of screening measures. It is, however a procedure which is more acceptable for some forms of measurement than others. For example, if we have devised a particular scale for measuring weight, say in grams, all we need to do to check the stability of our measuring device is weigh the same objects on it on two occasions separated by some period of time. In fact, most if not all measures of physiology or anatomy fall into this category and the procedure is highly acceptable because we are not sampling items from a larger universe of behavior. Similarly, there are certain measures of behavior where the problem of sampling from a larger universe of items does not occur; for example, in measuring perception of brightness or reaction time, in which the individual's performance is measured by repeatedly testing his brightness perception on the same machine or his reaction time to the same stimulus, the test tasks are defined so that sampling from a more extensive universe of behavior is nonexistent. Therefore, in all these types of measures, the repetition of the test over time is a perfectly acceptable way to determine its reliability.

However, in measures of human behavior, i.e. intellect, language ability, temperament, etc., correlating two sets of scores from the same test is not a highly desirable way of calculating reliability. There are several reasons for this lack of desirability, one of which has to do with what one form of a test actually represents. All single tests consist of a limited sample of items from a much larger universe of possible items; (think, for example, of the possible universe of items for a test of vocabulary). When we obtain an individual's test score, for most practical purposes we use it as representative of the individual's ability to respond to all of the items in our possible universe of items for that particular test. Thus, reliability is not only a measure of the consistency of individual behavior over time, it is also a measure of the *adequacy* of our sampling of items out of the possible universe of items. Obtaining two sets of scores on the same measure keeps the sampling of items constant, yet we know from the reliability studies of parallel forms of a test that a certain amount of error variance stems from differences in item sampling. Consequently, reliability coefficients calculated by the test-retest procedure may be expected to yield spuriously higher correlations than those based on parallel forms, because the error variance associated with item sampling has been omitted.

A second and perhaps more obvious reason why the test-retest reliability procedure is not always desirable stems from such factors as memory for particular items and practice effects. The impact of these particular factors will depend on the length of the test, i.e. the number of items, the distinctiveness of the individual items, and the length of the time interval between the two test administrations.

The final reason why this procedure is not always the most preferred has to do with the attitudes and motivation of the individuals involved in the testing. For example, if the test being evaluated is very long, tedious, boring, or requires intense amounts of concentration or rapid responding, the individual's attitudes and levels of motivation may change from the first to the second administration, thus lowering the correlation between the two administrations. With computer technology, it is now possible to randomize the order of items, or item options, from one test administration to the next providing, of course, the items are not arranged in a sharp difficulty gradient. Such randomization, although not very powerful in counteracting attitude or motivational factors, may often be quite successful in combatting memory sets or the memorization of specific items.

Procedure III: Subdivision of a single test into two presumably equivalent groups of items, each scored separately, and correlation of the resulting two scores.

This procedure is often called the internal consistency or split-half technique and consists of artificially subdividing the total test into two half-length tests and correlating the scores on each half. This single administration of one test and then extracting an estimate of its reliability by splitting into two halves is often used on measures that have been designed for research purposes or for practical situations where costs in time, personnel and/or materials are so high that preparing two forms, or administering the test twice, is economically out of the question. It is important to note, however, that this type of correlation coefficient does *not* give a reliability estimate for the full test, but for one only *half as long*. To obtain the reliability estimate for the full test, statistical formulae derived by Spearman-Brown must be used (see Jackson and Messick, p. 231, 1967 for their derivation).

There are at least two major characteristics of reliability estimation from part (half) scores that make it differ from two separate tests; the first is that the two parts are not separately timed, and the second is that the performances on these two parts are adjacent to each other or may even be intermingled in time. These two characteristics may often place limitations on split-half reliability coefficients. One major limitation may come if the test under evaluation is some form of speed test and one half score consists of the first half of the items and the other half score comes from the second half of the items. In this type of situation one cannot meaningfully compare the two scores because the individual's score on the second half of the test will depend, to a great extent, on how fast he completed the first half, i.e. the number of items he completes on the second half of the measure will strongly depend on how much time he had left to answer them. In general, reliability estimates for speed tests based on split-halves tend to be misleadingly high; hence, when selecting a speed test one should be alert to what the reliability estimate is based on. The other major limitation of split-half reliability coefficients is the fact that there is no time interval between the two test performances. In other words, not only are the two performances adjacent in time, but also they may even be intermingled (see following discussion on odd - even (alternate) item presentations). One of the consequences of an adjacent or an intermingled performance is that the fluctuations in performance over time (minute to minute, day to day or week to week), which are usually allocated to error variance, cannot be so allocated for a test whose two halves are being given at the same time. Hence, split test reliabilities of even unspeeded tests may be spuriously high, especially if the variance from time fluctuations is likely to be substantial.

There are four major selection procedures that may be used should we decide to employ reliability estimates from part scores. The first method we may use equates the two half tests for content and difficulty level. The idea here is to choose items specifically for each half so that they are as equivalent as possible. Items, then, would be selected so as to meet the specifications for the whole test, but within these limits, items would be assigned to either half on the basis of chance (random assignment). The reliability coefficient for the half test would then be based on the correlation between the two halves. It is possible to have a compromise between what is suggested here and the actual compilation of parallel forms. For example, we could prepare sufficient items for one test, but arrange them into two equivalent and separately timed halves. The halves could be administered consecutively in time or on separate days; the sum of the two halves would provide the total score for the measure itself. The advantages of such a compromise include less time and money spent on preparing two parallel forms, reduced administration time (for both examiners and subjects), and, if the two equivalent halves are given on different days, the opportunity to obtain an estimate of reliability which will include error variance for time fluctuations.

The second method we may use is to split the test in half on the basis of selecting alternate items. The most common procedure used is to have one half of the test made up of all the odd numbered items and the other half to consist of all the even numbered items. If the test consists of several successive items in one topic area, or if the items become progressively more difficult, then this procedure will automatically divide the items in an even manner. However, it should be noted that this method will only approximate equivalence in the two half tests. It also means that moment-to-moment fluctuations in efficiency or memory will tend to make performance on successive items more similar than on items more widely separated on the test. Hence, moment to moment fluctuations in efficiency, etc., which are usually attributed to error variance, will not occur and may thus contribute to a spuriously high reliability estimate.

A third method of splitting a test is a variation of the second procedure discussed, only this time items are selected on the basis of alternate *groups* of items. Quite frequently one may find measures that have a whole series of items closely related in content, i.e. items on a reading test all based on the same paragraph or passage. Whenever a group of items appear to share a specific or common content, it is preferable to put them together in one half or the other of the split halves, so that each half of the test is made up of alternate groups of *items*. One of the advantages of this procedure over the odd - even method is that it tends to account for more moment-to-moment fluctuations in efficiency and memory as error variance, and consequently the reliability coefficient is likely to be a more appropriate (less spurious) estimate of the test reliability.

The fourth and final method of splitting a test is by the first versus the second half procedure. Essentially this method was also devised in order to reduce a spuriously high correlation coefficient due to relatively short time fluctuations in performance not being accounted for by error variance. Although this method may avoid such correlated errors of measurement it produces other kinds of difficulties, especially if items become more difficult as the test progresses or if there is a systematic shift in content (from one topic area to another) somewhere between the beginning and the end of the test. In these types of situations, the two split halves are clearly not equivalent and, despite its shortcomings, it is usually preferable to use the odd - even procedure.

Procedure IV: Analysis of variance among items. This procedure essentially uses all the information available about consistency of performance from item to item within the test. It produces a type of reliability coefficient similar to those obtained through Procedure III (split-half methods) and has many of the same characteristics and limitations. It is essential in this procedure, as in split-half procedures, that *the examinee have the opportunity to consider and respond to each item.* If this does not occur, then item characteristics such as item difficulty, item variance and item intercorrelations may become so distorted as to be meaningless. Though individuals may, of course, deliberately not respond to specific items, they must have the opportunity and time to attempt each item; consistency of performance cannot be evaluated unless the subject has an opportunity to perform on the entire test.

Usually the most useful formula for estimating reliability coefficients from the relationship of item variance to total test variance is the Kuder-Richardson Formula No. 20 (which is available in nearly all standard textbooks on psychological statistics). Another formula (derived by Hoyt, 1941) which uses analysis of variance techniques for estimating test reliability via consistency of individual performance across test items, may also be employed. For detailed discussions of these methods see Thorndike (1967) and Stanley (1971).

It is important to note that the above procedure cannot be used if sheer speed is an important element in the taking of a particular test. In the case of speed test situations it is essential that reliability coefficients be obtained by correlating scores from two *separately timed* tests or half tests, rather than on scores from a test with a single time limit. The reason for this is that unless one splits the single test into two halves and gives them separately, one cannot separate out the differential effects of speed versus power (ultimate functioning ability). Thus, by splitting the test in half time-wise rather than item-wise (say fifteen minutes for each measure, providing each half is parallel in item content and difficulty), one is more likely to obtain a valid measure of the test's reliability.

One special kind of reliability procedure that should also be reported on in this chapter is the one usually referred to as *inter-rater reliability* or *inter-observer agreement*. This type of reliability coefficient is extremely important whenever a measure has a large number of items that require the examiner to make an observational judgement of whether the examinee passed a particular item or not. In this type of test situation we are concerned not so much about the reliability of the item per se but rather on the *reliability* of the examiners to judge *accurately* and *consistently* individual performance on each item. Inter-rater reliability is usually derived by having all the examiners who will be administering a particular measure observe and evaluate at the same time, a number of testees' performances on the given test. Their scores on each testee are then correlated and the resulting correlation constitutes the inter-observer reliability coefficient. Although personal bias and the so-called halo effect contribute to low inter-rater reliability, the most common problem related to examiner consistency has to do with item performance being poorly or ambiguously defined by the test constructor.

For those readers wishing to delve further and at greater depth into the realm of test reliability the author recommends the following: Cronbach, Gleser, Nanda and Rajaratnam (1971), Lord and Novick (1968), Stanley (1971), and Thorndike and Hagen (1977).

Chapter 4

VALIDITY

THE PRESENT CHAPTER ON TEST VALIDITY is again not meant to be an in-depth analysis of the concept of validity, but rather a general overview of the field and a discussion of the importance of test validation for any measures related to screening.

In the field of education and psychological measurement, a great deal has been written about the different procedures for validating tests, much of which is beyond the scope of this book; however, for those who would like to grapple with the more intricate details of validity the author suggests reading the following: American Psychological Association (1974); Campbell and Fiske (1959); Cronbach (1971); Cronbach and Meehl (1955); Ebel (1967); Payne and McManis (1967).

The concept of test validation is simply and best described by one of the most insightful researchers on the topic (Cronbach, 1971) as "the process of examining the *accuracy* of a specific prediction or inference made from a test score." Test validation may be described as a process of investigation; an investigation into the soundness of all the interpretations we may make about an individual's test score or performance.

Prior to the early 1950s, test validation consisted, almost exclusively, of checking a test's score against something else; usually an observation by an independent judge, or a test score on some other measure was used as an outside criterion. The merits of the test were then determined by how well (accurately) its score predicted to this criteria.

Since 1950 the concept of test validation has expanded to include not only predictive validity but also content and construct

70

validity (descriptive or theoretical interpretations); as well as considerable emphasis on the logical and procedural requirements for validation studies.

Before entering into a discussion of these different types of validation it is necessary for us to digress for a moment and consider some of the more general aspects of test validity. Basically, we may use specific measures for at least two purposes; to make decisions about the individual being tested and to describe him. In the first case, the decisions we make usually have to do with future events, i.e. some later level of performance, and so we are particularly concerned with criterion (predictive) validation; in the second case, descriptive tests rely most heavily on content or underlying constructs, so here we are more concerned with content or construct validity. This type of dichotomy is not meant to imply that for decision making we are solely interested in prediction and not content or underlying constructs (or vice versa), only that our major emphasis is on the test's ability to predict some later level of performance. The matter is complicated, however, by the fact that a measure may be used for both decision-making and descriptive purposes; for example, we may use, say, the Strong–Campbell Interest Inventory (1977) as a predictor of later job success and/or satisfaction, or we may use it descriptively to provide increased understanding to the individual about himself. The point being made here is that a single measure may be used in a variety of different ways, so when we talk about a test's validity, we are not necessarily talking about an overall estimate of its worth, but rather the validity of a particular interpretation for which it is being put to use. For example, we might use a reading test to screen children for entry into an advanced program, or for placement in a remedial class, or as a measure of effectiveness of a particular instructional program. Since the application of this reading test is based on three different interpretations, in order to use the test appropriately, we really need three different validity estimates. In other words, evidence that the test is an excellent screening measure for advanced training does not necessarily make it a valid measure for evaluating instructional effectiveness.

Another aspect of test validation that must be taken into account is that the estimate derived is not just of the measure itself, i.e. the test itself is only one element in the entire validation procedure; every aspect of the test setting and every detail of the test administration has to be taken into account. This is why a test manual is such an essential part of any published measure available, for it is in the manual that such factors must be spelled out with clarity and great detail. If a test manual is not printed or does not spell out *clearly* all the procedures involved in regards to setting, required examiner behavior, test administration, scoring, etc., then it becomes virtually impossible for another investigator to conduct a validation study accurately. Let us now turn to a discussion of the major empirical methods for determining a test's validity coefficient.

CONTENT VALIDITY

This type of validty is estimated on the basis of showing how well the content of the test (total number of items, observations or whatever) actually samples the class of situations or subject matter about which interpretations are to be made or conclusions are to be drawn.

In principle, the validity of the selection of items or observations as a representative sample should be judged without considering the persons to be tested *at all;* the focus should be specifically restricted to the test materials and the universe of items (item domain) from which the test materials or items were selected. Hence, if the content is validly selected and truly representative of the universe of items, then the test should be content-valid for persons of *all kinds.* One of the major difficulties encountered in attempting to achieve this goal is that although we may operationally (or behaviorally) define the domain of content for a given area, the actual universe of items is restricted to those samples of items already in existence together with those that we are prepared to write.

Another problem related to the content validity of a particular measure is that the content of a test is not necessarily a permanent state of affairs; items or tasks frequently reflect social events, accepted beliefs, or societal norms and values, and these, of course, frequently change with time so that sooner or later the test's items may become unrepresentative of the universe domain. Therefore, it is important that when selecting items the test constructor ensures that they are not only relevant and fit the definition of the universe of content, but also that the answers considered correct to such items have a high level of accuracy *as judged by* various experts in the field.

In the first edition of the American Psychological Association's *Standards for Educational and Psychological Tests and Manuals* (1966) is the following description:

> Content validity is especially important for achievement and proficiency measures and for measures of adjustment or social behavior based on observation in selected situations.

Such a description of content validity is just as true today as it was in 1966.

For anyone currently involved in preschool or developmental screening, one can readily see how important it is to know whether a particular screening measure has high content validity. For example, developmental screening tests frequently include a measure of language or social skills behavior. It is not usually clear how far such tests contain a representative sample of the universe domain for, say, language ability, as few of these measures have been subjected to any kind of rigorous content validation studies. The ease with which content validation studies may be carried out depends, in general, on the clarity with which the developer has specified his objectives and how unambiguous he has been in defining the test's task domain. For example, if, in the above discussion, we were using a developmental screening test for language ability, and if language was being measured by *vocabulary knowledge,* then the task domain for such a measure might be defined as *all* three to five letter words used in the 30,000 most frequently used words (as reported by Thorndike and Lorge, 1944). The total number of items and their relative frequency of usage is thereby known, so that the representative sample of words used in the measure could be easily determined. However, when we attempt to use a screening measure for social skills, we are in a task domain which is more subject to ambiguity and therefore much less clearly defined. In this case, the test developer would invariably have to have the task domain of social skills defined and determined by the pooled judgements of a variety of child experts, including, for example, child psychologists, child psychiatrists, speech and language specialists, etc. Whether the task domain has been clearly and easily defined or not, the best method of obtaining evidence on a test's content validity is through the examination of the test items (or tasks) by a series of competent and highly knowledgeable judges. Whenever appropriate, the most thorough examination usually occurs when these judges actually take the test themselves; in this way they are able to give very close and careful attention to the test's individual items.

Other evidence for a measure's content validity may be obtained by: (a) the test user himself, who, by comparing his own purposes and needs with a careful examination of the test's items draws conclusions on its suitability; and (b) a careful examination of the test's manual. If, for example, the manual provides detailed information about the unique characteristics of the test, defines the item domain sampled, plus clearly outlines the test developer's objectives, then the manual can be very helpful in determining for the user its content validity.

One final point of importance is that there is nothing in the logic of content validation that requires that the item domain, or that the sample of items selected be homogeneous in content. As long as the measure has a sufficiently large sample of items, there is no particular reason for the test to have high intercorrelations; hence, it is not appropriate for a test developer to report high item-test correlations as evidence of content validity. Similarly, the correlation of items with an external criterion is not really relevant to a test's content validity because in the validation of content we are trying to determine how well the items of the test *represent* the entire content universe (domain) of items in any given descriptive area.

CONSTRUCT VALIDITY

This type of validity is evaluated by investigating what *psychological qualities* a test measures. These psychological qualities invariably refer to a person's internal processes or states, i.e. such qualities as anxiety level, degree of insight, or ego strength, all of which are usually inferred from a person's behavior.

The rationale for construct validation developed out of personality testing (Cronbach and Meehl, 1955) and has been of increasing importance in validity studies ever since. If, for example, we are trying to measure a person's degree of insight, there is no unique pertinent criterion to predict to; neither is there a domain of content to sample. Usually, however, such a construct as insight has a theory of development behind it that has adequately derived the presumed nature of the trait, i.e. there have been enough investigations into the construct and enough support for its existence that it can be readily understood and defined unambiguously. If the score on our test of insight is indeed a valid manifestation of the trait, then its relationships to other variables should conform to certain theoretical expectations, i.e. should be related to other behaviors associated with the construct.

Construct validation requires the integration of many studies. There is no such thing as a coefficient of construct validity nor does a series of studies permit us to summarize a construct in any simple way. Construct validity begins when a test constructor claims that his test measures a certain construct. However, this claim is meaningless until he has elaborated the construct into a meaningful set of sentences, i.e. has spelled out the meaning of the construct. In a study by Grimes and Allinsmith (1961) the meaning of the construct, compulsivity, was spelled out in the following way:

> In summary, the compulsive person appears to have exaggerated conceptions about exactness and order, and is oriented motivationally and perceptually by these concerns. Compulsives are described as relatively rigid, preoccupied with small details, inhibited in spontaneity, conforming, perfectionistic, seeking certainty, and intolerant of the ambiguous or incongruous situation.

If a particular construct is taken seriously by the profession its validity is then challenged over and over again. The challenge usually comes in the form of a counter hypothesis, i.e. an alternative construct is proposed to account for all or part of the test behavior.

There are at least three major ways of evaluating a test's construct validity; correlational studies, experimental studies and logical analysis. *Correlational studies* are by far the most common and are based on the premise that individuals who score high on the test ought to score high (have high positive correlations) on other indicators of the same construct. These indicators may be other tests, ratings of every day behavior or reports regarding the social groups to which the person belongs. In other words, one would expect people who score high on a measure of compulsivity (as defined earlier) to be extremely neat and tidy or *meticulous* in appearance, make very good chartered accountants or I.R.S. investigators and be quiet and reserved at social functions.

These types of correlational studies are frequently called *convergence studies,* but at no time should one of the indicators used be taken as an absolute criterion or standard; rather, the test's construct validity should be based on correlational data from as many indicators as is feasible or practicable.

As Campbell and Fiske (1959) have previously pointed out; however, the demonstration of convergence across indicators is not sufficient evidence for high construct validity; what is also required is evidence demonstrating *discrimination* from other constructs; such discrimination requires that indicators of one construct have relatively low correlations with measures interpreted in terms of other constructs. In other words, our measure of compulsivity should correlate highly with such indicators as personal neatness and measures of rigidity and attention to detail; it should correlate at a relatively low level with indicators of such a trait as say impulsivity or flexibility.

Experimental intervention is another way to check on the construct validity of a test. In these types of interventions an experimental condition is set up so that a deliberate attempt is made to change an individual's test score to try and identify influences to which performances on the test may be sensitive. This experimental treatment may consist of special instructions, changes in time limits or the teaching of particular strategies. For example, an investigator may have a measure of social competence which he wishes to check for its susceptibility to faking. One way of doing this would be to take a large group of subjects, randomly assign one half of the group the test with the usual instructions and request the other half to complete the test in such a way as to create the greatest impression of social competence. If, after statistical analysis, there exists a significant mean difference between the two groups, then one has shown that scores on the test may be significantly affected by faking.

The third major way of evaluating a test's construct validity is through *judgement* and *logical analysis*. In this kind of evaluation a person who has a great deal of expertise in testing and measurement theory may be used as a judge to look over the measure in question in order to detect flaws or impurities which the test constructor may have overlooked. This type of logical analysis of content and format cannot be employed to refute or disprove a test's level of validity; it can, however, put forward a counter hypothesis whose relevance can then be verified empirically. For example, a judge evaluating a particular measure of spelling may point out that because the test only measures spelling through dictation, the usual interpretation of scores will be inappropriate for individuals who are hard of hearing or who have poor auditory discrimination.

The importance of construct validity in regards to screening measures varies according to what the test is attempting to screen; for example, in screening for vision and hearing, vocabulary level, or fine motor coordination, one is more likely to be concerned about the measures' content validity. However when using developmental screening measures for looking at social skills, cognition or reading readiness, one is much more concerned about construct validity. It should be obvious by now that content and construct validity are both important concepts that must be considered in the selection of a particular screening test; the degree of relative importance between the content and construct validity of such measures is merely for purposes of illustration; screening measures for such constructs as cognitive and social skills must have both high content and high construct validity.

If, after a large series of different investigations, the test developer has found little supportive evidence of the psychological construct his test is attempting to measure, he is faced with one of two major choices; he must either revise his original definition of the construct, or revise his test so that it becomes a significant measure of the construct he originally wished to measure. It is, of course, through this verification process that the test developer increases his own knowledge of the construct he wishes to measure as well as the usefulness of the test itself.

CRITERION-RELATED VALIDITY

This type of validity estimate compares test scores or predictions made from them with an external criterion considered to provide a direct measure of the characteristics or behavior in question.

We often use test scores for decision-making purposes; for example, in the field of education we may use them to select applicants for advanced training programs or to allocate students to different instructional programs. The decision made is essentially a choice between various *treatments* (here treatments may be considered as a particular training program, a career path or a specific therapeutic procedure). We may use test scores to *classify* people along various paths, say into architecture, engineering or fine arts. When alternative treatments are on some kind of progressive level of difficulty, say elementary, intermediate or advanced, our decision becomes one of *placement.* For example, we may decide that all high scorers (top 15%) on a particular test of mathematics should be placed at the advanced level, all those in the middle at the intermediate level and all those who score low (bottom 15%) at the elementary level. In a *selection* decision we either choose to *accept* the person for a particular program, therapeutic procedure or whatever, or we choose to *reject* him. In a fair number of situations decisions involving selection and classification may be combined.

Although we may make these decisions on purely subjective grounds, usually (and hopefully) we base our decisions, particularly when using test scores, on some kind of objective rule or rules. These rules are usually determined, in large part, by the *predictive validity estimates* of the measures we are basing our decisions on. These estimates are frequently based on the correlation between an individual's test score and some *subsequent criterion task.* These criterion tasks are standards which have been accepted by professionals in the field as providing direct measures of the behaviors or abilities to be predicted. For example, we might correlate a person's test scores on mechanical ability with his actual performance on a series of mechanical tasks (criterion measures) six months or one year later.

In theory, if not always in practice, the validation of an *objective* decision rule should be based on an experiment (or series of experiments) in which each person, *regardless of his test scores, is randomly assigned* to a particular treatment (for instance, using our previous example, to advanced, intermediate or elementary levels of instruction) and his performance outcome measured several weeks (or months) later. The joint distribution of these outcomes and the original test scores are then evaluated in order to determine what objective rule produces the best decision. In other words, if all the high scorers (top 15%) perform best in the advanced level of training and the middle scorers do best at the intermediate level and all the low scorers (bottom 15%) perform best at the elementary level, we know that the best decision rule to use for placement would be one employing specific test scores.

In all *predictive* validity studies, the outcome measure should follow *only* after some weeks or months have elapsed or some treatment procedure has been completed. Sometimes, however, when discussing the predictive validity of his measure, a test developer will include in the test's manual data on the test's concurrent validity. Concurrent validity *is* part of criterion related validity, but is *not* the same thing as predictive validity and should not be used to determine the validity of a test for decision making.

Briefly, concurrent validity refers to the collection of test score data and outcome measure data at approximately the same point in time; i.e. concurrently. For example, we could give a measure of mechanical ability to a group of mechanics on the job whose proficiency on mechanical tasks has already been established. The correlation between these test scores and actual performance scores on specific mechanical tasks would constitute the estimate of concurrent validity for the mechanical ability measure. The reason that we cannot use such a procedure to estimate the test's predictive validity is that we have no way of knowing how much a person's mechanical ability was influenced by his training and development in his job situation.

Preschool developmental (or any other) screening is a procedure used to enable someone (examiner, administrator, screening program director) to make a decision about a particular examinee. In a sense, any decision based on a screening measure is a choice among various alternatives; for example, the child's screening results may be considered normal, questionable or at-risk. If normal the child will simply be directed to a regular developmental program; if questionable or at-risk the child may be referred back for a second administration of the screening procedure, given other screening measures, or referred to a specialist or series of specialists for complete diagnostic evaluation. When we consider a child's screening test as normal we are *predicting*, in effect, that the child will progress normally and will not require any assistance or special programs in the future. On the other hand, when we consider a child's screening test as abnormal we are *predicting* that the child will not progress normally unless he receives a complete diagnostic evaluation to determine the specific nature (causes) of his disorder coupled with a subsequent treatment program to completely alleviate (whenever possible) his disability.

It is probably true to say that screening essentially involves a combination of *selection* and *classification* decisions. Initially, we select out those examinees who are considered normal on the basis of their screening test scores; of the remaining examinees, we may classify them as questionable (requiring rescreening and perhaps referral for further evaluation), or at-risk (requiring diagnostic evaluation and, if diagnosed as disabled, intensive or extensive special treatment programs). Actual placement decisions, however, are more the concern of the diagnostic specialists than of the people involved in the screening program.

Although, on the surface, predictive validation may appear to be a rather straightforward process, there are a variety of factors which have to be considered when evaluating a test's predictive validity estimate. For example, as discussed earlier, predictive validity is an estimate of how well an individual (given a particular score on a specific test) will perform on some later criterion task. Although this criterion task is the *standard*, which has been accepted by various professionals in the field, the *level* of success in reaching that standard may be subject to disagreement. For instance, it may be agreed that an acceptable criterion standard for estimating the predictive validity of a measure of managerial ability is salary level after three years on the job. The disagreement may involve what salary level constitutes *success*: $25,000 per year, $35,000 per year, $50,000 per year. Another related problem has to do with the fact that a particular measure may be used to predict several different, but equally relevant, criterion tasks. Here, for example, we may employ a screening measure to predict a successful level of general physical development, social success in nursery school, academic success in primary school and freedom from behavior problems. Because our screening measure is likely to correlate differently with each of these criterion tasks, our measure may have several different predictive validity estimates (coefficients). Hence, just as we discussed for construct validity, unless our screening measure is specifically used to predict to just one single criterion task, it *cannot* be defined as having a *single* predictive validity coefficient.

Several other factors that may affect the predictive validity coefficient itself must also be considered. For example, the actual time period between test and criterion task administration may seriously affect the level of correlation. It is well known that the longer the period between test and criterion measure, the lower the relationship is likely to be. This result comes about primarily because chance factors (error variance) can affect both test and criterion performance over long periods of time; another variable that also may affect the correlation is increased attrition rate of subjects as the time span increases. In other words, over long periods of time between test and criterion measure the subjects tested become harder and harder to locate so the attrition rate becomes higher and higher. Attrition rate, as was mentioned earlier, is an important reason for selecting a large enough sample of subjects to begin with.

Another problem that may affect the predictive validity of a measure, although indirectly, is related to local validation and extrapolation. Unless the measure to be used is actually going to be employed in the geographic region it was validated in, the test user is going to have to use extrapolation in judging the adequacy of his test results for the population he used it on. Extrapolation is called for whenever a test user employs a measure on a population which is not identical to the one used for the purpose of validation; it is also necessary to use extrapolation for another reason and that has to do with the nature of predictive validity studies themselves. Frequently, predictive validation of a measure may take anywhere from one to five years; consequently, by the time the measure is on the market and being used extensively, the conditions under which the data were collected, as compared with the current situation, may have changed substantially. Obviously, the greater the similarity between the conditions at validation and the present, the less extrapolation that is required; however, for all predictive tests the data collected for validation may only be used for so long before more current validity studies will be required (if only as a check on its present adequacy). In the long run, moreover, the accumulation of data from long-term follow-up studies should, in effect, indicate how well various types of early criteria were related to long-term outcomes or performances.

This point is of particular importance when the scores on a given predictor test are correlated with another measure (say an achievement test) at the end of a period of time, such as a course or a school year. Suppose, for example, in validating a preschool screening measure's ability to predict later reading achievement, we correlate screening scores with scores on a reading test at the end of grade one, a very common and convenient procedure. Usually, the reliability coefficients of group tests of reading achievement are of only modest proportions at the best of times and this reliability is decreased even further if the reading test is scored by a variety of first grade teachers because different teachers tend to use different bases for judging reading achievement. If such a procedure is our short-term (early criterion) measure, then the relationship between it and long-term measures of reading achievement (which provide estimates of more permanent gains) may be very important in our overall evaluation of the preschool screening test's ability to predict. For example, if scores on our early criterion measure are significantly related to the scores on our long-term criterion measure, then we can expect that if our preschool screening test predicts well to the early criterion, it should also predict well to the long-term one. We will pursue the discussion of this topic in more detail in Chapter 5.

Another factor that may affect a screening test's predictive validity is the reliability of the criterion measure itself. Criterion measures like predictive measures are not infallible; they are subject to errors of measurement and unreliability. In terms of the former (errors of measurement), they operate in just the same way for criterion measures as they do for test-retest reliability coefficients and are due essentially to random errors of chance. Hence, the predictive validity coefficient of a particular test will be low to the extent that either the test itself or the criterion measure is unreliable or has high errors of measurement. The unreliability of the criterion measure may stem (in addition to errors of measurement) from a variety of sources, one of which is the previously mentioned differences in agreement over what constitutes level of success on the criterion; another has to do with how truly representative the criterion is of a universe of potential outcomes (criteria) that may be used as a measure of a test's ability to predict. The extent to which a test developer or investigator considers his criterion an adequate one will determine, in part, its level of reliability.

Finally, a test's predictive validity may be affected by *criterion contamination*. This type of problem varies in significance depending on the types of criterion tasks used; however, any validation procedure that employs judges to evaluate criterion performance can be prone to it. Simply speaking, it occurs whenever the judges involved have access to the individual scores on the predictive test. By prior access to such scores, judges' evaluations of performance on the criterion measure may be *contaminated*. Screening tests validated in preschool or school situations are particularly prone to such contamination whenever teachers' ratings or judgements are used to evaluate criterion performance and they have already seen the scores on the screening measure.

As we have mentioned earlier one of the prime objectives of using a screening measure is to select out those examinees who may be considered as questionable or at-risk. How does one go about determining the predictive validity of a screening measure when the major objective is selection? The best procedure is to pair predictor and criterion measure scores for a representative sample of subjects. Because, in our present example, we are using a measure to predict the presence or absence of particular disabilities, our criterion measure may well be ratings of the actual presence or absence of specific disorders as determined by a specialist or team of specialists. Thus, the correlation between scores on our screening measure and ratings by diagnostic specialists becomes our predictive validity coefficient for the selectiveness or *power* of our screening test. A similar procedure could be used if we were using our screening measure for classification purposes. In this type of screening, we might classify, on the basis of screening test scores, examinees into three classes; no risk, some risk and high risk. The ratings of the specialists could also be divided into these three categories and our validity coefficient will be the correlation between scores on our screening and outcome measures.

Notice that in determining these validity coefficients for both selection and classification purposes, those examinees whose screening scores indicated no risk were included in the study. This is important because we not only want to know how good a predictor our screening measure is for selecting or classifying people at-risk, we also want to know how many people it *may miss,* i.e. those examinees whose screening scores indicate no risk, but when evaluated by a team of specialists actually are rated as having a particular disability. The total number of these individuals will, of course, determine the false-negative rate for the screening measure.

After this fairly lengthy discussion on validity, one may well ask the question: what constitutes an adequate or acceptable level of validity? There is, of course, no simple answer to such a question, but a series of *it depends* types of answers. For example, if we know that a particular screening measure selects examinees such that all of them with scores in the at-risk category invariably are found to have a disability, that can be completely alleviated through appropriate treatment procedures, then we might consider the costs of testing minimal in view of the improved outcomes for the people so detected. This would hold true even if the validity coefficient for the measure was not very high (for example .5) because it was found that the measure did not detect *all* of the people who were at-risk.

Another *it depends* answer is related to the importance of the decision that has to be made. For instance, a screening or other measure that has only a modest validity coefficient may be well worth using if it not only provides information that is otherwise unavailable but will also minimize errors in decision making. Obviously, the most serious errors connected with decision-making are those that cannot be reversed at some later time or can only be reversed at great cost, either financially or to the person involved. A good example of this situation might be in screening for deafness in very young children. Although many of the screening measures in this area have only modest validity coefficients, any measure that can help us to minimize our error rate in screening potentially deaf young children is well worth using because the costs of not using it (loss of language ability, retarded cognitive development, drastically reduced communication skills) are extremely high. Cost factors, hit rates and a test's level of usefulness or *utility* will be discussed more fully in Chapter 5.

Before closing our discussion on test validation, some brief mention should be made of *face validity*. The face validity of any measure has to do with the extent to which it seems relevant, or appears to be measuring something that is important and of high interest. It does *not* refer to a validity coefficient, but is simply related to the surface appearance of the test or the test items. The test may be considered (rated) high in face validity, but actually be a completely invalid and unreliable measure; frequently, tests or ratings published in popular magazines fall into this category. This is not to deny that face validity is totally unimportant. Obviously, all tests should appear relevant, interesting and convey to the examinee that they are measuring something of importance, if for no other reason than to motivate the subject to complete the test. A measure, however, that has high face validity is not necessarily empirically valid or reliable.

Chapter 5

MEASUREMENT AND UTILITY
FACTORS SIGNIFICANT TO
SCREENING MEASURES

ONE OF THE MOST FUNDAMENTAL ISSUES related to screening has to do with accuracy of prediction for specific target groups. Any decision made on the basis of scores or ratings on specific screening measures will, in a sense, only be as sound as the measures themselves. When we consider using a specific screening test or even a series of tests, it is very helpful in our selection of any given measure to have information concerning certain strengths or weaknesses which underlie it. This chapter attempts to bring together, at a relatively unsophisticated level, information on a variety of measurement variables.

MEASUREMENT SENSITIVITY AND MEASUREMENT SELECTIVITY

As we have already learned from information discussed in previous chapters, the measure that has a perfect reliability co-efficient or a perfect validity coefficient, i.e. correlations of 1.00, has yet to be developed. Therefore, because of a test's error variance, no score (or rating) on a specific measure will be a per-fect predictor of later performance or outcome. Such a state of affairs means, for our purposes, that when we have to make a decision about which examinees should be classified as at-risk or as developmentally normal, some of the time our decision is going to be just plain *wrong*. In view of this universal happening, we would obviously prefer to use a screening measure that will enable us to keep our decision errors down to an absolute minimum. It is at this point that we must consider a measure's level of *sensitivity* and *specificity*.

In simple terms, a test's sensitivity level is directly related to the number of false-negatives that were reported on the validation studies; specificity level, on the other hand, is directly related to the number of false-positives reported on the validation investigations. What do we mean when we talk about a test's false-positive or false-negative rates? The number of false-positives reported for a given measure simply refers to the number of examinees who were identified as at-risk on the predictor test (screening measure), but who, when evaluated on an outcome measure (diagnostic test, diagnostic - team rating, or other outcome measure), at a later date, were found *not to have* a particular disability or disorder. The number of false-negatives reported on the same measure refers to the number of examinees who were identified as *normal* on the screening test, but who were later diagnosed as having a particular disability. The following two-by-two contingency table, using data from an actual study (Barnes, 1978), illustrates the false-positive and false-negative plus the true-positive and true-negative rates for a sample of preschool children tested on a screening measure for reading disability (The Jansky Screening Index; Jansky and de Hirsch, 1972).

As can be seen from the table, the false-positive, false-negative, true-positive and true-negative rates are given as simple percentages and hence do not require a sophisticated knowledge of mathematics to compute. As we can see from the example, the screening measure (JSI) identified thirty-nine preschoolers as at-risk who were later found to have *no* indications of reading disability (as tested on a criterion measure of reading) three years later. These thirty-nine examinees, then, constitute the total number of *false-positives* for the screening measure. One hundred and one children were identified on the JSI as normal and three years later were found to have no reading disabilities. These children constitute the number of *true-negatives*. Sixty-three children were considered at-risk on the JSI and three years later were found to be reading disabled; these children, then, make up the number of *true-positives*. Conversely, twelve preschoolers who were initially identified as *normal* on the Jansky Screening Index were in fact found three years later to be *reading-disabled*. These twelve examinees make up the total number of *false-negatives* for the Jansky Screening Index. As briefly mentioned earlier, the false-positive and false-negative rates for a particular screening measure are not only critical in terms of enabling a screening examiner to make the least number of decision errors, but also may significantly contribute to cost factors (both financial and humanistic).*

Table III

FALSE-POSITIVE AND FALSE-NEGATIVE RATES
FOR THE JANSKY SCREENING INDEX

PREDICTIVE MEASURE

JSI

Outcome Measure Gates Reading Test	*Normal*	*At-Risk*	
Normal	101	39	140
At-Risk	12	63	75
	113	102	215

False-Positive Rate $= \dfrac{39}{140} = 27.86\%$

False-Negative Rate $= \dfrac{12}{75} = 16.00\%$

True-Positive Rate $= \dfrac{63}{75} = 84.00\%$

True-Negative Rate $= \dfrac{101}{140} = 72.14\%$

---

*A screening test's false-positive/false-negative rates should not be confused with a measure's over- under-referral notes. As Table III indicates, the over-referral rate for the JSI is $\dfrac{39}{102}$ or *38.24* percent while the under-referral rate is $\dfrac{12}{113}$ or *10.62* percent. Translating these figures into words, they indicate that if all children identified on the JSI as at-risk had been referred to diagnostic evaluation 38 percent of them would have been evaluated unnecessarily; while, conversely, 12 percent of the children classified as normal should have been referred, but were missed.

Any discussion of a measure's false-positive and false-negative rates usually includes a discussion of the measure's hit-rates. In a way, the hit-rates simply tell us how many examinees the test identified correctly, i.e. as either at-risk or not at-risk. For example, if we use the same data as above, the hit-rates for the Jansky Screening Index are as presented in Table IV.

Table IV

PREDICTIVE HIT-RATES FOR THE JANSKY SCREENING INDEX

PREDICTIVE MEASURE

JSI

Outcome Measure Gates Reading Test	*Normal*	*At-Risk*	
Normal	101	39	140
At-Risk	12	63	75
			215

Hit-Rate for Reading Disability $= \dfrac{63}{75} = 84.00\%$

Hit-Rate for Normal Reading Disability $= \dfrac{101}{140} = 72.14\%$

Overall Hit-Rate $= \dfrac{164}{215} = 76.28\%$

What we can see from this example is that our screening measure (JSI) correctly identified sixty-three preschool children out of a total of seventy-five children who, three years later, were considered to be reading disabled (true-positives); an accuracy rate for predicting reading disability of 84 percent. On the other hand, the JSI correctly identified 101 preschool children out of a total of 140 children who, three years later, were considered to be of at least normal reading ability (true-negatives); an accuracy rate of 72.14 percent. The overall hit-rate is simply a composite of the total predictive accuracy of the screening measure; it combines, in the above example, all those children who were correctly identified as at-risk with all those preschoolers who were correctly identified as normal (63 plus 101) and divides them by the total number of children screened (215). This gives an overall accuracy rate for the JSI of 76.28 percent.

On the surface, these hit rates may appear very impressive; however, the actual predictive power of a screening measure cannot be based on the above simple derivation of hit-rates; it must also be refined to take into account *conditional probability values.* Furthermore, one must also closely scrutinize the measure's false-positive and false-negative rates, for, as mentioned earlier, they indicate certain cost factors related to misidentification.

What is being argued here is that one cannot simply evaluate the accuracy of a particular screening measure on the basis of just one index, i.e. reliability coefficient, validity coefficient, hit-rates, false-positive rate, false-negative rate or whatever. What one has to do is evaluate a screening test's worth on the basis of a variety of indices in order to get some idea of its overall *utility.*

PREDICTIVE UTILITY AND CONDITIONAL PROBABILITY VALUES

In order to determine a screening measure's overall predictive utility, we must not only know how reliable (consistent) it is and how well its scores correlate with various criterion measures (validity), but also we must know something about its hit-rates, false-positive and false-negative rates and whenever possible the *prevalence rates* of the disability or disorder to be predicted. For whenever we attempt to pick out people as at-risk for some disorder, we enter the world of probability theory. The idea of applying Bayesian Probability Theory to measures involved in prediction was first discussed by Meehl and Rosen (1955) in an article looking at antecedent probability and the most efficient use of cutting scores or predictive tests. (For a more recent article in this area, which specifically refers to screening measures, see Satz and Fletcher, 1979.) Although we will look at other methods of how to select out, in an optimal way, at-risk examinees, i.e. regression analysis and expectancy tables, one of the most commonly used methods is to establish a particular cutting score on both the screening test and the criterion measure. For example, in the previous illustrations, where data on the Jansky Screening Index was used, the cutting score for determining at-risk was any score below the mean; similarly, the cutting score for determining reading disability on the criterion measure (Gates Primary Reading Test) was a grade level score of 2.2 or less. Needless to say, the screening measure's hit-rates and false-positive and false-negative rates may be drastically changed depending on where the cutting scores on the test are placed. The following example, shown in Table V from actual data reported by Barnes (1978), may help clarify this point.

Table V

FALSE-POSITIVE, FALSE-NEGATIVE AND PREDICTIVE HIT-RATES
FOR JANSKY SCREENING INDEX
WHEN TWO DIFFERENT CUT-OFF SCORES ARE SELECTED

Example 1: JSI Cut-Off Score $=$ Below $\overline{X}$

PREDICTIVE MEASURE

JSI

Outcome Measure Gates Reading Test	*Normal*	*At-Risk*	
Normal	94	64	158
At-Risk	1	7	8
			166

False-Positive Rate $= \dfrac{64}{158} = 40.51\%$

False-Negative Rate $= \dfrac{1}{8} = 12.50\%$

Hit-Rate for Reading Disability $= \dfrac{7}{8} = 87.50\%$

Overall Hit-Rate $= \dfrac{101}{166} = 60.84\%$

Table V (Continued)

Example 2: JSI Cut-Off Score = -1 Standard Deviation

PREDICTIVE MEASURE

JSI

Outcome Measure Gates Reading Test	Normal	At-Risk	
Normal	143	15	158
At-Risk	1	7	8
			166

False-Positive Rate $= \dfrac{15}{158} = 9.49\%$

False-Negative Rate $= \dfrac{1}{8} = 12.50\%$

Hit-Rate for Reading Disability $= \dfrac{7}{8} = 87.50\%$

Overall Hit-Rate $= \dfrac{150}{166} = 90.36\%$

From the above illustration one can see that the false-positive rate and the overall hit-rate of the JSI is improved substantially when the cutting scores on the screening measure are moved from below the mean to below minus one standard deviation from the mean. Obviously, for purposes of accurate prediction if for no other reason, the efficient screening examiner attempts to select those cutting scores that will decrease the number of false-positives and false-negatives to an absolute minimum.

Let us return to the issue of probability and how it relates to measurement in screening and predictive utility. The issue of the predictive utility of a measure has only recently been discussed at any length in regards to screening and diagnostic measures. (Satz, Fennell and Reilly, 1970; Satz and Fletcher, 1979); however, it is an important concept that is vital to the determination of a screening test's (or screening battery's) actual value for early detection purposes.

The whole idea behind predictive utility is to evaluate the actual accuracy rates, i.e. valid-positives and valid-negatives of a measure in relation to the actual if known, or estimated prevalence rate of the disorder or disability which is to be predicted for in the general population (or at least for the population for which the measure has been designed). In our illustrations on the JSI, the valid-positive rate and the valid-negative rate would be evaluated in relation to the known incident or base-rate for reading disability. When it is known or can be accurately estimated, usually through independent epidemiology studies or large-scale sampling of the general population, a measure's predictive utility can be computed directly by using the principle of inverse probability or Bayes Theorem. However, the value assigned to such a calculation will depend on the individual decision maker. In other words, the *value* given to the predictive utility of any given screening measure is often highly *subjective* (regardless of what the statistical calculation may be), and is frequently dependent upon simple individual preferences or personal bias, which probably explains why so many screening measures may continue to be used because they are subjectively felt to be highly useful, but whose actual worth in terms of calculated predictive utility may be extremely low. This is an important point, which we shall return to in a later discussion. Thus, when base rates for a given disorder are available, one can easily determine the conditional probability values for each of the measure's valid-positive (at-risk) and valid-negative (normal) signs. For example, the Bayesian formula for computing the conditional probability value for a valid-positive (at-risk) sign is as follows:

$$\text{Conditional Probability Value for Valid-Positive Sign} = \frac{\text{Base-Rate for Reading Disability (Valid-Positive Rate)}}{\substack{\text{Base-Rate for Reading Disability (Valid-Positive Rate)} \\ + \\ \text{Base-Rate for Normal Reading (False-Positive Rate)}}}$$

Let us work out the conditional probability values for the data on the JSI. The base-rate estimate for reading disability varies depending on the population screened; for example, for white, middle class, suburban students, it tends to be around 0.20 (20%); whereas for students from low socioeconomic levels in urban-ghetto schools, it tends to be around 0.35 (35%). We will use this latter incident rate for the JSI data presented in Table VI because the population of students screened was primarily from a low socioeconomic area who went to urban-ghetto schools.

Table VI

CONDITIONAL PROBABILITY VALUES FOR THE JANSKY SCREENING INDEX
WHEN THE BASE-RATE FOR READING DISABILITY IS ESTIMATED AT 0.35

PREDICTIVE MEASURE

JSI

Outcome Measure Gates Reading Test	Normal	At-Risk	
	Valid—Negative Rate	False-Positive Rate	
Normal	101 (0.721)	39 (0.279)	140
	False-Negative Rate	Valid-Positive Rate	
At-Risk	12 (0.160)	63 (0.840)	75
			215

Conditional Probability Value for Valid-Positive Sign
$$P(PR/+) = \frac{0.35\,(0.840)}{0.35\,(0.840) + 0.65\,(0.279)} = 0.62$$

Conditional Probability Value for Valid-Negative Sign
$$P(GR/-) = \frac{0.65\,(0.721)}{0.65\,(0.721) + 0.35\,(0.160)} = 0.89$$

Now, what do these statistics tell us about the predictive utility of the JSI? The first probability value, for valid-positive sign, tells us that out of every 100 children that were found to be at-risk, our prediction would have been correct for sixty-two of them and the other thirty-eight children would have turned out to be average or above average readers three years after screening. What does the second probability value, that for valid-negative sign, tell us about the JSI's predictive utility? It indicates that out of every 100 children found to be normal, our prediction would have been accurate for eighty-nine of them and the other eleven would have turned out, three years later, to be disabled readers.

Before looking at what such conditional probability values mean in the way of costs, it is perhaps helpful for general information purposes to show what conditional probability values may occur when the incident rate for a particular disability is very low. Let us imagine, for purposes of illustration, that the base rate for reading disability in the general population is 0.03 (3%). What difference would this make to the predictive utility of the JSI? Let us see:

$$\text{Conditional Probability Value for Valid-Positive Sign } P(PR/+) = \frac{0.03\,(0.840)}{0.03(0.840) + 0.97(0.279)} = 0.09$$

$$\text{Conditional Probability Value for Valid-Negative Sign } P(GR/-) = \frac{0.97(0.721)}{0.97(0.721) + 0.03(0.160)} = 0.99$$

Obviously the incident rate makes a very significant difference when it is low. In the above case, our predictive accuracy has dropped from 0.62 or sixty-two children out of every 100 correctly identified as at-risk, to 0.09, or nine children out of 100 correctly identified. It is true that our predictive accuracy has increased for the correct identification of able readers (from 0.89 to 0.99); however, the major purpose of our screening measure is not to identify good readers, but to pick out children who will be disabled readers.

It is in this context that one can see the critical importance, in any screening endeavor, of *knowing* or having at least an accurate estimate of, the base-rate or prevalence of the disability to be predicted.

In the light of the examples given, let us now look at the various cost factors involved in the decision-making process. Costs may be broken down in a variety of different ways but for discussion purposes we will look at three major categories: human, financial and manpower-time costs. Although these three cost factors have been separated out for purposes of discussion, they are, in fact, nearly always interrelated in one way or another.

For most of us involved in health, education or other behavioral sciences, human costs are of prime significance. The extent of human costs in any screening program will depend mainly on the predictive accuracy of our screening decisions. This accuracy will also feature greatly in the financial and manpower cost areas, too. By way of a concrete example, let us consider the data already presented (Table III) on the JSI. The false-positive rate of this screening measure was found to be approximately 0.28 (28%), so the *specificity* rating will be 1.00 - 0.28 or 0.72 (72%). However, when we calculate the conditional probability value (in order to allow for the prevalence of reading disability in the population) we find that this specificity level drops to 0.62 (62%). In terms of human costs, this rate means that 38 percent of the children considered at-risk will either be sent for full diagnostic work-ups or may be referred directly to early intervention programs. The human costs here are mainly ones related to the creation of unnecessary parental and child anxiety, plus the other human costs that go with being mislabeled and perhaps singled out as abnormal or handicapped by peers, teachers and administrators. What about financial and manpower costs? Both of these could be substantial; the cost of diagnostic services or early intervention programs varies depending on the underlying disability looked for but can be very substantial. The manpower-time costs will be directly related to the number of examinees referred who really do not require diagnostic or early intervention services (in our example 38 percent of all preschoolers considered at-risk). As the number of specialists involved in both diagnostic services and intervention programs are invariably in short supply, these manpower-time costs may be extremely significant.

What about the costs incurred when a screening decision is made that an examinee is not at-risk but in actual fact he is later found to have the disability? These are what we referred to earlier as the false-negatives and in our data on the JSI, the false-negative rate was found to be 0.16 (16%). Hence, the *sensitivity* of our measure is 1.00 - 0.16 or 0.84 (84%). In many ways, the human cost factors here are even more devastating than for the false-positives. This is because, in the case of many disorders or disabilities, remediation or treatment programs may be much less effective if the disorder has gone undetected for several years. For example, the human ramifications of a child not having a serious reading disability detected until the second or third grade may be such that the child never does learn to read adequately, with the result that he never feels educationally competent, may fail or repeat one or more grades, perhaps drops out of school early, or does not graduate and finally may become either delinquent or marginally employable. These are not necessarily invariant consequences for every reading disabled individual, but for many they represent truly significant human costs. The financial and manpower-time costs may be equally substantial; for example, when an older child does not perform well in school he may be referred to a variety of specialists for a series of diagnostic work-ups before his reading disability is finally uncovered. Similarly, remedial programs for older children may be more costly in terms of the materials and equipment required. Also, in cases where the disability prevents employability or creates delinquent behaviors, the financial costs to the community may be very substantial. Manpower-time costs are substantial in both unnecessary specialist consultations and also in the use of remedial or treatment specialist's time. In other words, a child with a reading disability left undiscovered and untreated until grade three may require 100 percent more of a reading specialist's time than if the disability had been discovered at the end of kindergarten.

This discussion now brings us to *decision analysis*. In simple terms, decision analysis refers to an analysis of all the factors or variables that we can think of that will influence the decision (in our case a screening one) that we have to make. All procedures used in decision analysis will contain elements of subjective judgement (professional opinion) as well as personal values; however, it is the position taken here (and by many others in the field) that wherever and whenever possible, scientific or statistical analysis be used to either substantiate, or, at the very least, be used as an addition to, subjective judgement. By this we mean that whenever we decide to use a given screening measure and make decisions on the basis of individual scores, we do not neglect or disregard statistical information about the test's reliability and validity coefficients or knowledge about the measure's false-positive and false-negative rates or its conditional probability values. All of these factors should play a part in our ultimate decision. For example, supposing we subjectively place a high weighting on human costs, especially as they are related to parent and child anxiety over being labeled as at-risk, then we would certainly want to compute the screening measure's false-positive rate and the conditional probability value for valid-positive sign. However, if we are more concerned about long-term costs to both the individual examinee and society at large, we would want to compute the test's false-negative rate and also the conditional probability value for valid-negative sign.

Although well beyond the scope of this book, there are various methods for actually computing specific financial costs related to particular screening decisions (see Reinke, 1969; Gay, Coons and Frankenburg, 1978). One or two additional comments should be made, however, about cost factors. One of the problems faced by decision makers in the realm of screening is the actual subjective judgement of assigning units of cost. Frequently, there are significant differences of opinion, in the area of screening objectives, between health and behavioral sciences professionals, management and administrative personnel, the individual consumer and the general public. For example, health professionals and health management personnel may want to reduce treatment costs, whereas the public at large may prefer to keep loss of productivity through absenteeism over health disability to a minimum while the individual consumer may prefer to satisfy his own pleasures and ignore the health hazards that are related to smoking, the excessive consumption of alcohol and the sustained over-indulgence in the consumption of junk food.

Another cost problem faced by decision makers in screening is not only judging the relative costs of treatment or remediation, depending on the type of screening program employed (partial or total mass screening), but also how many of the examinees screened as at-risk will actually report for a diagnostic evaluation or enter an early intervention program. This latter factor is particularly important in some instances because the treatment costs or the actual physical costs to the individual may escalate substanially the longer an at-risk examinee remains undiagnosed or untreated. A good example of this type of cost is reported by Hatfield (1979) in the area of preschool vision screening, where out of 14,579 children referred for professional diagnostic evaluation, one-third of them did not show up for their scheduled appointments.

As Acheson (1963) has previously pointed out, the selection of disabilities to be screened in a particular program should take into account certain criteria. For example, does the disorder occur frequently in the general or specific population, i.e. what is the prevalence or base rate? Does the disorder present a risk to life or is it sufficiently incapacitating to have serious effects on the person's later life? Are there specific and highly identifiable signs which indicate fairly reliably that the disorder is present? If a sign is highly identifiable, is it economical to screen for on a mass basis and will the measure used be physically or psychologically unobjectionable to the examinee? Once the disorder is detected, are there effective treatment programs available to cure it or at least alleviate its symptoms?

EXPECTANCY TABLES AND REGRESSION ANALYSIS

In an earlier discussion we talked about the importance of cutting scores in making selection decisions and reducing our errors of prediction to a minimum. The actual determination of appropriate cutting scores on screening measures frequently can be made through the use of an expectancy table, where the data (scores) on the predictive measure and criterion measure are grouped in tabular form. An example from the scores on the JSI and Gates Primary *B* Reading Test (based on data reported by Barnes, 1978) is given in Figure 2.

As can be seen from the Figure, the predictor scores on the JSI are given on the bottom of the table and the criterion (outcome) scores are given on the side. A grade level of 2.3 or more is considered a normal score; while a score of 2.2 or less is considered to be an indication of reading disability. The total number of subjects in the study was 215 and the correlation (predictive validity coefficient) between the JSI and the criterion measure (Gates Primary B Reading Test) was .72. The cutting score for the JSI was above or below the mean, or a JSI total raw score of

thirty-two and above or thirty-one and below. When all preschoolers with JSI scores of thirty-two and higher were selected
as normal ($N = 113$), 101 of them would have been successful
readers by the end of their grade two year and twelve of them
would have been disabled readers. The ratio of 101 to 113 or 89
percent is referred to as the *success ratio* for preschoolers selected
as normal on the predictor test. Conversely, of the preschoolers
whose total index scores on the JSI fell at thirty-one or below
and who were selected as at-risk ($N = 102$), sixty-three of them
would have been disabled readers at the end of grade two and
thirty-nine would have been successful readers. The ratio of
sixty-three to thirty-nine or 62 percent is referred to as the *failure ratio* for preschoolers selected as at-risk on the predictive
measure.

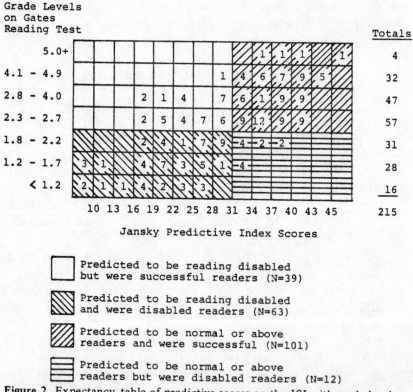

Figure 2. Expectancy table of predictive scores on the JSI with grade level on
the Gates Primary B Reading Test.

Another way of arranging an expectancy table for the same data as previously illustrated is seen in Figure 3.

Probability of Reading Level Achievement

JPI Index Scores	1.2	1.2-1.7	1.8-2.2	2.3-2.7	2.8-4.0	4.1-4.9	5.0+
47 - 49							1.00
44 - 46						1.00	
41 - 43				.14	.41	.41	.05
38 - 40			.07	.32	.32	.25	.04
35 - 37			.07	.40	.30	.20	.03
32 - 34		.15	.15	.33	.22	.15	
29 - 31		.04	.38	.25	.29	.04	
26 - 28	.14	.23	.32	.32			
23 - 25	.20	.20	.07	.27	.27		
20 - 22	.11	.38	.21	.26	.05		
17 - 19	.29	.29	.14	.14	.14		
14 - 16	1.00						
11 - 13	.50	.50					
<11	.40	.60					

Figure 3. Expectancy table of grade level reading achievement according to total scores on the Jansky Screening Index.

This type of expectancy table shows data in terms of the probability of achieving a particular reading level given a specific total score in the JSI. For example, from this table one can see that if a preschooler earned a total score of forty-three on the screening measure, his chances of achieving a reading grade level of 5.0 or higher at the end of grade two are quite low (0.05 or five chances in 100); the probability of him achieving grade levels of 4.1 to 4.9, 2.8 to 4.0, and 2.3 to 2.7 respectively is 0.41, 0.41 and 0.14.

The advantages of expectancy tables are that they can be easily understood by people with no training in statistics, can be constructed by anyone who may be involved in follow-up studies and, because of their visual properties, can be easily used in determining what the optimal cutting score on a screening measure should be.

One way of summarizing statistics from an expectancy table is through regression analysis. This kind of analysis is depicted by a *trend* or *regression line*, which shows the relationship between predictor measure X and outcome (criterion) measure Y. Regression analysis and the function of trend lines are particularly useful in the evaluation of predictive measures for practical purposes, especially when examinees, on the basis of their screening scores, may be placed in two or more different programs and we wish to obtain the greatest beneficial outcome possible for each person.

Before giving a practical example to illustrate this point, let us first find out how to determine regression or trend lines. In a direct and perfect linear relationship (which, so far, has never been discovered in the social or behavior sciences), a change in variable X is always accompanied by a constant change in variable Y. Let us say that for predictive test X and for outcome measure Y we have the following relationship among scores:

Predictor (X)	1	3	5	7	9	11	13	15
Outcome (Y)	2	6	10	14	18	22	26	30

Here we observe that the rate of change in Y scores for changes in X scores is:

$$\frac{Y_2 - Y_1}{X_2 - X_1} = \frac{4}{2} = 2$$

and that this rate of change is the same no matter which pair of X and Y scores we may select. We call such a relationship linear because when we draw a trend line all the pairs of X and Y scores fall on a straight line (see Figure 4) and the slope of the line drawn in Figure 4 thus shows the rate of change in Y scores for changes in X.

Because, in our example, there is a perfect linear relationship between X and Y scores, and because we know the slope of the line, we are in a position to predict the value of any Y score from the value of any X score. For example, when $X = 11$, $Y = 2 \times 11 = 22$; and when $X = 5$, $Y = 2 \times 5 = 10$ and so on.

As mentioned earlier, such perfect linear relationships just do not occur in the social or behavioral sciences; nevertheless, it is possible to make relatively accurate predictions about Y from a knowledge of X. By postulating an approximate straight line relationship and measuring how far off from this postulated straight line the data (scores) actually fall. Whenever we use this type of approximation, we are employing *regression analysis,* which is usually expressed algebraically as $Y^1 = A + B\,(X)$; where $Y^1 =$ *predicted* values of $\dot{Y}$ (rather than actual values) and A and B indicate the constants of the Y intercept and slope when we sample a group of individuals from a given population.

Variable Y

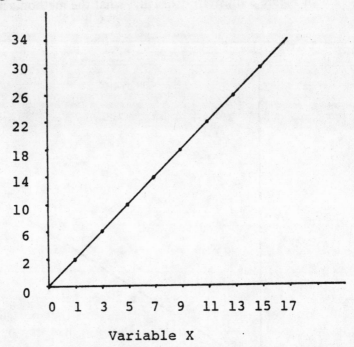

Variable X

Figure 4. Hypothetical regression line showing the relationship between X and Y variables, when the relationship between X and Y is perfectly linear.

Let us now provide numerical values for the regression equation $Y^1 = A + B\,(X)$. The actual data, listed previously in Figure 2, is from a study evaluating the effectiveness of a preschool screening measure to predict later reading disability. Before performing

the statistical analysis, it is important to consider that we calculate
the regression line which will provide the *best fit* for the two sets
of scores. Essentially, we want our estimate of Y to be as close
to the actual value of Y as possible over the long run. The best
procedure to use for this purpose is the method of *least squares*.
A regression line computed by this method will produce a line
such that the vertical distances of the actual Y values from the
predicted (Y^1) values will be at a minimum. Thus, by using the
method of fewest squares, the trend line found is one that will
minimize the squared differences between the predicted (Y^1)
values and the actual Y values. The hypothetical data plotted below in Figure 5 illustrates, visually, what the method achieves.

Variable Y

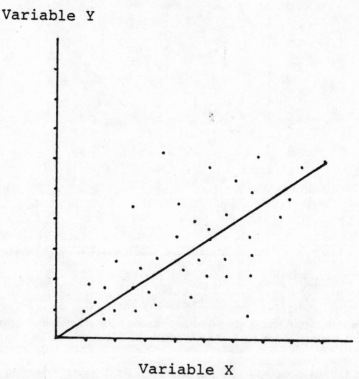

Variable X

Figure 5. Hypothetical regression line showing the relationship between X
and Y variables when the relationship is linear and moderately positive.

As will be recalled, our formula for Y^1 was $Y^1 = A + B (X)$ and in order to derive the regression line, we must provide numerical values for A and B; we have numerical values for X, for they are the scores on our predictive (screening) measure. The formulas for A and B are as follows:

$$B = \frac{N \sum XY - (\sum X)(\sum Y)}{N \sum X^2 - (\sum X)^2}$$

$$A = \overline{Y} - b(\overline{X})$$

If we use the data from Figure 2 and make the necessary statistical calculations we have:

$$B = \frac{2355928}{3305826} = 0.71 \quad \text{and}$$

$$A = 19.46 - 0.71(31.15) = -2.66$$

The result of our equation gives: $Y^1 = -2.66 + 0.71 (X)$, which means that the line that fits the data on the JSI by least squares better than any other line has A approximately equal to -2.66 and B approximately equal to 0.71. As can be seen in Figure 6, the constant A (-2.66) is the point at which the line crosses the Y axis; while the constant B is the slope of the line, or the degree to which the estimated value of Y changes with a change in X.

The regression analysis illustrated on the next page was on one sample of preschool children assessed on the JSI; such an analysis can only be used, however, if the following assumptions are met: (1) the relationship between X and Y variables is linear and not curvilinear; (2) the distribution of each Y for given values of X is normal; (3) the variances of X and Y are equal; and (4) the error variables for X and Y are independent, i.e. not correlated.

The use of regression analysis is particularly useful when the range of scores on the X and Y variables is restricted or narrow, because it provides a more general description of the X, Y relationship. Regression slopes are also invaluable when one is using a specific measure for placement purposes. For example, supposing we used a screening measure for assessing general development to place children into a home enrichment program or structured day care program in order to maximize their general development and we wish to evaluate the effectiveness of our decisions. Our outcome measure here might be pediatricians' ratings of overall development. The hypothetical example (see Figure 7) shows us how regression analysis can quickly give us a picture of the two different programs and their effectiveness given certain scores on the predictor (screening) test *X*.

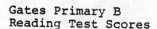

Gates Primary B
Reading Test Scores

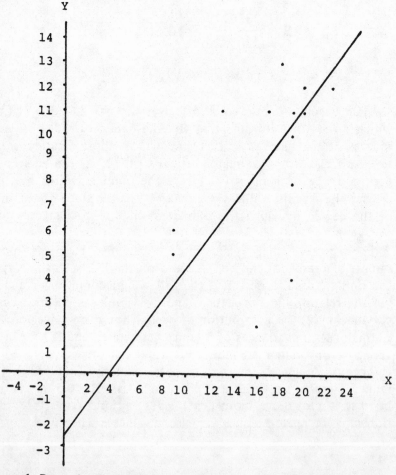

Figure 6. Regression line showing the relationship between JSI total scores and scores on the Gates Primary B Reading Test.

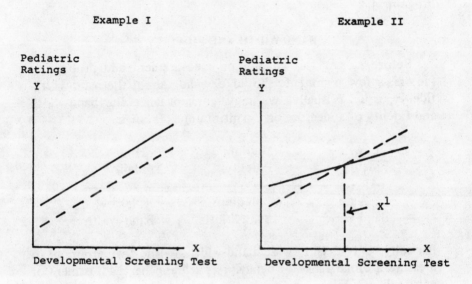

Program A = ——————— (Home Enrichment)

Program B = - - - - - - - (Structured Day-Care)

Figure 7. Hypothetical regression line showing the relationship between predictive screening measure X and outcome measure Y for two different preschool programs.

In Example I we see that Program A achieves better average outcomes than Program B at all values of X studied; while in Example II we see that the regression lines cross at the point indicated by X^1. Thus, our decision rule, if the first example was true, would be to assign all children to Program A in the future; however, if the second example were true, we would want to assign all children whose X scores exceed X^1 to Program B and all others to Program A.

BAND-WIDTH AND FIDELITY

Before closing this chapter on measurement and probability factors, a few comments should be made about the band-width-fidelity issue. Visually, we may conceptualize the band-width and fidelity of a measure on a continuum as follows:

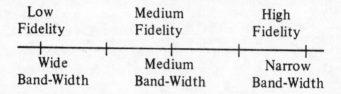

Low Fidelity	Medium Fidelity	High Fidelity
Wide Band-Width	Medium Band-Width	Narrow Band-Width

Basically, a test with wide band-width is one that attempts to measure a broad range of behaviors, such as general adjustment or personality; while a narrow band-width test is one that attempts to measure one very specific area of behavior such as fine-motor coordination or special ability. In relationship to band-width there tends to be a fidelity factor such that the broader the band-width, the more noise or distortion in the system; that is the lower the fidelity or conciseness of the test. In other words, when we decide to employ a test or multi-score battery that attempts to measure wide or general areas of behavior, there is a cost factor involved because of a certain loss of precision. This cost factor rarely occurs in the measurement of highly specific (narrow) behaviors because of the opportunity to sample the behavior more extensively in a given period of time and because it is usually easier to construct a precision instrument to measure one aspect of behavior than many aspects of behavior. The problem that we are faced with, however, is that when we use a very narrow band-width test, we are usually restricted to making no more than two or three decisions, whereas with a broad band-width measure we may have less precise measurement, but our decision-making may be relatively unrestricted. Our choice of specific measures, then, is governed by the kind and number of decisions we wish to make;

if we are only required to make a single decision, then our choice should be for a measure that will give us the most dependable answer for our efforts, i.e. a measure with narrow band-width and high fidelity. If, on the other hand, we have a wide variety of questions to be answered or decisions to be made, then we should look for a multi-test battery of wide band-width but with as much fidelity as possible. Thus, for any given decision situation, the ideal compromise is between variety of information (band-width) and clarity and dependability (fidelity).

As a general rule, we can say that (1) when many decisions have to be made, it is usually more profitable to divide the testing time among several measures than to concentrate on just one test; (2) when time and money are limited, the measures selected should be the ones most related to providing information for the most important, rather than all, of the decisions to be made; (3) the number of tests used and the amount of time devoted to each test should be optimally distributed, i.e. where each test contributes equally, then time should be distributed equally across tests; if the contribution of each test is unequal, then the bulk of the time should be spent on those measures that make the maximum contribution. For a more detailed discussion of this issue, see Cronbach and Gleser (1965).

Section III
Selected Preschool Screening
Measures

Chapter 6

MEASURES OF HEARING
AND VISION

HEARING

HEARING, MORE COMMONLY called auditory functioning in the research literature, is one of the most well-developed systems present at birth in the human organism. It is, of
course, one thing to know that a system is well-developed phys-
iologically at birth and something else again to determine how well
that system functions. In the screening of hearing in neonates
and very young infants the examiner is hampered by a variety of
factors including the neonate's lack of sophistication in indicating when an actual stimulus has been heard as well as the state
the infant is in when screened (alert and actively wakeful to deep
sleep). Other factors that may influence the infant's reaction to
auditory stimulation are such environmental variables as room
temperature, brightness and directness of light and noise level
(Cohen and Gross, 1979). However, there does appear to be a
developmental sequence of sound detection which goes from general reflexive behavior in new-borns (eye blinks, stirring movements) to head turning (laterally and up and down) in later infancy.

Although the incidence of deafness or serious auditory deficit
is at least one in every 2,000 births (Northern and Downs, 1974),
mass screening for auditory deficits in young infants and children
under the age of two years is not, currently, very extensive for
several reasons, the major one being the difficulty in training
volunteer or paraprofessional examiners to achieve reliable screening results. This difficulty, of course, is related to the variability

of interpretation of young infant behaviors. When one is measuring, on a mass basis, a young infant's ability to detect sound, one is dependent on such behaviors as head turning, eye shifting, eye widening and so on and these kinds of movements are difficult to define precisely, so what may constitute a head movement for one examiner may not be so classified by another examiner. Another major factor that influences reliability in early auditory screening is that some of the above behaviors may not yet be a consistent part of the young infant's behavioral repertoire; hence, the absence of lateral head moving in response to an auditory stimulus (bell) may mean a deficit in hearing, or simply that lateral head movements have not yet developed in the particular child being assessed.

Such a state of affairs does not mean that auditory screening in infancy has been abandoned. The major ways such screening has been carried out is well documented by Northern and Downs (1974) and consists of the application of a high risk register and the use of a variety of noise makers (squeeze toys, bells, rattles, etc.) to determine if the infant displays any form of orienting response to such stimuli.

There is now considerable evidence to suggest (Hardy, 1965; Bergstrom, Hemenway and Downs, 1971; Downs and Silver, 1972) that the use of a high risk register may be an extremely useful tool in the early identification of potential or actual auditory impairment in children under two years of age. The measurement of auditory deficit or potential deficit through the use of various noisemakers is, however, subject to the kinds of examiner problems discussed earlier; namely, the reliability with which screening examiners can identify specific orienting responses to particular sounds and whether the lack of such orienting responses is due to auditory deficit, inattentiveness, poor motivation, or simply the absence of particular orienting responses in the young infant's behavioral repertoire.

Because of the lack of standardized screening measures available for very young infants, the auditory screening tests reviewed below are primarily for children between the ages of two and five. In this age range auditory screening programs attempt to pick out those children with potential hearing problems both conductive, sensorineural or a combination of both. According to Northern (1975), conductive impairment may be the result of problems in the external ear canal, the middle ear cavity or the tympanic membrane; however, whatever the origin, the result is an interference with sound transmission through the air conduction pathway. Sensorineural impairment, on the other hand, is invariably the result of damage to either the fibers of the auditory nerve or the sensory cells of the organ of Corti within the Cochlea itself. Whatever the cause, the major long-range objective of auditory screening at the preschool level is to prevent serious social, speech and language communication disorders from occurring or to catch the disorder at a time when it is more amenable to treatment. The actual prevalence of significant hearing loss in young children appears to vary between 3 and 5 percent (Anderson, 1967; Osborn, 1970; Weber, McGovern and Zink, 1967).

The tests most commonly used for such purposes are the VASC, pure-tone audiometry, acoustic impedance audiometry or otoscopic examination. These auditory screening measures are reviewed below; however, ostoscopic testing has been excluded because it requires the use of the pneumatic otoscope, an instrument requiring considerable professional and clinical training.*

In view of the general paucity of research reported on auditory screening measures, the reader is advised that none of these measures meet all of the 1974 A.P.A. *Standards for Educational and Psychological Tests;* hence, when such measures are to be used for mass screening, the findings should be carefully evaluated over considerable time periods.

Pure-Tone Audiometry

Audiometric screening utilizing the pure-tone audiometer has been in use now for over twenty-five years, and although it has been widely accepted as a reliable and valid measure the author has been unable to find a single comprehensive evaluative study on its use with children between the ages of two and five.

---

*This situation may well change in the near future due to an increasing shortage of otolaryngologists and the fact that a recent project by Wood (reported on by Northern and Downs, 1974) has demonstrated that well-trained nonmedical personnel can perform reliable and valid pneumatic otoscope examinations.

A report by Young (1975) on the use of the pure-tone audiometer for play audiometry provides no information on validity and reliability, while a similar report on pure-tone audiometric screening for children four years of age and older indicates that although test-retest reliability for children over six years of age approaches 100 percent, for children between the ages of three and six the reliability coefficient is closer to 0.9. In terms of validity, Young reports that

> Pure-tone audiometric screening also has excellent validity in conductive hearing losses which exceed the screening levels and in finding those individuals who have high-frequency sensorineural hearing loss. However, pure-tone screening tests may miss as much as 50 percent of the mild to serious otitis media cases.

Unfortunately, despite these very positive comments Young does not provide any references or actual data to support such statements. The one study reporting on the test-retest reliability of pure-tone measurement in preschool children (Mencher and McCulloch, 1970) indicates that in an investigation of twenty-nine kindergarten-aged children who failed pure-tone screening on initial testing, only 10 or 34 percent failed the same measure on retesting. Although the sample of children assessed in this study is woefully inadequate, such a finding if replicated on a larger sample does not speak well for the consistency of pure-tone screening measures when used on preschool-aged children. However, in the area of school screening the evaluation of pure-tone audiometric screening is much better and in light of the scarcity of evidence for the use of pure-tone audiometers in preschool children, some brief discussion will be made on the findings of Melnick, Eagles and Levine (1964) and Moghadam, Robinson and Cambon (1968).

In the Melnick et al. study an entire school population ($N = 860$) was subjected to audiometric threshold tests, pure-tone screening and pneumatic otoscopic examinations. When one uses diagnostic threshold testing as a criterion measure for evaluating pure-tone screening on school-age children, the results of Melnick et al.'s study provide the following findings summarized in Table VII.

Table VII

PREDICTIVE AUDITORY SCREENING OF SCHOOL-AGE CHILDREN USING THE PURE-TONE AUDIOMETER

PREDICTIVE MEASURE

Pure-Tone Audiometric Ratings

Outcome Measure Threshold Hearing Test	*Normal*	*At-Risk*	
Normal	704	13	717
At-Risk	21	122	143
			860

Specificity $= \dfrac{704}{717} = 98.18\%$

Sensitivity $= \dfrac{122}{143} = 85.31\%$

False-Positive Rate $= \dfrac{13}{717} = 1.81\%$

False-Negative Rate $= \dfrac{21}{143} = 14.69\%$

Source: Melnick, Eagles and Levine, 1964.

Table VII illustrates that the specificity of pure-tone screening equals 98 percent; while the sensitivity of such screening equals 85 percent. The false-positive rate is 2 percent while the false-negative rate is 15 percent. In evaluating these findings in regards to the value of pure-tone screening for school-age children one can see that the false-positive rate is very acceptable (2% of the children classified as at-risk on audiometric screening had no hearing disorder); however, the false-negative rate is substantial (15% of the children classified as having a hearing loss were missed on the screening test).

In a study of 6,055 elementary school children (grades one to six), Moghadam, Robinson and Cambon (1968) found, on initial pure-tone screening, a total of 212 children who had a hearing loss of fifteen decibels or more in an average of five frequencies (250, 500, 1,000, 2,000, and 4,000 cps). For purposes of retesting four to six weeks later these 212 children were matched with 212 control children who on the initial screening were found to have no hearing loss. On retesting the authors found that only 62 percent of the original hearing-impaired children were still at-risk, while 16 percent of the non-hearing impaired children (control group) were found to have a hearing difficulty. With a 54 percent misclassification rate such a finding suggests that the test-retest reliability of pure-tone audiometers, at least in this study, is at the chance level. Thus, on the basis of the above two studies, the sensitivity of pure-tone audiometric screening and the reliability of pure-tone audiometers, at least in school-age children, leaves a great deal to be desired.

Basically, pure-tone audiometry may be employed for two specific purposes; it may be used as a simple screening technique to select out those children with actual or suspected hearing losses from those children with normal hearing acuity, or it may be used for audiometric threshold testing, which is the measurement for precise hearing acuity at a variety of frequencies at specific octave intervals (usually from 250 to 8.000 Hz). In the case of screening, the generally accepted criterion for referrals (Northern and Downs, 1974) is a failure to respond to twenty-five decibels (American National Standards Institute) at any frequency. For detailed accounts of the procedures used in both play audiometry and direct pure-tone audiometric testing, see Northern and Downs (1974) and the report by Young (1975).

The greatest problems in using both play audiometry and pure-tone audiometric testing in children under six years of age fall into three major areas. The first problem area involves the preschool child himself; such personal characteristics as inattentiveness, uncooperativeness, fear, noncompliance or extreme timidity will all affect the reliability and accuracy of the test findings. The second problem area has to do with examiner characteristics, screening examiners who are poorly or inadequately trained in the use of the audiometer, who are lacking in patience and understanding of child behavior, or who simply fail to achieve adequate rapport with preschool children may markedly influence any child's performance. The final problem area is related to the reliability of the instrument itself. Pure-tone audiometers, although carefully built, are often subjected to a great deal of carrying back and forth when used in audiometric screening programs. One of the consequences of such movement is a loss of calibration and a failure to meet reference levels and standards set by ANSI. Not only must the instrument be handled with care, but it should also be subjected to regular maintenance and acoustic calibration tests (at least twice per year) by a trained technician. In fact, even newly purchased audiometers should be tested for calibration and accuracy before being used in case they have been damaged in shipping.

Verbal Auditory Screening for Children (VASC)

This measure was developed by Griffing, Simonton and Hedgecock (1967) as a method of screening for potential hearing loss in preschool children. The test items consist of four randomized lists of the same twelve spondee words which are recorded by the same male voice on a tape cartridge and played on a modified tape deck (which can be calibrated). The first word in each list is presented at fifty-one decibels and each word thereafter at a declining four-decibel rate until the last three items, which are presented at fifteen decibels. The child's hearing is evaluated by having him point to a picture (on a board in front of him) which he believes represents the stimulus word presented. According to the authors, the screening test measures hearing in a range from one hundred to fifteen Hz and can be administered to two children at the same time.

The evidence on the measure's reliability and validity is meager. Griffing et al. (1967), in the original test construction study, evaluated 175 preschool children on the VASC and then administered pure-tone audiometric tests on all those who failed as well as on every third child who passed. Although five of the nine children who failed the VASC were found to have hearing deficits on pure-tone testing, one cannot accurately evaluate the overall efficiency of the measure because only one third of the normal children were given the criterion measure. Furthermore, such a study provides no evidence on reliability of the test as the VASC was only given once and the test items were not subdivided in any way, so no internal consistency analysis could be performed.

The only other study so far reported on the reliability or validity of the VASC was one conducted by Mencher and McCulloch (1970). In this study, fifty-three kindergarten children (twenty-eight boys and twenty-five girls between the ages of 5.5 and 7.5 years) were administered the VASC and pure-tone audiometric testing on two consecutive days. The criterion for failure on the VASC was less than two correct responses out of three on the last three words presented at the fifteen decibel level, while the criterion for failing the pure-tone test was: (1) an inability to hear or respond to any two frequencies between five hundred and four thousand Hz above twenty-five decibels; and (2) any hearing loss above twenty-five decibels at six thousand Hz. The results of the study are summarized in Tables VIII and IX.

As can be seen from Table VIII, the false-negative rate in the initial screening was 90 percent, which is a totally unacceptable level for any screening measure. As to the test-retest reliability of the VASC (Table IX), the sample of children studied is really too small to draw any meaningful conclusions from; however, of the four children originally considered at-risk on the VASC and confirmed by pure-tone audiometric screening, only one (out of the three available at recall) or 33 percent was considered still at-risk and confirmed as hearing disabled on retesting. In fairness to the authors of the VASC, this low retest finding may be in part due to the unreliability of pure-tone audiometric screening for preschool-age children.

More recent predictive studies on the VASC by Ritchie and Merklein (1972) and Neal (1974) essentially have reported similar findings. For example, Ritchie and Merklein evaluated the screening efficiency of VASC on a sample of 162 preschool children between the ages of 4.0 to 5.9 years of age. The hit-rate for hearing disability, evaluated on a criterion measure of pure-tone audiometric testing, was 51.2 percent; the false-positive rate was 4.1 percent and the false-negative rate was a substantial 48.8

percent. Neal's (1974) study was on a sample of ninety-seven educable mentally retarded children between the ages of 6.7 and 15.5 years of age. Again the criterion measure was pure-tone audiometric testing and the hit-rate for hearing impairment was a very low 25 percent, while the false-positive rate was zero and the false-negative rate was a staggering 75 percent.

Table VIII

PREDICTIVE AUDITORY SCREENING OF PRESCHOOL CHILDREN USING THE VASC

PREDICTIVE MEASURE

VASC

Outcome Measure Pure-Tone Audiometry	Normal	At-Risk	
Normal	23	1	24
At-Risk	26	3	29
			53

Specificity $= \frac{23}{24} = 95.83\%$

Sensitivity $= \frac{3}{29} = 10.34\%$

False-Positive Rate $= \frac{1}{24} = 4.17\%$

False-Negative Rate $= \frac{26}{29} = 89.66\%$

Source: Mencher & McCulloch, 1970.

Table IX

ONE DAY RETEST RELIABILITY OF THE VASC
ON A SAMPLE OF PRESCHOOL-AGE CHILDREN
ORIGINALLY CLASSIFIED AS AT-RISK ON PURE-TONE SCREENING

PREDICTIVE MEASURE

VASC

Outcome Measure Pure-Tone Audiometry	*Normal*	*At-Risk*	
Normal	19	0	19
At-Risk	9	1	10
	28	1	29

No change in At-risk classification
(VASC) from $time_1$ to $time_2$ $= \frac{1}{3} = 33.34\%$

No change in normal classification
(VASC) from $time_1$ to $time_2$ $= \frac{26}{28} = 92.86\%$

Source: Mencher & McCulloch, 1970.

Because Ritchie and Merlein (1972) tested their preschool subjects twice on the VASC and calculated a phi correlation coefficient of 0.73, one might use this finding as an estimate for the test-retest correlation of the VASC itself. However, such an interpretation must be made with a great deal of caution for two major reasons; first, the two administrations of the VASC, although counterbalanced for order effects, were only separated by a few moments in time and secondly, the subjects assessed in the study were not a stratified random sample of preschool-aged children.

Thus, on the basis of these rather limited research findings, it must be concluded that the VASC requires a great deal more research before it can be considered a valid and reliable screening measure of preschool hearing.

Acoustic Impedance Audiometry

The use of the electro-acoustical impedance bridge in many ways does not meet the usual criteria for inclusion in a review of measures for screening; however, it is briefly included here because of its increasing use in the United States for the screening of hearing in preschool children and because it is now becoming more acceptable to have it administered by nonprofessionally trained personnel.

In essence, according to Northern and Downs (1974), "Impedance audiometry is an objective means of assessing the integrity and function of the peripheral auditory mechanism." Basically, such a procedure has been used as a diagnostic instrument to determine such things as existing pressure in the middle ear, eustachian tube function, the mobility of the tympanic membrane, acoustic reflex thresholds and a variety of other functions of the ear. The technique is reported by many professionals in the field to be very helpful in the hearing examination of young children when it is hard to perform adequate otoscopic examinations or establish valid hearing thresholds. Normative test values for children of various ages have been reported by Brooks (1969, 1971), Robertson, Peterson and Lamb (1968), Jerger (1970) and Keith (1973).

The actual number of studies evaluating impedance audiometry in preschool children is quite small; however, in testing the hearing of forty newborns, Keith (1973) found the test-retest reliability of the impedance technique to be approximately .85. Probably the most comprehensive study in the area is by Jerger, Jerger and Mauldin (1974) who extensively evaluated 398 children under six years of age using impedance audiometry. They reported, among other things, that while 55 percent of the group could only be successfully examined on pure-tone audiometric tests, 77 percent of the group were successfully examined through the use of impedance methods.

From the point of view of mass preschool screening, the use of impedance audiometry has several drawbacks, some of which include the use of sensitive and somewhat delicate equipment, the necessity of an appropriate testing environment, very well-trained screening examiners and the back-up services of audiologists and otolaryngologists. Another problem is that in order to determine the impedance meter's validity as a screening measure, one requires very sophisticated diagnostic outcome measures, of which impedance audiometry has been a prime example; hence, one is then left with either an individual case study approach or the surgical confirmation of a specific hearing disorder. Despite these drawbacks, impedance audiometry does have some real advantages including a very short administration time and the fact that one does not have to elicit the young child's active participation in the hearing examination, only sufficient cooperation to permit the wearing of headphones and the establishment of an airtight seal in the child's ear.

Screening Tests for Young Children and Retardates (STYCAR)

Although the battery of screening tests developed by Mary Sheridan in Great Britain is predominantly used for vision screening, one part of the STYCAR may be used for hearing (Sheridan, 1969). Unfortunately, only one recently published study by Feinmesser and Tell (1976) has reported on the STYCAR with a large group of children and the subjects in this investigation were children between the ages of five and six months of age. Out of a total of 15,071 children screened, STYCAR correctly identified 59 percent of those children defined (through total audiological evaluation) as hearing impaired. The false-positive rate was 2 percent and the false-negative rate was a substantial 41 percent. As this study was carried out on an Israeli population seen at the Hadassah Audiological Center, it is difficult to determine whether such findings could be generalized to a population of North American children.

VISION

Vision is not as fully developed at birth as auditory sense, and in the first eight weeks of life the human infant seems to have relatively poor visual acuity and visual accommodation (ability of the lens to reflexively change its shape relative to the distance of an object). The eyes appear to lack binocular convergence. However, it is also true to say that until very recently these visual characteristics were very difficult to evaluate accurately primarily because of the problems and limitations set by the restricted behavioral repertoire of neonates and young infants. The picture has changed somewhat in the last five years due in part to improved research methods and in part to more sophisticated measuring devices, notably the measurement of evoked potentials and the corneal reflection technique (see Cohen and Gross, 1979), for a more detailed discussion of this last technique).

In essence, the measurement of vision in infants and young children before they acquire language is pretty well limited to a variety of behavioral responses, many of which are not very precisely defined. The behaviors may include visual inspection, preference, selection, orientation, attention or fixation, as well as the previously mentioned corneal reflection and the direct observation of an infant's eye or his coordinated eye and head movements in response to a given stimulus.

There are at least three major problems related to actual visual screening in young infants; one is the problem previously discussed on audition, namely, the variability and consistency of specific responses in the infant's behavioral repertoire; the second is the problem related to examiner inter-rater reliability, which is always a problem when trained volunteers and paraprofessionals are being asked to make judgements concerning the occurrence or nonoccurrence of specific behaviors. A third major problem has to do with the variability of research findings on the actual development of perception in infancy. The problem here is that in order to screen for something in infancy (to see if it is present or absent) one has to know rather precisely when it occurs in the developmental process. For example, the recent work on vision in infancy by Bower (1974, 1977) has tended to indicate that many aspects of the visual process are present and functioning at a much earlier age than was ever believed possible; however, much of Bower's work is quite controversial and is still subject to verification by studies replicating his research findings.

Whatever the needs may be for visual screening in early infancy, the present author believes that because of the problems discussed above, coupled with the need for sophisticated equipment (for measuring evoked potentials and corneal reflection) and a testing environment that is isolated and meets certain controlled conditions (lighting, heating, soundproofing, etc.), the screening for early visual defects on a mass basis should probably be restricted to a few well-equipped facilities with trained professional and/or technical staff. Such a position is not meant to negate the importance of neonatal or early infant visual screening but is taken to ensure that those children requiring early screening will receive it under the best possible conditions.

Basically, vision screening programs for preschool children may be divided into three categories of visual problems; amblyopia, refractive errors and strabismus. Amblyopia or reduced visual acuity is due to a prolonged lack of stimulation of the retina or suppressed retinal imagery in one eye. Both of these conditions tend to result from strabismus and refractive errors, particularly if one eye has a significantly greater refractive error than the other (Barker and Barmatz, 1975). The prevalence rates for amblyopia tend to vary with age (Downing, 1945; Oliver and Nawratzi, 1971); for example in children under the age of two the rate is approximately 0.5 percent; between three and four years of age it is about 1.0 percent, while in children between four and six it is between 1.5 and 2.0 percent. Fairly recent studies in the area of treatment of amblyopia (Gunderson, 1970; Oliver and Nawratzi, 1971; Rosenthal and Von Noorden, 1971) have indicated that the most effective treatment effects are found to occur between four and six years of age; hence, the importance of early visual screening programs for children below school age.

Refractive errors such as myopia, hyperopia and astigmatism make up by far the most common eye disorders found in preschoolers. The prevalence of refractive errors in children between two and one-half and six years of age is reported by Woodruff (1972) to be around 14 percent. This prevalence rate is considerably higher than the 6 percent rate reported earlier by Hatfield (1967); however, these differences may be due to sampling errors or examiner differences as the 652 children in Woodruff's study were, to a certain extent, preselected, while the Hatfield results were based on a national mass screening program involving 64,223 children between the ages of three and six.

Strabismus, or ocular muscle imbalance, results in an inability to align the eyes and thus fuse the images perceived by the two eyes. Next to refractive errors it is the most common visual problem found in preschool children. According to Francois (1961) strabismus is frequently familial and as Pratt-Johnson, Lunn, Pop and Wee (1968) report, may often be found associated with large refractive errors. The actual prevalence of strabismus in children varies between one and four percent, with the highest rate being found in five year olds. (Duke-Elder, 1973; Foote, 1954; Hatfield, Barrett and Nudell, 1967.) The effectiveness of treatment is similar to that of amblyopia in the sense that the earlier the disorder is treated, the more positive the outcome (Arnott and Calcutt, 1970; Gunderson, 1970. Barker and Barmatz (1975) indicate that for the detection of congenital strabismus, the optimal age for screening is sometime before two years of age; while for acquired strabismus the ideal age is between four and five.

The most comprehensive mass screening programs for vision in preschool age children have been sponsored and coordinated by the National Society for the Prevention of Blindness (Hatfield, 1967, 1979). In reporting on these programs Hatfield states that of the 156,252 preschool children screened in 1965-1966 only 64,223 had sufficient data on them for statistical analysis and of this total number of children 3,741 were referred for complete visual diagnostic workups. However, only 2,457 (66%) of these referrals actually turned up for their appointments, and of those that were professionally examined approximately 19 percent had no vision problems, 58 percent had refractive errors, 15 percent had amblyopia, 7 percent had muscle imbalance conditions and one percent had other significant eye problems. The findings of the National Society's program for the years 1974-1975 are remarkably consistent with these earlier findings. For example, out of the 331,330 children screened, 14,579 of them were referred for diagnostic evaluation and almost 33 percent of them did not show up for their appointments; however, of all the children who were professionally examined, approximately 22 percent had no vision problems, 54 percent had refractive errors, 12 percent had amblyopia, 11 percent had muscle imbalance conditions and one percent had other significant eye problems. In addition to the pioneering efforts in the area of early visual screening made by the National Society for the Prevention of Blindness, two government reports (Savitz, Reed and Valadian, 1964; Lin Fu, 1971) have both stressed the importance of large scale visual screening programs for children over the age of thirteen months. Lin Fu's report reiterates the tremendous importance of cooperation and coordination among health professionals, community agencies and volunteer organizations if large scale vision screening programs are to be successful in any given community. He also points out the need for the careful selection and training of screening examiners together with the need for adequate follow-up of those children identified as at-risk and referred for diagnostic evaluation. Savitz et al., on the other hand, point out that such early visual screening programs would not only help in the earlier discovery of poor vision but would also provide much needed information on the prevalence rates of visual disorders and further clarification as to what constitutes normal vision in children under six years of age. This latter point is of considerable importance because one of the great difficulties in preschool vision screening is that workers within the field have not yet reached common agreement as to what constitutes normal visual acuity in children between the ages of three and eight (Lippman, 1971), although Woodruff (1972) has provided considerable data on visual acuity in children under six years of age. Another problem, as reported by Borg and Sundmark (1967), has to do with their findings that when children are retested for vision, either on the same measure or on different measures, there is a progressive improvement in their visual acuity. Possibly related to this phenomenon is the finding of Lippman (1969) that the actual visual acuity of children tends to consistently increase with increases in age. One of the ramifications of this finding in regards to preschool vision screening could be a substantial false-positive rate, i.e. large numbers of children detected as at-risk on initial screening who, on later ophthalmological examination, are found to have normal vision. Two other factors that appear to affect the

testability of young preschoolers are the distance from the child
to the test chart (10 feet, 15 feet, 20 feet) and the number of
letters or symbols to a test line. Savitz, Valadian and Reed (1965)
indicate that testability tends to decrease with an increase in test
distance; while more than forty years ago Berens (1938) reported
that the presentation of a single letter or symbol was less confus-
ing to young children than the presentation of a whole test line,
a finding that has been reconfirmed in the work of Lippman
(1969).

In terms of the types of measurements used, Doster (1971)
indicates that the most basic and worthwhile screening measures
for vision are the test for visual acuity, particularly the Snellen-
type charts, coupled with parent and examiner observations and
direct inquiry into any visual complaints the child may have. In
regards to the reliability of such wall charts, Gordon, Zeidner,
Zagorski and Uhlaner (1954) have shown that the test-retest reliability of such wall charts as the Army Snellen or the Modified
Landolt Ring for the measurement of visual acuity is not as high
as that of such measures as the Bausch and Lomb Ortho-Rater,
although the correlation between the two methods is very high.

In the implementation of any large scale visual screening program the recommendations of the National Society for the Prevention of Blindness should be given serious consideration. These
recommendations include a basic minimum screening procedure of
assessing all kindergarten children for *distance visual acuity*
through the use of the Snellen E symbol chart. In addition to this
basic minimum procedure the society also suggests that other
screening measures may be added such as the *Plus Lens Test for
Hyperopia*, a *muscle balance* test and, for other children, *depth
perception* tests. For three and four year olds the society recommended the use of the Snellen E chart and isolated letters at a 20
foot distance, plus a careful and thorough attempt to locate,
amongst the children screened, those with amblyopia.

According to Hatfield (1979):

> Tests for muscle imbalance, and excessive hyperopia are generally
> considered low yield tests and may result in an excessive number
> of over-referrals. In addition, testing for muscle imbalance is dif-
> ficult and requires screeners with a high level of competency to

obtain accurate results. Also, there is no scientific evidence, at the present time, that establishes the value of the Plus Lens Test.

As a minimum, Hatfield recommends that eye screening should be carried out at three age levels; the newborn, six months, and three to five years of age.

In general, the problems related to vision screening in preschool-age children, apart from those associated with the actual reliability of the test equipment itself, include a frequent lack of standardized conditions (lighting, exact distance, printed instructions, etc.), variability in the training of examiners, the reliability of the examiner's observations and the sometimes substantial difficulties in actually testing young children, particularly those between the ages of thirty-six and fifty-four months. One other significant problem which has been pointed out by Sloane, Dunphy, Emmons and Gallagher (1954) is that even under ideal testing conditions and the employment of professional and experienced eye examiners, it is extremely rare in the measurement of visual acuity and heterophoria for distance or closeness to find *identical agreement* across examiners.

The most commonly used measures for visual screening are reported on below; just as in the case of screening measures for hearing, the evidence on the reliability and validity of these tests is anything but substantial and like hearing tests none of them meet all of the A.P.A. *Standards for Educational and Psychological Tests* (1974).

Allen Picture Card Test

This screening measure developed by Allen (1957a; 1957b) consists of seven pictures (a telephone, a man on a horse, a man driving a jeep, a house, a Christmas tree, a bear and a birthday cake) together with a plastic lorgnette occluder. The test was essentially designed for those preschool children who are not able to respond appropriately to either the Illiterate *E* or the Sjogren Hand tests. Initially, the pictures are presented at close range so that the child may identify them; the child is then moved back to a distance of twenty feet and one eye is occluded. Each picture is then presented and the child is requested to identify them first with one eye and then with the other eye. A four-year-old is considered at-risk if he is unable to recognize the majority of the pictures at a distance of fifteen feet.

The one major evaluation carried out so far on the Allen Picture Cards was conducted by Taubenhaus and Jackson (1969). The children in this study consisted of 422 three- to six-year-olds who were tested twice on the Allen cards one week apart. The test retest reliability was .84, which indicates that the short-term consistency of the measure is fairly good. The validity study compared the Allen test with the Illiterate *E* and found a positive correlation of .91; however, the level of agreement in the at-risk category varied between .41 and .50, which means that at least half of the children identified as at-risk on the Allen test were not so identified on the criterion measure (Illiterate *E*). However, as the validity data on the Illiterate *E* test is far from prolific, it is difficult to evaluate the meaningfulness of such correlation co-efficients. One of the advantages of the Allen test is that it is well liked by the majority of the preschoolers who have so far been screened (Woodruff, 1972); it is also easy to administer and in-expensive as it can be given by trained volunteers (Frankenberg, 1970). The test's major disadvantages are that it is not as optically precise as say the letters on a Snellen chart and the evidence on its validity, particularly when using ophthalmological examinations as criterion measures, is virtually nonexistent.

Illiterate *E* Test

This test is a measure of visual acuity at a 20 foot distance; it is essentially the same as a Snellen Letter Test, but only uses the letter *E*. Basically, the Illiterate *E* was designed for screening young children (or adults) who had not yet learned the alphabet; the basic task of a child is to indicate either verbally or by pointing which position the letter *E* is in after each presentation. Although the standard distance for administering this test is 20 feet, it can be modified so that test distances of 10 to 15 feet may be utilized.

As with the Allen Picture Card Test, most of the data on the Illiterate *E*'s reliability comes from the study by Taubenhaus and Jackson (1969). These authors found that the reliability of the measure increased with increasing age; for example, at three years of age it was .80; at five to six years of age it was .85. Again, these reliability coefficients are reasonably good for five- to six-year-olds, but leave a great deal to be desired at the three-year-old level.

Although there have been a variety of studies reported in which the Illiterate *E* test has been used (Lippman, 1969, 1971; Oliver and Nawratzi, 1971a, 1971b; Keith, Diamond and Stansfield, 1972; Woodruff, 1972), none have been reported on that have been directly designed to evaluate the predictive validity of the test. Indirectly one can use the published reports on the large scale screening programs sponsored by the National Society for the Prevention of Blindness, but one must be extremely cautious in doing so because these programs did not randomly select children from the general population nor did they follow up on many of the children screened. In fact, they did not follow up on *any* of the children who passed the screening test; thus, one has no way of checking on the test's false-negative rate. The lack of extensive reliability and validity data is indeed unfortunate because the Illiterate *E* test has certain advantages over some of the other vision screening measures. For example, as it only uses one letter, the child does not have to know the alphabet in order to respond; it also takes less time to train the children and its administration time is relatively short. Furthermore, especially when it is administered at a distance of ten feet, it compares favorably with the STYCAR in its untestability ratio (the ratio of children who are unable to learn the test or who are unable to be screened, Lippman, 1971).

The test's major disadvantage is directly related to the child's ability to indicate direction; as the development of directionality varies from child to child and is particularly unstable in children under four, the test has specific limitations for children in this age-group.

Sjogren Hand Test

This screening measure, developed by Sjogren (1939) many years ago, is in many ways similar to the Illiterate *E* test. The major difference is that the visual symbol is a hand rather than a letter of the alphabet. The administrative procedure is almost identical, with the child being asked to indicate in what direction the fingers of the hand are pointing. In the usual procedure the stimulus card is presented at a distance of six meters starting with the largest figure. The examiner records the child's responses right down to the smallest figure the child can recognize.

Taubenhaus and Jackson (1969) reported a test-retest reliability coefficient of .92, while the overall relationship between the Sjogren and the Illiterate *E* was .94; however, the level of agreement in the at-risk category was only .54. Other studies on the Sjogren Hand Test have tended to look at untestability ratios (Keith, Diamond and Stansfield, 1972) and home vision screening carried out by parents (Press and Austin, 1968); there have been no studies so far reported in the literature that address the issue of screening results with later ophthalmological examinations. The advantages and disadvantages of the Sjogren Test are essentially identical to the Illiterate *E*, except that because only the fingers on the Sjogren Hand Test meet Snellen's requirements, it cannot be interpreted in exactly the same way as a Snellen Letter Chart; i.e. the fingers approximate the visual acuities of Snellen letters, but are not identical to them.

The Screening Tests for Young Children and Retardates (STYCAR)

These measures were developed by Sheridan (1969) over an extended period of time. The vision test for three- to five-year-olds consists of seven single letters (*A, H, O, T, U, V, X*) which are presented at a distance of 10 feet and the child is requested to match the letter the examiner is presenting. These letters have been designed to match closely the Snellen equivalents to the Illiterate *E* Test.

One of the great problems in evaluating the STYCAR is that there appear to be *no* published reports on the test's reliability and validity. To be sure, Sheridan (1969) reports that thousands of children have been screened and referred for diagnostic work-ups on the basis of the test's findings, but none of this work has been published. The research work on the STYCAR that has been published (Lippman, 1969, 1971; Keith, Diamond and Stansfield, 1972; Woodruff, 1972; Sheridan, 1974) tends to indicate that it produces higher acuity scores than other similar screening measures (Illiterate E, Michigan Preschool Test, Sjogren Hand Test and the Beale Collins Picture Test), is faster to administer, has the lowest untestability ratios and does not require a mature sense of directionality. However, despite these very positive findings, one is forced to reserve judgement on the actual effectiveness of the STYCAR until at least some data on its reliability and validity have been reported.

Chapter 7

MEASURES OF SPEECH AND LANGUAGE

THE ACQUISITION OF SPEECH AND LANGUAGE is what makes human beings relatively unique in the animal world. Needless to say, language acquisition is not something that is achieved overnight; however, it does appear to begin soon after birth and although it develops throughout a person's lifetime, the essential components appear to be mastered during the first ten years of life.

At the present time most speech and language experts tend to believe that language acquisition is directly related to a child's general cognitive development and that language acquisition is not really possible until a certain level of cognitive development has been achieved. Such a statement is not meant to imply that cognitive development is the only factor necessary for language acquisition; in fact, Cromer (1976) and Slobin (1973) have both argued that specific linguistic mechanisms (ability to attend to the order of words, or the ability to attend to the ends of words) may also be essential to the acquisition of language.

Although, at the present time, it does not seem possible to specify precisely what the cognitive prerequisites for language actually are, much speculation has arisen from Piaget's idea that during the first two years of life, cognitive development is directly related to the child's active exploration of his environment (including objects, people, events and their various interrelationships). This exploration and the resulting learning experiences provide the child with the understanding that the world is made up of objects and that these objects have permanence, even if they are not always visible. According to Cohen and Gross (1979) the child also learns from these experiences such things as: (1) spatial relations, or the idea that objects exist in both time and space; (2) means — ends, or that objects may be used or manipulated in order to achieve certain goals, i.e. the child learns to use a wooden spoon or other object to reach something (cookie) which he cannot reach with his hands. He may also, of course, utter the word *cookie* while his mother is watching and hence obtain the same objective; (3) imitation, or the reproduction of other people's behavior. Here, the modelling of parents' and siblings' behavior is well known including, of course, their verbal behavior; (4) play, or the ability to produce representational (symbolic) behavior, which is usually well illustrated by eighteen to twenty months of age through such behaviors as feeding stuffed toys (dolls, monkeys, etc.) with a spoon, arranging certain functional objects together (cup, spoon, dish, plate), or chaining object schemes together in sequence, i.e. feeding the toy doll, undressing it, putting it to bed and covering it with blankets; and (5) communicative intentions, or preverbal attempts by the child to obtain an adult's attention either for purposes of acquiring something (a cookie, a toy, etc.) or to show the adult something, i.e. a horse in a field or a dog on the street. Communicative intentions are felt by Bates (1976) to be exceedingly important in language acquisition because she believes they provide a major reason for talking.

In their detailed discussion of language development sequences, Cohen and Gross (1979) have postulated that language acquisition follows a developmental process beginning with the production and comprehension of lexical meaning, followed by the production and comprehension of relational meaning and ending with the production and comprehension of grammatical form, and that within each one of these major language development categories, there exists a series of sequences from simple to more and more complex acquisition of language usage. For example, in the case of lexical (word) production, the child appears to go from a basic vocabulary of ten different words at a mean age of fifteen months to a basic vocabulary of fifty different words at a mean age of twenty months, and in the last two months of the sequence (from mean age fifteen to mean age twenty months) there is a substantial *spurt* in additional words acquired. Furthermore, this word production sequence accelerates at an even greater rate, so that between twenty and thirty months of age the child's vocabulary has increased from fifty different words to 450.

A similar process is noted in regards to lexical comprehension; in this sequence the child progresses from a rather inconsistent or unstable comprehension of approximately a dozen words at twelve to sixteen months of age to a stable comprehension of approximately two hundred to three hundred words by twenty-four months of age. This estimate is based on very old data (Smith, 1926) so may not be representative of children's word comprehension today.

In regards to the production of relational meaning, one finds that the child progresses from single-word utterances (mean age approximately fifteen months) to successive single-word utterances i.e. cookie, mommy (mean age approximately nineteen months) to word combinations that possess relational meaning, i.e. eat, mommy, cookie (mean age approximately twenty-two months). By twenty-four months of age the emergence of two-term semantic relations used to code relational meaning, i.e. more apple or mommy shoe, and by thirty months of age three- and four-term semantic relations have emerged, i.e. boy hit ball.

Comprehension of relational meaning, although somewhat limited to begin with, appears to emerge at around sixteen months of age, i.e. the child can comprehend the difference between *give me the cookie* and *show me the cookie*, and by approximately twenty-four months of age the child appears capable of comprehending various semantic relations accurately at least 80 percent of the time.

It is interesting to note here that over forty years ago Stinchfield and Young (1938) proposed a critical developmental period for language acquisition. This *speech readiness period,* which occurred between nine and twenty-four months of age, Stinchfield and Young maintained was the period that children were the most receptive to language learning. For a more comprehensive discussion concerning the relationship between speech development and critical periods, see Lillywhite (1958).

The production of grammatical form does not appear to get under way much before twenty-four months of age and seems to consist of mastering four basic categories of linguistic development; sentence elaboration (development and acquisition of noun phrases and verb phrases), inflectional development (inflection of nouns and verbs), interrogative sentences (the formation of more and more complex questions) and negative sentences (from adding no or not to a two-word utterance at age twenty-four months as in *no John eat*, to the inclusion of "don't" or "can't" at thirty-six months as in *"he can't play,"* to the flexible use of negatives as in *"isn't it a nice day"* at age forty-eight months).

In the comprehension of grammatical form, Cohen and Gross (1979) maintain that children do not tend to develop the ability to comprehend on the basis of word order until the ages of thirty-six to forty-two months. Because such comprehension seems to develop, relatively speaking, at a somewhat later age than the production of grammatical form, one has to be cautious about evaluating a child's comprehension of word order. This is particularly true for a couple of reasons, one being that the child's spontaneous speech may give the impression that he understands word order at a much higher level than he actually does, and secondly that apart from direct questions that require a verbal response or specific commands that demand compliance-type behavior, many language forms do not impose any kind of requirements for either verbal or behavioral responses.

Before reviewing the available screening measures for speech and language, several general comments should be made about language acquisition and development, and all of them revolve around the importance of the environment in which the child grows up and the interactions that occur between himself and the other significant persons in his life.

In the initial stages of language development it appears that children tend to develop different types of vocabularies; for example, some children may develop vocabularies which contain many different objects, while others may have vocabularies with few objects but with many words related to feelings, needs or social relationships. Furthermore, as Nelson (1973) has shown, the first fifty different words that children acquire are remarkable in their lack of similarity, i.e. very few words were shared by even 50 percent of the children she studied. Similarly, Bloom and

Lahey (1978) have more recently observed that although children may talk about the same general categories of things, such as food or drink or toys, the words that they use to talk about these things are based directly on their experiences in the world in which they live and the active contact that they have had with those objects.

Although a child's early use of words and his comprehension of them both seem to be related to specific objects and events in his own living environment and to perhaps unique contexts within that environment, his responsiveness to the spoken word may vary depending on his level of interest, attention and the frequency with which words are spoken to him; such responsiveness may also be strongly related to the amount of reinforcement (verbal or otherwise) that the child receives while interacting with others at a verbal level.

Although language has been shown to develop sequentially, with most children reaching certain linguistic levels at approximately the same age, the actual type of language acquired and the rate of progress made on an individual basis may fluctuate widely, with some children making much more rapid progress than others. These differences it is generally believed stem from a variety of factors, the most important of which include: the kind of provisions made in the home for language stimulation, the type of parent-child interaction, the cognitive style of the child's parents and the actual needs the child has for using language. Also, in view of the importance of cognitive prerequisites to language, the actual conceptual development, i.e. particularly cognitive enrichment the child has undergone prior to acquiring language may significantly influence the language acquisition of the individual child.

For purposes of discussion, we may divide language development into two main parts; *receptive,* the ability to *decode* or the process of translating language stimuli, and *expressive,* the ability to *encode* or the process of transmitting language stimuli. The assessment of receptive language in young children has concentrated primarily on selective listening (Friedlander, 1971). So far, Friedlander has looked at such variables as loudness, language redundancy, speaker identity and signal-to-noise ratios. He has found that when children with normal language are compared to language-impaired children (nondeaf children with diffuse disorders of speech development) on a task of watching and listening to a storyteller on television, the language-impaired group shows the same level of high interest when the storyteller is totally incomprehensible as when he is clear and easy to understand. As there are still no really good screening measures on receptive language, further studies of this type are necessary in order to delineate the specific components of receptive language that need to be measured.

The measurement of expressive language has been subjected to a somewhat broader range of empirical research than receptive language. Most of the research, however, has focused on the child's ability to repeat sentences or other grammatical structures presented to him. Several researchers in the field (Fraser, Bellugi and Brown, 1963; Menyuk, 1963; Lowell and Dixon, 1967; Heber and Garber, 1971) have shown that a child's ability to repeat sentences is related to his performance on measures of language comprehension and production. Furthermore, research by Bernard, Thelen and Garber (undated) has shown that in the assessment of expressive language, it is important to obtain samples of a child's free speech patterns, i.e. repetitive utterances, single-word utterances, vocabulary range, etc. These authors have also shown that the quality of free speech production is very much higher in children who come from language-enriched environments.

By the age of thirty-six months, most children have mastered the pronunciation of new sounds, speak in short sentences, have a fairly extensive vocabulary and have some mastery of English syntax. One of the problems in the field of speech and language, however, is the definition of what constitutes abnormal speech development. In order to talk about speech deviations one must have a set of norms or standards for normal speech patterns and in North American societies, such standards as have been proposed are usually as varied as the authors defining them (Drumwright, 1975).

The problem here has been an apparent lack of operational definitions for language deficit. Although Milisen (1957) discusses a variety of deviations in speech, such as articulation disorders, rhythm disorders, voice disorders and so on, he does not provide the reader with an operational definition of what constitutes a normal or standard speech pattern. In general, Drumwright (1975), reports that "children with speech disorders exhibit articulation errors and language deviations which are inappropriate for their ages and which do not decrease significantly as they mature." It is a problem to know at what point of developmental maturity one should intervene in regards to both screening and treatment.

Another difficulty encountered in screening preschool-age children for speech and language difficulties is the general lack of data on prevalence rates. Although there have been some studies reported for kindergarten and elementary school aged children (Roe and Milisen, 1942; Milisen, 1957; Perkins, 1971), the base-rate data for preschool children is not only quite sparse, but also seriously outdated (Templin and Steer, 1939; Templin, 1953). Templin's (1953) data indicates that of 300 children between the ages of thirty-six and seventy-two months who were assessed on the Templin Non-Diagnostic Articulation Test (1947), between 18 and 25 percent of them had articulation problems as measured by an articulation diagnostic test, with the higher rates being found for children between thirty-six and forty-eight months of age.

The speech and language measures reviewed below are the ones that appear to be the most widely used and reported on. Like the screening measures for vision and hearing, they do not meet all of the *essential* requirements of the APA *Standards for Psychological and Educational Tests* and caution should be used in applying them for mass screening purposes.

DENVER ARTICULATION SCREENING EXAM (DASE)

One of the major aims of the developers of the DASE is to "reliably differentiate between normal and abnormal development in a disadvantaged population of children ranging in age from two and one-half to 6 years." (Drumwright, Van Natta, Camp and Frankenburg, 1973). This articulation screening measure, which consists of thirty sound elements, is administered by a trained nonprofessional and the child's task is to repeat those words spoken by the examiner. The screening examiner then evaluates the child's sound production and also makes a judgement on the child's overall intelligibility for connected speech. Any child whose score falls below the fifteenth percentile or whose connected speech is judged to be inadequate is considered to have failed the screening test and is referred for a diagnostic evaluation.

The standardization sample for the DASE consisted of 1,540 preschool children of lower socioeconomic status (Anglo, black and Mexican Americans), all of whom lived in metropolitan Denver, Colorado. For purposes of data analysis, only 1,455 children were included (the rest were eliminated because they had failed to respond to four or more of the test items). The children were divided into age-groups at six-month intervals and were assigned as equally as possible in terms of sex and socioeconomic/racial backgrounds. As no statistical differences were found between sexes or cultural backgrounds at any of the age levels, norms of performance were pooled within each age-group.

The test-retest reliability for 110 subjects who were read-ministered the test four to eight days after initial assessment was .95. The validity of the screening measure was evaluated by using the Hejna Articulation Test (Hejna, 1959) as a criterion measure. One hundred and fifty subjects participated in the study and the proportion of children who were both identified as at-risk and confirmed as at-risk on the criterion measure was 88 percent; while the proportion of children identified as normal on both the screening measure and the criterion test was 91 percent. Although both these ratings are very good for a screening test, it must be remembered that the criterion was another test of articulation and not an actual diagnostic evaluation, so the criterion here is only as good as its own reliability and validity coefficients.

By and large, the DASE appears to be a very promising screening measure of articulation. However, apart from the original standardization study by Drumwright, Van Natta, Camp and Frankenburg (1973) there have been no further reliability and validity studies that this author can find in the published literature. Another potential disadvantage, at least for mass screening purposes, is that the DASE has been specifically designed and standardized for use with disadvantaged preschoolers and has only been used on one sample of children from an urban population. One of its main strong points is that it has been constructed to be used by people not professionally trained; other advantages are that it is inexpensive and can be administered in approximately fifteen minutes. (For a second analysis of the DASE, see Peterson, 1978.)

THE NORTHWESTERN SYNTAX SCREENING TEST
(NSST)

The NSST was designed by Lee (1971) to specifically identify children between the ages of three and eight years who are delayed in syntactic development. The test allows for comparisons between the receptive and expressive uses of language.

The measurement of receptive language is carried out through picture selection in response to forty spoken sentences (given in pairs), while expressive language is measured through sentence repetition in response to forty stimulus pictures (also given in pairs). Each correct response is given a score of one; hence, a perfect score would be forty for each of the two parts of the test.

The test was standardized on 242 children between the ages of three and seven years and eleven months, of whom 111 were males and 131 were females. The children were divided into six-month age levels and came from middle and upper class families where "standard American dialect was spoken." (Lee, 1971). The author admits that the norms established for the test are tentative as they are based on a very small and homogeneous sample of children (Lee, 1970).

Of all the language measures reported on, the NSST is the one that has had the most evaluation from a research point of view. For example, Ratusnik and Koenigsknecht (1975) studied the test's internal consistency and report that in three different samples of preschool children (those showing normal language development, impaired language development and mentally retarded development) the "NSST assessed consistently the syntax and morphology used by children with atypical language development." The authors report further that in a differential item analysis across the three different groups of children, twenty-nine of the forty receptive language items revealed significant differences in performance, while thirty-nine of the forty expressive language items produced significant differences in performance. One other significant finding was that the normal language development group achieved a mean expressive language score just above the seventy-fifth percentile when compared with the norms developed by Lee (1970).

In a study of response patterns to the NSST by kindergarten-age children, Larson and Summers (1976) reported that in comparison to Lee's norms for the NSST, their population fell below the twenty-fifth percentile for both receptive and expressive portions of the test. Two possible explanations given by the authors are that by including lower socioeconomic children in their sample, the levels of syntactical performance was reduced and/or that there exists "a general population-wide difference in grammatical proficiency in differing geographic areas." Whatever the reason, such findings indicate the need for cross-validational studies across different populations in order to establish appropriate national norms for the NSST, or failing the completion of such studies, the development of local norms wherever the test is to be carried out for screening purposes.

The one other area of research that is seriously lacking is in the region of reliability and validity studies. There has been no published research on the test-retest reliability of the NSST, nor have there been any predictive validity studies reported. Some indirect support for the validity of the NSST is reported in studies by Lee (1970) and Prutting, Gallagher and Mulac (1975). In Lee's studies, she reports that "children already enrolled in speech and language development programs in clinics and in public schools regularly fall below the tenth percentile on either or both portions of the test."

In a similar vein, Prutting et al. found that twelve language-delayed children between the ages of 4.3 and 5.11 all scored below the tenth percentile in the NSST norms. (For other critical analyses of the NSST, see Arndt, 1977; Byrne, 1977; Lee, 1977; Fontana, 1978; and Logue, 1978).

THE TEMPLIN-DARLEY TESTS OF ARTICULATION

The Templin-Darley Tests consist of three separate but related measures: a 141-item diagnostic test, a fifty-item screening measure, and a forty-three item test called the Iowa Pressure Articulation Test. The following comments are restricted to the fifty-item screening measure only.

The fifty items used for the screening measure were selected in a study (Templin, 1947) of 100 preschool-age children that assessed their ability to produce 113 speech sound elements. These fifty items were then administered to 480 white children between three and eight years of age divided up into eight sub-samples of sixty children each at age levels 3, 3.5, 4.0, 4.5, 5, 6, 7 and 8; these 480 children, selected from fourteen public schools and twenty-one nursery schools in the Minneapolis-St. Paul region, constituted the normative group for the first edition of the test, which was published in 1960. The second edition, published in 1969, had a normative sample of sixty children varying in age from three to eight years, who also came from the Minneapolis-St. Paul area. Each item in the screening test consists of a drawing that has been designed to elicit a spontaneous utterance of a particular stimulus word. The response the child makes to each item is either scored correct or is recorded as a substitution, an omission, a distortion, a nasal emission or a non-response. The child's performance is then compared to the norms for his particular age-group, and his score may be classified as average, accelerated or retarded relative to his peers.

It is clear that the authors of the Templin-Darley Screening Test have taken a considerable amount of care in constructing the test and in publishing the test manual; however, the evidence for the test reliability and validity is not very substantial. For example, the one study on test-retest reliability reported by Templin (1953) was carried out on fifty-seven nursery- and kindergarten-age children (tested eight days apart) and reported correlation coefficients of .93 to .99. However, not only is this study now almost thirty years old, but also it assessed a very small number of children and has never been replicated.

In regards to validity, there have been no published reports on the test's predictive utility, although Battin (1975) reported, in a review of the measure, that it tended to generate over-referrals; however, he provides no data to support this statement. Templin (1953) suggests the screening test is valid because it correlates .64 with chronological age and .71 with mental age, but the correlations tell us nothing about the test's predictive ability when compared with diagnostic evaluations for articulation disorders.

In general, empirical evidence in support of the efficacy of this measure is very slight and what there is of it is very old. There have been no cross-validational studies carried out and the norms for the 1969 edition are based on a very small sample of children between the ages of three and eight. Although the authors of this measure have made some real attempts at constructing a worthwhile articulation screening measure, they have not been very successful in carrying out the kind of validity and follow-up studies which are required to demonstrate the real value and utility of a screening test.

Chapter 8

MEASURES OF
GENERAL DEVELOPMENT
Gross and Fine Motor Control,
Personal–Social Skills and
Cognitive Development

GROSS AND FINE MOTOR DEVELOPMENT

IN GENERAL, THE DEVELOPMENT OF coordinated movement is both sequential and orderly; it appears to progress in direct relationship to the maturation of the child's central nervous system. Periods of learning when the child seems to most easily learn a new motor skill are subject to considerable individual variation; thus, the normal period for walking may range from ten to eighteen months. Actual development of the child's neuro-muscular system seems to follow three basic principles: (1) movement control proceeds in a cephalocaudal direction; in other words, from head to foot, i.e. the control of the head and neck occurs before control of the arms, which occurs before the control of the feet; (2) movement development proceeds from flexion to extension and then in combination. In other words the very young infant starts out in a state of relative flexion (all parts of the body are drawn together) and then progresses to extension (straightens out legs, raises head above the backline) and then through the practice of extension movements learns new flexion movements, so that he ultimately combines patterns of extension and flexion to form controlled mature movement; (3) movement progresses from reflexive to volitional control; in other words, although at birth and in the first few months of life the infant's movement patterns are dominated by reflexes, gradually over time and in conjunction with maturation of the neuromuscular system, this reflex behavior is replaced by automatic reactions, which in turn support the final development phase known as volitional control, i.e. deliberate, planned and directed movement by the child.

Not much needs to be said about reflexive behavior (for a detailed discussion see Cohen and Gross, 1979) except to point out that primitive reflexes have a lot to do with much of an infant's early movement, and although sometimes obscure, their functions obviously are important both in terms of survival (sucking reflex) and for preparing the infant for later movement development.

Automatic reactions appear to fall somewhere between reflexes and volitional movement control in terms of sequence, and play an important role in the development of volitional movement. In essence, automatic reactions are *unthinking* responses in our movements in that they automatically respond to an individual's movement needs. Each automatic reaction, as it appears in sequence, is more sophisticated than the one before it, and all comprise essential prerequisites to later volitional movements. These movements include such reactions as *righting reactions* (a child's response when out of alignment with his own body or with gravity); *equilibirum responses* (an automatic response when pushed off balance); and *protective extension,* i.e. when righting or equilibrium responses have not been effective, protective extension reactions take place in response to actual falling.

Volitional movement, as mentioned earlier, represents the conscious and deliberate control of bodily movement. It does not occur very much before one year of age primarily because it requires the integration of a variety of movement skills. Such physical attributes as strength, flexibility, balance and physical coordination, together with development of the central nervous system, physical maturity and personal motivation, all contribute to the volitional control of movement.

The early development of fine motor control is, of course, contingent in many respects on gross motor development. In the first year of life, probably the most important adjuncts to fine motor development are vision, reaching and grasping. *Vision* is important for location and motivation; *reaching,* although essentially a gross motor skill, is an integral component in the development of fine motor movement and control; and *grasping* and *releasing* are obvious and essential to the development of fine motor skills. In regards to the latter two factors, the development of grasp invariably precedes releasing movements by several months.

Sequentially, fine motor development in the areas of reaching and grasping proceed from proximal to distal, i.e. from areas closest to the trunk of the body, shoulders, upper arms, to those areas furthest removed from the trunk, such as fingers and toes. Hence, reaching is a proximal movement response, while grasping, which develops at a later time than reaching, is a distal movement response. Grasping and ultimately hand control involves a very complex series of movements which requires coordination of the shoulder, upper arm, elbow, wrist and, of course, the fingers and thumb. This developmental sequence for fine motor skills requires greater and greater control over movements that take place between the elbow and the wrist and which involve both pronation and supination of the forearm. In other words, a turning or swiveling of the forearm from a palm-upwards position (supination) to a palm-downwards position (pronation).

In terms of grasping and hand control behavior, the developmental sequence here is from the ulnar palmar to the radial digital. In other words, initially the infant learns to grasp objects by pressing them into the palm of his hand and gripping them with the small, ring and middle fingers (ulnar palmar grasping); gradually he acquires the ability to hold objects between his thumb, his index finger and whatever other fingers are required given the size of the object (radial digital grasping). The development of the grasp response proceeds from the grasp reflex, to the ulnar palmar grasp, the radial digital grasp, the scissors grasp and ultimately to the most precise grip of all, the pincer grasp, which involves the thumb and index finger alone.

From about the age of one year, the development and refinement of fine motor control depends on the continuing successful integration of not only gross motor and fine motor skills,
but also the maturation of the central nervous system, perceptual
and cognitive skills and human motivation.

PERSONAL AND SOCIAL SKILLS

The development of personal and social skills, like many other
regions of development, appears to progress in a sequential fashion, although the age ranges often tend to be wider because many
of the areas to be discussed are subject to training and experiential effects.

In terms of personal skills the five areas that tend to be most
dominant are: independent feeding, self-toileting, dressing, grooming and self-management of independent activities. It must be
remembered that progress in acquiring these skills is also dependent upon development in other areas; for example, one cannot expect a child to feed himself if he has not mastered the
grasping response or has good control over the movements of the
forearm (pronation and supination). Similarly, successful self-
toileting requires adequate control over the sphincter muscles
and so on.

It goes without saying that the acquisition of these five major
skills allows the child to function more and more as an independent person; through this acquisition process, the child also
learns a great deal about the expectations, norms and values unique
to his own culture. The interesting thing about acquiring these
skills is that they are taught primarily in the child's home with
very little regard for *structured* training, *formalized* educational
techniques, or *standardized* curricula. In fact, in North American
society, the child is expected to have mastered all of these skills
before entering the public school system.

In terms of training for self-feeding, the usual sequence after
weaning is a progression from cup feeding to finger feeding and
finally self-feeding using various pieces of cutlery. Some of the
secondary aspects of teaching a child to feed himself concern
parent-child interactions; for example, feeding behavior is one set
of responses that the child has ample opportunity to observe.

The kind of model his parents provide may be very significantly related to the kinds of feeding responses he learns. Similarly, the amount of parental assistance he receives when first starting to drink from a cup or use a knife and fork may well influence the speed at which he learns self-mastery.

Children vary widely in learning bowel and bladder control. It is usual for bladder control to precede bowel control with a regular toileting schedule being the last thing acquired in the sequence. The nature and quality of parent-child interactions can be very influential in the acquisition of these skills and many regressions may occur before final mastery is achieved. This is particularly true if parents make an issue of the process because the regulation of one's bowel or bladder is one thing a child has total control over, whether his parents like it or not.

The progression in dressing and grooming proceeds from having the young infant enjoy his bath to such sophisticated motor skills as shoe tying and the manipulation of zippers and buttons. The usual sequence in dressing goes from an initial cooperativeness in being dressed (about twenty-four months), to putting on his own pants, shirts, socks, etc. (at about thirty-six months), to tying shoe laces and manipulating buttons (at about five years of age). Grooming proceeds from washing hands and face (around thirty-six to forty months) to brushing teeth (about forty-eight months), to combing and brushing hair (between five and six years of age).

The self-management of independent activities probably begins with imitative behavior; from the imitation of mother or father carrying out a variety of household tasks, to manipulating doors, handles (about thirty months), to helping with household tasks (putting things away, dusting, helping in the garden, around thirty-six to forty-eight months), to putting toys away neatly and performing simple errands (around five years of age), to answering the telephone and being able to provide information to others about himself (somewhere between five and six years of age).

The development of social skills probably begins with the child's cognitive acquisition of object permanence (knowledge), although the significance of early attachments (bonding), particularly with the mother, must also be considered as a major variable in the ultimate acquisition of social skills.

In the intial phase of development, the child's social responsiveness tends to be indiscriminate in that although the young infant can discriminate faces from other objects, he does not seem able to discriminate between *familiar* and *unfamiliar* faces. He does, however, use a variety of signaling behaviors (smiling, crying, vocalizations) to activate adult behavior in order to bring the mother and other principal caregivers into close proximity.

These early attachment behaviors are of vital importance to the later bond between the child and his parents, which in turn is of prime importance to the child's overall social development. In fact, Erickson (1976) has reported that early attachment behaviors between parent and child are essentially circular in nature. In other words, the infant's attachment to the mother (or father) is in part dependent upon the parent's reaction to the infant; the parent's reaction, in turn, is based to a considerable extent on the infant's temperament and behavior. The continuation of this process and its resultant behaviors, will, of course, determine to a significant degree, the development of the final relationships between parents and child.

In the second phase of development (around three to six months) the infant shows through a variety of behaviors the ability to discriminate his mother and other essential caregivers from other people. At around seven months of age, with an increase in locomotive abilities, the infant becomes more active in initiating the seeking out of proximity and social contact. He now may actively follow, approach or cling to significant adults in his environment and these contact behaviors become more clearly *goal directed*.

Bowlby (1969) has proposed that at around the third year of life, the child becomes capable of differentiating himself from others to the extent that he can now differentiate social interactions separate from himself. At this point in his development, he is now not only capable of reciprocal social relationships with other close family members, but also is able to start to form attachment relationships with his peers. Many of these new attachments are formed and reinforced within a variety of different play activities, both within unstructured situations (home, neighborhood, park) and more structured situations (day care center, nursery or cooperative preschool settings).

There appears to be little doubt about the fact that a child develops a great deal of social skill in play situations and in the content of the play engaged in. The general sequence of play behavior appears to progress along a dimension of increased social involvement, from preference for solitary activities (around age two to three years) to highly sophisticated social (cooperative) play at five to six years of age (Parten, 1932; Barnes, 1971). It is generally felt that as the child's cognitive abilities continue to develop and mature, he becomes more *ready* to try out increasingly sophisticated social interactions, i.e. he becomes less involved in body exploration and movement control and more interested in social activities and other people.

Essentially, then, the child acquires more sophisticated social skills through specific developmental sequences related to social interactions and relationships. Initially he progresses through early attachment to parents and other significant caregivers until strong and consistent bonds have been achieved. Next, he learns greater and greater social discriminations until he is capable of discriminating self from others. Finally, the child, through many learning opportunities, particularly in play situations, enters into the realm of goal-directed relationships in which he not only chooses friends, but becomes increasingly able to share objects and activities, and also gradually acquires emotional understanding (sensitivity) of the feelings of others.

EARLY COGNITIVE DEVELOPMENT

The development of cognition is an extremely complex process and so far we have no screening measures of cognitive capabilities, at least for the first few years of life; therefore, at the present time we are frequently required to *infer* cognitive functioning from the child's behavior. The model of cognitive behavior most frequently used for this process is the one developed by Piaget over the last thirty years or so and is based on his extensive observations of child behavior. According to his model, the process of cognitive development continues over a long period of time, and through repeated interactions with his environment, the infant gradually develops his ability to think rationally, conceptually and symbolically. Adaptive changes in his thinking (cognition) occur through the process of *accommodation* (ideas or concepts gradually conforming with external objects) and *assimilation* (the interpretation of events and/or objects according to one's own way of thinking).

The first two years of life are described by Piaget's model as the period of *sensorimotor development*. Although it is difficult to determine whether the infant, during this period, is actually capable of manipulating internal images or symbols, there is substantial evidence to suggest that he is capable of recognition and anticipation of specific and recurring objects and events and his behavior is sufficiently predictive to suggest that he *knows* something about them.

This sensorimotor period covers six stages of development where the infant goes from a simple sucking and mouthing of objects to the differentiation of objects, the successful searching of objects, which have been screened from view, and the ability to imitate models who are no longer present. Hence, at each stage the infant progresses at an increased level of behavioral organization, which allows him to respond in more sophisticated and complex ways, leading him to the gradual development of concepts that ultimately give older and meaning to the objects and events in his life.

Perhaps the most important of these concepts is *object permanence,* which permits the infant to deal more and more with objects and other people as independent aspects of his own perceptual and motor activities, i.e. objects and experiences become differentiated from his own actions and behavioral patterns and he gradually comes to *know* that specific objects and events are not just an extension of himself. Other important concepts the individual infant learns about in the sensorimotor period are such things as the organization of objects in space, means-ends relationships, causality and object organization.

Screening measures of general development are usually employed to select out those children who may be at-risk for some significant future disability associated with developmental delay. The actual quantitative extent of a child's developmental delay is rather difficult to define as a preschool child at any age may develop in a somewhat inconsistent or sporadic fashion; i.e. in spurts or periods of slow development. It is recognized, further, that most, if not all children, have some transient problems at later periods of their lives (Campbell and Camp, 1975). Hence, Campbell and Camp have suggested that "developmental screening be performed when the child is between 1 and 2½ years of age, again at 3 years, after speech is well developed, and at 5 years, prior to school entrance."

Significant developmental delay has been attributed or linked to a wide variety of factors including genetic/biological anomalies, pre- and perinatal care and such environmental variables as parental education, poverty, social deprivation and the emotional stability of the child's parents or major caregivers. It is hypothesized that some of the long-term effects of developmental delay may be retardation in intellectual and social functioning, speech and language disorders, behavioral and emotional instability and serious mental disorder. In regards to this latter factor, there is now substantial evidence to suggest that the degree of psychopathology is directly related to the quality of the child's family environment (Anthony, 1970; Werner, Bierman and French, 1971; Werner and Smith, 1977; Cools and Hermanns, 1978).

Although identifying a child on a screening measure as at-risk for general development is usually done through a comparison of the child's performance relative to his normative group, such a procedure leaves much to be desired for a variety of reasons. For example, we do not yet have any *national* norms as to what constitutes adequate or normal general development. Furthermore, although many of the developmental screening tests have normative data associated with them, most of these norms are restricted to certain target populations and very specific geographic locations (Thorpe and Werner, 1974). A related problem has to do with the fact that although many of these screening tests purport to measure the same thing, namely, general development, the general level of agreement (correlation) across measures is subject to substantial variability and may range from .46 to .98 (Caldwell and Drachman, 1964) and from .86 to .92 (Frankenberg, Camp, and Van Natta, 1971). In conjunction with these problems is the difficulty in specifically determining what a developmentally delayed preschool child is at-risk for. This difficulty is more substantial in some developmental areas than in others; for example, many general developmental screening measures have subtests in areas such as language and gross/fine motor abilities, and significantly delayed performance in these areas may have a very disabling effect on the child in terms of adequate communication skills and later school performance. However, significant delay in personal-social skills, self-identity or self-sufficiency is more difficult to evaluate and may be more related to a child's later personality development or temperamental characteristics than to significant disabling conditions; i.e. psychopathology or serious behavioral problems. In fact, as Campbell and Camp (1975) point out: "Despite the efforts of many investigators to relate factors in early childhood to later development of psychiatric disorders, very little has been done to weld this information into a viable tool." Such a point must be given serious consideration in view of the fact that a child may be identified as at-risk on the basis of failing only one or two subtests on a general development screening measure.

Another problem that must be taken into account when evaluating the impact of developmental delay on later performance is how that later performance is measured and its relative level of precision. For example, if a child is at-risk in the area of visual acuity there are a series of refractory diagnostic procedures which utilize rather precise standardized measuring devices to determine the existence, nature and extent of the child's potential visual difficulties. However, when we enter into the realm of general developmental screening, the outcome or criterion measures generally used are characterized more by their diversity than by their homogeneity and/or precision. For example, the relationship between a preschool child's score on a developmental screening test and his later ability to function may be measured by such things as a battery of psychological tests, a pediatric examination, referral to a psychiatrist or an educational specialist for diagnosis, repeating or failing a grade in school, teacher ratings, observations of deviant or acting-out behavior, or performance on other, more individualized scales of child development. This diversity in outcome measurement leads to considerable difficulty in the evaluation of screening measures of general development. For example, Smith, Flick, Ferris and Sellmann (1972) showed that a combination of various prenatal, perinatal and postnatal events successfully predicted a child's performance on a battery of psychological tests at age seven. However, the relationship between a specific child's performance on this battery and his actual functioning level in say reading, spelling, arithmetic, writing or nonacademic activities is not reported on and as the relationships between scores on psychological tests and actual functioning in real life situations is frequently less than perfect, it is not clear from this study (and others like it) what this combination of predictor variables actually predicted in the way of *specific* disability or disorder. This statement is not meant to deny the validity of using psychological tests as criterion measures for developmental screening, but is made to emphasize the importance of getting the constructors of general developmental screening measures to define what a developmentally delayed child on their particular measure is at-risk for.

Of course, in any measurement of a child's general development, one of the main uncontrolled variables is his *home environment,* and it is interesting to note in our review of developmental screening measures that only a few test developers have paid serious attention to this variable. Such a state of affairs is indeed unfortunate, for as Sameroff (1974) and Lewis (1980) have pointed out, there is now considerable evidence to support an interactional model for the identification of risk factors in young children. Such an interactional model postulates that later disabling conditions (antisocial-deviant behavior, language disabilities, psychopathology, etc.), comes about through the interacting of the biological and temperamental characteristics of the young child, his principal caregivers and the social/economic quality of his physical environment. One of the major ramifications of this model may be that to ensure the most successful early identification of developmentally at-risk children the best method may not be to simply screen the preschool child on a general developmental screening test, but to broaden the screening data base to include direct observation of the child's behavior in his home, together with measures of his mother's level of anxiety, the social, educational and economic levels of his family and the degree of psychopathology of his parents (Meier, 1973; Bijou and Peterson, 1974; Sameroff, 1974; Garmezy, 1976; Werner and Smith, 1977).

The final problem that must be included in any discussion of general developmental screening has to do not with the measures themselves but with actually getting parents and other principal caregivers to bring their preschool children in for testing. In many health settings, the percentage of children seen for developmental screening may be as low as 50 percent of the total number eligible, despite active mass media campaigns and other ways of notifying parents about some of the clinics. One possible solution to this problem may be *outreach clinics* (Richmond, 1969) specifically designed to identify and introduce into the system of preventive health care those individual families who are most in need of screening services, but who have not yet participated in them, either because they don't know about them, or because they lack personal motivation. Another type of solution might be the development of well constructed developmental screening tests that may be administered by parents; a third alternative may be to carry out the screening program in the child's home, particularly if the family is reluctant to bring the child into the community health setting. This last approach is an alternative that has already been actively implemented by Bradley and Caldwell in their development of the Home Inventory.

While reading the following selected review of developmental screening tests, two points should be kept in mind. The first is associated with a measure's test-retest reliability, for in the measurement of development, especially in early childhood, the organism changes very rapidly; therefore, the longer the period between the first and second administration of the test, the lower the reliability coefficient is expected to be. The second area of concern is related to the issue of validity. Because many constructors of general developmental screening tests have not defined what specific disabilities their tests are supposed to predict, many of them, in validating their measures, have used the approach of correlating their tests' scores with a whole variety of disabilities, including learning disorders, behavioral problems, cognitive deficits and psychopathology.

Although most screening measures of general development (and those on preacademic readiness to be reviewed in the next chapter) do not meet all of the essential requirements of the A.P.A. *Standards for Educational and Psychological Tests,* there is frequently a noticeable improvement, when compared with measures previously reviewed, in the way that the tests have been constructed, and the more rigorous efforts that have been made by the developers to provide data on reliability and validity.

THE DENVER DEVELOPMENTAL SCREENING TEST (DDST)

The DDST consists of 105 items divided into four subtest areas; gross motor (thirty-one items), fine motor (thirty items), language (twenty-one items) and personal social skills (twenty-three items). It covers an age range of from birth to six years and children are classified as *normal* (no failures), *questionable* (one failure in one subject area) and *abnormal* (two or more failures in at least one subtest area). The test was standardized on 1,036 normal children between the ages of two weeks and 6.4 years, whose families reflected the occupational and ethnic characteristics of the Denver, Colorado population.

Since the introduction of the DDST by Frankenburg & Dodds (1967), the test has been revised, Frankenburg, Dodds & Fandal (1970), and has been the subject of a considerable amount of research, both in North America and other parts of the world, including Japan (Ueda: 1978, 1980), the Netherlands (Hermanns, 1978) and the Phillipines (Williams, 1980). Within North America a wide variety of studies (Sandler, Van Campen, Ratner, Stafford and Weismar, 1970; Frankenburg, Camp and Van Natta, 1971; Frankenburg, Camp, Van Natta, Demersseman and Voorhees, 1971; Frankenburg, Goldstein and Camp, 1971; Thorpe and Werner, 1974; Barnes and Stark, 1975; Frankenburg, Dick and Carland, 1975; Camp, van Doorninck, Frankenburg and Lampe, 1977; van Doorninck, Dick, Frankenburg, Liddell and Lampe, 1976; van Doorninck, 1978) have been carried out looking at both the reliability and predictive validity of the DDST.

In general, the reliability studies have produced test-retest correlations ranging from a low of .66 to a high of .93 depending on the child's age (Frankenburg, Camp and Van Natta, 1971). However, according to the authors' report some items are more stable than others and when one looks at the data, one sees that most of these stable items (63 percent) are the ones requiring the mother to report on her child's behavior. By and large, the reliability studies have been carefully done; however, the results are frequently based on small samples of children that have not been randomly selected nor stratified for socioeconomic status.

The validity studies have primarily looked at two aspects (concurrent and predictive); in the studies on concurrent validity (Frankenburg, Camp and Van Natta, 1971; Frankenburg, Goldstein and Camp, 1971), scores on the DDST have been compared to scores on the Stanford Binet Intelligence Test, the Revised Yale Developmental Schedule, the Bayley Infant Mental and Motor Scales and the Cattell Infant Intelligence Scale, and the correlation coefficients have ranged from .84 (Bayley Motor Scale) to .97 (Cattell Infant Intelligence Scale). The data for the hit rates and false positive/false negative rates are shown in Table X. Although the false-positive and false-negative rates are rather high (24.31 percent and 26.79 percent respectively), their high magnitude may in part be a reflection on the fact that a relatively high proportion of the items on the DDST are scored as passed according to the mother's report of the child's behavior, whereas all items on the Stanford Binet and the Bayley scales are scored according to the child's observed level of performance. However, the specificity and sensitivity of the DDST and its false positive/false negative rates diminish substantially if one reanalyzes the data omitting those subjects who fall into the borderline or questionable categories, as illustrated in Table XI.

As one can see, the specificity of the test increases to 95.14 percent, the sensitivity to 88.24 percent, the false-positive rate drops to 4.86 percent, while the false-negative rate is reduced to 11.76 percent.

The two predictive studies by Camp, van Doorninck, Frankenburg and Lampe (1977) and van Doorninck, Dick, Frankenburg, Liddell and Lampe (1976) have both looked at performance on the DDST with later school performance; where school performance has been defined as abnormal (poor achievement, intense behavior problems and an I.Q. of less than eighty) or normal

Table X

**PREDICTIVE VALIDITY OF DDST SCORES WITH SCORES
ON THE BAYLEY INFANT MENTAL AND MOTOR SCALES (BIMMS)
OR THE STANFORD-BINET (S-B)**

PREDICTIVE MEASURE

DDST

Outcome Measure BIMMS or S-B	*Normal*	*At-Risk*	
Normal	137	44	181
At-Risk	15	41	56
			237

Specificity $= \dfrac{137}{181} = 75.69\%$

Sensitivity $= \dfrac{41}{56} = 73.21\%$

False-positive Rate $= \dfrac{44}{181} = 24.31\%$

False-negative Rate $= \dfrac{15}{56} = 26.79\%$

In order to reduce the data to fit into a 2 X 2 contingency table, the Abnormal and Borderline categories from the original study by Frankenburg, Goldstein & Camp (1971) have been combined.

Table XI

**PREDICTIVE VALIDITY OF DDST SCORES WITH SCORES ON THE BIMMS
OR THE S-B WHEN Ss SCORING IN THE BORDERLINE OR
QUESTIONABLE CATEGORIES ARE OMITTED**

PREDICTIVE MEASURE

DDST

Outcome Measure BIMMS or S-B	*Normal*	*At-Risk*	
Normal	137	7	144
At-Risk	2	15	17
			161

Specificity $= \dfrac{137}{144} = 95.14\%$

Sensitivity $= \dfrac{15}{17} = 88.24\%$

False-positive rate $= \dfrac{7}{144} = 4.86\%$

False-negative rate $= \dfrac{2}{17} = 11.76\%$

Source: Frankenburg, Goldstein & Camp, 1971.

Table XII

**PREDICTIVE VALIDITY OF DDST SCORES
IN SCREENING FOR SCHOOL PROBLEMS**

PREDICTIVE MEASURE

DDST

Outcome Measure
School Problems   *Normal*   *At-Risk*

	Normal	At-Risk	
Normal	17	11	28
At-Risk	8	29	37

65

Specificity $= \dfrac{17}{28} = 60.71\%$

Sensitivity $= \dfrac{29}{37} = 78.38\%$

False-positive Rate $= \dfrac{11}{28} = 39.29\%$

False-negative Rate $= \dfrac{8}{37} = 21.62\%$

Source: Camp, van Doorninck, Frankenburg & Lampe, 1977.

Table XIII

**PREDICTIVE VALIDITY OF DDST SCORES
IN SCREENING FOR SCHOOL PROBLEMS**

PREDICTIVE MEASURE

DDST

Outcome Measure School Problems	Normal	At-Risk	
Normal	32	28	60
At-Risk	19	72	91
			151

Specificity $= \dfrac{32}{60} = 53.33\%$

Sensitivity $= \dfrac{72}{91} = 79.12\%$

False-positive rate $= \dfrac{28}{60} = 46.67\%$

False-negative rate $= \dfrac{19}{91} = 20.88\%$

Source: van Doorninck, Dick, Frankenburg, Liddell & Lampe, 1977.

(average or better achievement, no behavior problems and an I.Q. of more than eighty). Table XII illustrates the data from the Camp et al. (1977) study, while Table XIII provides the data from the van Doorninck et al. (1977) study. The data for abnormal and questionable has again been combined for these 2 X 2 contingency tables.

As can be seen from the tables, the false positive/false negative rates for the Camp et al. study were 39.29 percent and 21.62 percent respectively; while the false positive/false negative rates for the van Doorninck et al. study were 46.67 percent and 20.88 percent respectively. These rates together with the test's specificity and sensitivity are again very high, but can be substantially reduced if one again leaves out all those subjects classified as Borderline or Questionable. For example, for the Camp et al. data, specificity and sensitivity increases to 89.47 percent and 100.00 percent respectively, the false positive rate drops to 10.53 percent, while the false negative rate is reduced to zero. Although the data for the van Doorninck study shows a similar increase in specificity (to 88.89 percent) and a corresponding drop in the false positive rate to 11.11 percent, there is a subsequent decrease in sensitivity (to 62.00 percent) and an increase in the false negative rate to 38 percent.

Although the results of these validity studies provide considerable support for the utility of the DDST as a screening measure, the studies themselves are not without some drawbacks. For example, the samples used are rather small and are not representative of the general population, but consist of nonrandomized groups of children from the Denver metropolitan area. Furthermore, the van Doorninck et al. study is particularly weighted with children from lower socioeconomic status families. Another problem is the validity of using I.Q. tests as current criterion measures, when in the past Frankenburg and Dodds (1967) have clearly stated that the DDST is not an intelligence test. A final concern is that the validity studies do not, in general, provide very much support for the Questionable scoring category of the DDST; in fact, the predictive utility of the measure is substantially improved when that category is dropped from the identification process of at-risk children.

Two cross-validation studies have also been carried out on the DDST (Frankenburg, Goldstein and Camp, 1971; Barnes and Stark, 1975). The study by Frankenburg, Goldstein and Camp (1971) was essentially a replication of their original concurrent validation study but with a new sample of 246 preschool-age children. Table XIV summarizes the data for those children who are identified as normal and abnormal (the Questionable/Border-line group has been omitted from this table, as the inclusion of this group again decreases the predictive validity of the DDST).

Table XIV

CROSS-VALIDATION OF THE PREDICTIVE VALIDITY OF DDST SCORES WITH SCORES ON THE BIMMS OR S-B

PREDICTIVE MEASURE

DDST

Outcome Measure BIMMS or S-B	*Normal*	*At-Risk*	
Normal	162	6	168
At-Risk	0	12	12
			180

Specificity $= \dfrac{162}{168} = 96.43\%$

Sensitivity $= \dfrac{12}{12} = 100.00\%$

False-positive Rate $= \dfrac{6}{12} = 3.57\%$

False-negative Rate $= \dfrac{0}{12} = 0.00\%$

Source: Frankenburg, Goldstein & Camp, 1971.

For this cross-validation sample, the test's specificity and sensitivity were extremely high, while the false-positive rate was 3.57 percent and the false-negative rate was zero.

The study by Barnes and Stark (1975) was on a stratified random sample of 226 British Columbia preschool children between the ages of two weeks and 6.4 years. Despite the fact that this sample of children came from a semi-rural population with families differing significantly from the Denver area in occupation, the intercorrelations between the Denver norms for the DDST and the norms collected by Barnes and Stark were .99 for each of the four subtest areas. Significant occupational class differences were found for some groups; for example, children from craftsman families seemed to consistently perform at a higher level than children from professional families. One other finding was the DDST's ability to discriminate across age levels. The results of an internal analysis of test performance across each of eight age-groups indicated that only one subtest area failed to significantly discriminate and that was in the fine motor area between age-groups seven to nine months and ten to twelve months. All other age-groupings in all four subtest areas were significantly different from each other. Thus, the distribution of scores in the four developmental subtest areas does appear to be significantly related to chronological age.

Significant occupational class differences were also reported between a cross-sectional sample of Anglo children, when compared with an Anglo sample of low SES families (Frankenburg, Dick and Carland, 1975). In this study, the authors report that up to the age of twenty months low SES children seem to be *more advanced* than cross-sectional SES children; however, by twenty-four months of age this process is reversed and the cross-sectional SES children perform at a more advanced level. The one exception to this finding is in the area of personal-social development where the low SES children consistently perform at a more advanced level. Finally, in a study of 104 Negro and Puerto Rican children between the ages of four and six, Sandler, Van Campen, Ratner, Stafford and Weismar (1970) found significant differences between their sample and the original DDST normative sample.

To date, the DDST is one of the most comprehensively researched screening measures so far developed; there are, however, still some areas of concern. One is that there are few representative national norms for the North American continent, another that there are few longitudinal studies on its predictive validity. Related to this latter factor is the problem of knowing what an abnormal score on the DDST means in terms of later disability. Some evidence has been cited (Camp, van Doorninck, Frankenburg and Lampe, 1977; van Doorninck, Dick, Frankenburg, Liddell and Lampe, 1976) to suggest that an abnormal DDST predicts to later educational and school behavioral problems; however, in an unpublished study of eighty-five preschool-age children screened on the DDST and followed up until the end of the third grade (Barnes, 1980) only five or 31.25 percent of the total number of children classified as at-risk were later identified in the school system as having behavioral and/or educational problems, and although the false-positive rate for this study was a low 9.46 percent, the false-negative rate was an incredible 68.75 percent. Thus, the consequences of delayed development, as measured on the DDST, are still somewhat uncertain. Such ambiguity constitutes a serious predictive problem if one of the major purposes of using the DDST is to identify children at-risk for specific disabilities at a point in time when treatment will be both more effective and economical. A final concern has to do with those children who score in the Questionable category. The evidence so far suggests that for purposes of predicting later disabilities this category is not very effective. Perhaps the best procedure to follow in these cases is to watch the children carefully over time and to reassess them at periodic intervals.

Despite these concerns, the DDST is a widely used screening measure and the developers have produced a test, which in many ways, has been designed to be used by trained paraprofessionals. The test manual is well written and instructive and the test materials are easy to administer and inexpensive. The developers are to be commended, further, for their continuing research efforts to make the DDST an increasingly effective screening measure.

HOME OBSERVATION FOR MEASUREMENT OF THE ENVIRONMENT (HOME)

In view of the significant relationship between preschool development and the environment in which the child lives, the screening measure that focuses on observations of the child's early home experiences provides an important tool in the screening process. Although the HOME takes approximately an hour to administer by a carefully trained person and thus is not very suitable for mass screening programs, it is reviewed here because, as pointed out earlier, an assessment of the child's environment might in the long run prove to be a more powerful predictor of children at-risk than many of the screening measures currently designed to identify developmental delay.

In its present format, the HOME Inventory, developed by Caldwell and Bradley (undated), consists of two subscales; one form covers the period of time from birth to three years of age, while the other form is designed for children aged three to six years. The zero to three subscale assesses six areas of the child's environment (emotional and verbal responsivity of the mother, avoidance and restriction of punishment, organization of physical and temporal environment, provision of appropriate play materials, maternal involvement with the child and opportunities for variety in daily stimulation), while the three to six version covers eight areas (stimulation through toys, games and reading materials; positive social responsiveness; physical environment conducive to development; pride, affection and warmth; stimulation of academic behavior; modeling and encouragement of social maturity; variety of stimulation; and physical punishment).

The HOME manual reports reliability coefficients for both forms of the inventory; unfortunately, there is no discussion of the demographic make-up of the standardization sample selected or in the case of the three-to-six subscale, the actual size of the sample used. However, for the zero-to-three subscale, using a sample of 174 children, Caldwell and Bradley (undated) report an internal consistency coefficient for the total scores of .89 and for a sample of ninety-one children, test-retest correlations of .62 (for a six-month time interval), .64 (for an eighteen-month time interval) and .77 (for a twelve-month time interval). For the three-to-six subscale, on a sample of unknown size, the authors report an internal consistency coefficient for the total scores of .93 and a test-retest correlation of .70 (for an eighteen-month time interval). In regards to the test-retest correlations, both subscales show substantial stability considering the time span between test-retest administrations.

The bulk of the validity studies on the HOME Inventory have essentially focused on the relationships between HOME scores in the first year of life and scores on the Bayley MDI at six and twelve months and Stanford Binet scores at thirty-six and fifty-four months of age (Elardo, Bradley and Caldwell, 1975; Bradley and Caldwell, 1976a; Bradley and Caldwell, 1976b; Bradley and Caldwell, 1978; Bradley, Caldwell and Elardo, 1977, 1979). One study has looked at the relationship between HOME scores at twenty-four months and ITPA scores at thirty-seven months of age (Elardo, Bradley and Caldwell, 1977) and another study looked at the relationship between three- to six-year-old HOME scores and socioeconomic status factors (Bradley and Caldwell, 1979). In general, the results of these studies tend to indicate relatively low correlations with Bayley MDI scores, but moderate to high correlations with Stanford Binet and ITPA scores and measures of socioeconomic status associated with maternal and paternal education. The data from one study that looked at the specific prediction of I.Q. at thirty-six months from HOME scores given at six months of age (Bradley and Caldwell, 1977) is illustrated in Table XV. As can be seen from this table, the Inventory's specificity and sensitivity is 78.12 percent and 100.00 percent respectively, while the false positive rate is 21.88 percent, and the false negative rate is zero. Another study, by Ramey, Mills, Campbell and O'Brien (1975) showed that the HOME Inventory could successfully discriminate between *normal* and *at-risk* homes for the purposes of identifying developmental delay in children under three years of age.

The HOME Inventory has been in existence now for fifteen years and has undergone two revisions; it was officially published in 1981. The developers of this inventory together with other researchers in the field have carried out a total of thirty-one studies on its reliability, validity and its relationship to other variables (Bradley, 1980). Probably the major weakness in its development has been that it has not been standardized on a large stratified random sample of the general population of children from birth to six years of age. It has also not been subjected to any cross-validation research and many of the samples that it has been used on have been small in size, predominantly black and from low socioeconomic families. Thus, the normative data currently available may be totally unsuitable for use in the screening of middle and upper-middle class families. The other disadvantage to its use as previously mentioned is that in its present form it is not very adaptable for mass screening due to its one-hour administration time. This latter disadvantage may soon disappear if the HOME Screening Questionnaire (HSQ) fulfills its early promise (see Chapter 10 for a review of the HSQ). However, despite these reservations, the HOME Inventory is by far the best developed screening measure currently available for evaluating a preschool child's home environment, and for those low SES children who, when screened for developmental delay, fall into the questionable category, it is the follow-up measure of choice.

Table XV

**THE PREDICTIVE VALIDITY OF HOME INVENTORY SCORES
AT SIX MONTHS OF AGE WITH SCORES ON THE STANFORD-BINET
INTELLIGENCE TEST (S-B) AT THIRTY-SIX MONTHS OF AGE**

PREDICTIVE MEASURE

HOME

Outcome Measure S-B	*Normal*	*At-Risk*	
Normal	25	7	32
At-Risk	0	12	12
			44

Specificity $= \dfrac{25}{32} = 78.12\%$

Sensitivity $= \dfrac{12}{12} = 100.00\%$

False-positive Rate $= \dfrac{7}{32} = 21.88\%$

False-negative Rate $= \dfrac{0}{12} = 100.00\%$

Source: Bradley & Caldwell, 1977.

THE MINNESOTA CHILD DEVELOPMENT INVENTORY
(MCDI)

The MCDI is a developmental screening measure based on the mother's observations of the child's behavior. It is designed for children between the ages of one and six years and consists of 320 descriptive statements of child behavior in the areas of general development, gross motor, fine motor, expressive language, comprehension conceptual, situation comprehension, self-help and personal-social. The items were selected from a total item pool of approximately 2,000 statements and the 320 most age-discriminating items were chosen for the standardization process. The standardization sample consisted of 796 children from white upper-middle class families who resided in the community of Bloomington, Minnesota. The manual (Ireton and Thwing, 1974), which is well written and clearly illustrated, provides detailed information on each of the eight developmental scales as well as data on the intercorrelation of the scales and their reliability.

The split-half reliability coefficients reported in the manual are given for specific age groups, and in general range from the middle .60s to the high .80s and low .90s with a median of .79; however, the coefficients for age-groups below one year are not as high (median = .65). The intercorrelations across the eight scales at three selected age-groups (twelve to seventeen months, thirty to thirty-five months, and fifty-four to fifty-nine months) are quite substantial especially at the youngest age level.

The test developers do not report on the amount of time required to complete the inventory, nor do they provide details on the MCDI's validity in the manual, but a study by Ireton and Thwing (1979) on a sample of 109 white preschool-aged children showed that below normal scores on the general development, fine motor, expressive language and comprehension conceptual scales were related to below average scores on psychological tests in the areas of expressive language, fine motor performance and intelligence. A study by Ullman and Kausch (1979) found that preschool children attending a head start program were considerably more developmentally delayed, as measured on the MCDI, than were children attending a regular nursery school program. One study on the prediction of reading skill at the end of the kindergarten year was carried out by Colligan (1976). In this investigation, fifty-nine children were screened on the MCDI before entering kindergarten, and at the end of their kindergarten year were assessed on the Lippincott Reading Readiness Test, the Metropolitan Reading Readiness Test and the Wide Range Achievement Test. The results indicated substantial correlations between the MCDI subscales of general development, fine motor and conceptual comprehension, and scores on the LLRT, MRRT and WRAT, especially for girls. However, for predictive purposes there are some problems with the study, including a very small N (twenty-eight males and thirty-one females) and the fact that the predictive validity of many reading readiness tests administered in kindergarten is low compared to actual reading achievement later on.

Despite the author's very careful work in developing the MCDI, there are several factors that must be carefully considered before using this measure for mass developmental screening. First, the normative data provided in the manual is based on one sample of children from an upper middle class community in the state of Minnesota. The applicability of these behavioral norms cannot, as pointed out by the authors, "be considered representative of white preschool-aged children in general . . . the norms represent a standard of development that is achievable under relatively favorable environmental circumstances." Secondly, as pointed out in an earlier chapter, the accuracy of a child's developmental performance, when based on parental observations, may be subject to considerable bias and inconsistency, particularly as all scale items on the MCDI are answered on a yes-no basis. Thirdly, although the test developers report split-half reliability coefficients, there is no evidence provided in the manual on the test's stability over time (test-retest reliability) and one should also be concerned about any test that purports to measure eight separate areas of development with intercorrelations as high as those reported for the MCDI. Finally, there is only one published report so far on the measure's predictive validity. Although some evidence is provided for concurrent validity, the children used were not randomly selected from the general population but were a *clinical* sample referred to a child psychology clinic for a variety of developmental problems.

Many of these concerns may well be alleviated as more research reports on the MCDI become available; however, until this happens one must be very careful about using the Inventory for mass screening purposes. Despite these cautions, the MCDI is one of the most promising developmental screening tests to emerge in the last few years because it seriously attempts to identify developmental delay on the basis of parental observations. And, as has been stated before, such a procedure, if free of response bias, provides a measure of child development based on much more extensive behavioral samples than can normally be achieved in a formally administered ten to fifteen minute developmental appraisal. For another review of the MCDI see Goodwin (1978).

Chapter 9

MEASURES OF ACADEMIC READINESS

IN A SENSE, THE DEVELOPMENT OF preacademic skills is simply an expansion and refinement of earlier general developmental skills, with particular focus on the areas of fine motor ability, intellectual/cognitive development and emotional maturity; in other words, those skills and abilities that are prerequisites to the three *Rs* (reading, writing and arithmetic) and other aspects of the school curriculum. The basic objective of screening for preacademic skills is to identify, as soon as possible, those preschoolers who, for whatever reasons, do not seem to be adequately developing those skills necessary for later academic success.

READING READINESS

There is little disagreement among educators or developmentalists concerning the importance of reading, both as a highly developed cognitive skill in its own right and as a precursor to the acquisition of many other learning skills necessary for adequate development in adolescence and adulthood. The major objective of screening for future academic achievement is, of course, to identify critical readiness skills (or the lack of them) so that the preschooler can be provided with the appropriate intervention programs (Zaeske, 1970; Zeitlin, 1976).

In general, because of their importance to nearly all facets of later learning, reading and a preschool child's readiness for reading are considered to be very significant factors in the level of academic success a person may achieve throughout his life. In view of this fact, the findings of Satz, Taylor, Friel and Fletcher (1979), from their very comprehensive study on the developmental and predictive precursors of reading disability, indicated that "cultural, linguistic, conceptual and perceptual skills all play an important role in forecasting later reading achievement." They pointed out further that parental reading skills and socioeconomic status may also play very influential roles in preparing children for later reading achievement.

Although there exists a variety of measures available for the screening of reading readiness, this kind of concept is rather global in nature and frequently involves the identification of a series of important subskills. Hence, a great deal of the research on reading readiness has been concerned with certain critical skill areas and the issues surrounding their development rather than concentrating on a normative-developmental approach to reading in general.

The major skill areas may be divided into the following parts:

1. *Auditory:* Research over the last decade has clearly shown that the area of audition contains several skill areas important to success in reading. These include *auditory discrimination,* which involves the discrimination of sounds as well as phonemes, single words, nonsense words and consonant differences. *Auditory blending* and *auditory segmentation,* which includes synthesizing syllables or phonemes into words when these component sounds are presented orally (blending), and, conversely, splitting words into their respective syllables and phonemes (segmentation). *Rhyming,* or the ability to either recognize when words rhyme or actually to be able to rhyme words together. *Auditory memory,* or the recall of words or sounds in the oral sequence presented.

2. *Visual:* In the visual area, the two major skills most relevant seem to be *visual discrimination,* including the perception and discrimination of various shapes and geometric forms. However, although readiness training programs have frequently utilized such tasks, there is now considerable evidence (Wingart, 1969; Robinson, 1972; Smith and Marx, 1972) to suggest that such training programs may be of limited value. On the other hand, there is increasing support for the idea that visual discrimination of *letters* and *words* is of substantial importance to the development

of later reading skills. (See Barrett, 1965, for a review of the research in this area.) Specifically, such tasks as matching letters, together with the identification of letters, their relative positions in words and their order within words, all seem to be relevant factors in later reading acquisition. In fact, one of the most consistent research findings in the area of reading acquisition is persistently high correlations between the successful identification of letters and later success in reading achievement. The second major skill in the visual area is that of *visual memory,* or the selection and matching of a previously observed stimulus letter or word.

3. *Auditory-Visual:* The integration of two senses (vision and audition) would appear to be a logical prerequisite to later reading ability. However, the research in this area is somewhat conflictual for two reasons; one is the fact that as yet we have no clear-cut developmental evidence as to when such intersensory integration takes place and the second is that we do not really know how such intersensory integration is uniquely related to reading. Perhaps what can be said in this area is that the actual matching of verbal utterances with their respective visual representations, i.e. words is probably an important intersensory skill to acquire for later reading.

4. *Language:* Although the relationship between reading and language goes as far back as the 1930s (Durrell and Sullivan, 1937), it has been extremely difficult to determine what specific language behaviors are developmentally significant to later success in reading. In other words, as Weaver and Kingston (1977) have recently pointed out, the dependency between reading and oral language has not yet been specifically identified.

5. *Rate of Learning Words:* Learning rate for words has, for many years, been considered a fairly powerful predictor of later reading achievement (Durell, 1956; Gavel, 1958; and Nicholson, 1958). However, there are several procedural problems in testing learning rates that have to be kept in mind; these include the types of words selected, word similarity and the time intervals between word teaching and testing for retention. All of these factors can and do influence the child's rate of performance.

6. *Concept of Reading:* Two factors seem to be important here. One has to do with the child's own expectations about

what reading is all about, i.e. his understanding of the purpose of reading and its function in his life. The belief here is that the more the child understands the purpose and function of reading, the more he may be motivated to learn to read. The other important factor is related to the child's basic understanding of words, letters and sounds and how they are related to the written language. It is generally believed that the more a child *understands* what words are and how they may differ from letters and sounds, the more *ready* he may be to learn to read.

7. *Reading Interests:* No discussion of reading readiness would be complete without some reference to the importance of the child's own interests and their relationship to reading acquisition. Although we must be careful to define what we mean when we talk about the child's interests and particularly how those interests are measured, it seems that given the opportunity, listening to stories of high interest value may serve as an important motivating factor in getting children to learn to read. Also, we should be aware of the fact that a child's interests and preferences may be markedly influenced by the environment in which he lives and the current trends and events in his society. Right now, for example, we are still deeply involved in space exploration, and of course, there has occurred a corresponding proliferation of television programs on the same topic.

Although the major emphasis in this section on reading readiness has been on specific skills and skill development, two other areas of importance also stand out. One is that in any assessment or screening for reading readiness one must not overlook information on the child's hearing, vision and general development. The second factor has to do with the child's home environment, not only in terms of the availability of reading materials and being read to, but also his parents' own levels of reading skills, interests and years of formal education, all of which seem to be related in some way or another to reading acquisition.

Readiness for Writing

Preparation for writing activities seem to be influenced by such factors as hand preference, the gripping of writing tools and scribbling and other graphic representations. Much of the research in this area has been carried out by Gibson and Yonas (1968) and Gibson and Levin (1975), who indicate that not only does scribbling begin in the second year of life, but that such behavior is reinforcing as well as good training for finger manipulation and control over writing instruments. Furthermore, there appears to be a developmental sequence or progression for children in this area as they go from scribbling to controlled strokes, to letter and number writing and finally to name and word writing.

Although Durkin (1963; 1966) has provided some evidence to suggest that for certain children who are early readers, scribbling and copying may lead to reading, it is usually only when such activities are accompanied by encouragement and adult questions and answers concerning reading activities that they may lead to early reading.

Readiness for Mathematics

As in early cognitive development, the model used most extensively for the development of premathematical skills is the one derived from the child observations of Piaget and his co-workers and covers the age range of two to six years of age. This period of development is usually referred to as the preoperational stage. (For the most up-to-date and articulate discussion of this whole period of development see Flavell, 1977.)

The child's cognitive development throughout this stage is a continuation and refinement of the cognitive processes acquired in the sensorimotor period. Perhaps the one major characteristic that best describes the child's performance on cognitive tasks in the preoperational stage is that it is *perception-bound*. That is to say that the child's judgements are heavily reliant on *perceived appearances* and he has great difficulty in making *inferences* about reality. He tends to center his attention on just one feature of a stimulus object or event; i.e. height or color, and in experiments on transformation will pay the closest attention to the *final state* of an event or object. For example, if twelve blocks are arranged close together and then transformed into a long row of blocks, the child will focus on the final state of the transformation and say there are more blocks than in the first arrangement.

The sequence of development during the preoperational period begins with the child performing simple *classification* tasks. He starts out by classifying familiar objects and events, putting toys in the toy box and clothes in the clothes closet; he then progresses to the point where he can place all square blocks together in one pile and all round objects in another. This classification sequence is followed by one of *ordination* or the identification and placing of objects in *serial position.* This process begins with the child being able to group objects according to size or height and ends with him being able to place objects in specific serial position; i.e. first, third, and so on.

The concept of *cardination,* naming objects by number, follows next in the sequence and begins with the child *subitizing* or estimating small groups of objects (one to three) accurately without actually counting each one. The importance of subitizing lies in the fact that it provides the child with opportunities to practice his counting skills, i.e. he makes an estimate and then counts the objects to see if his estimate is correct. Accuracy of estimation is also aided by *rote counting;* although, of course, simple rote counting is of limited value by itself, it becomes increasingly useful if it is paired on a one-to-one basis with the actual counting of objects.

The fourth step in the developmental sequence of preoperational cognition is the one involving the child's understanding of number sets and set comparisons; more commonly called *set concepts.* In this part of the developmental process, the child learns to make judgements about sets of objects to the extent that he is able to work out which set of objects has more or less than, or the same number as another set of objects. Mastery of set concepts is, of course, essential to the child's later ability to solve addition- and subtraction-type problems.

The final step in this preoperational stage is some basic understanding of the concept of *conservation.* Essentially, conservation of number is the ability to understand that the actual quantity of number remains *unchanged* even when subjected to a wide variety of transformations which may appear to affect the quantity. Until this concept is mastered, Piaget maintains that the child will basically lack the true understanding of the logic involved in addition and subtraction. The tasks most commonly used to measure conservation are ones in which two sets of objects of equal number are presented and then an irrelevant transformation is performed, i.e. the elements of one set are expanded by increasing the length of the row and the child is asked if the two sets are still the same, or if the one set which was transformed now contains more. Mastery of conservation tasks, as can be imagined, takes a long time to acquire and does not tend to be completed until the child is around seven to eight years of age. It is based, according to Piaget, on many years of extensive experience in situations where the child is frequently being called upon in every day life to make conservation-like judgements. For a much more in-depth analysis and discussion on the early development of pre-academic skills, see Cohen and Gross (1979).

Despite the fact that in North America most children are expected to attend the first grade from about the age of five years eight months, there is a great deal of individual variability as to a child's actual readiness for academic learning and his level of social and emotional adjustment to school attendance and classroom routines. After many years of debate, there is now increasing acceptance of the fact that intellectual, emotional and neurophysiological development occurs in an uneven manner within and across children and that although many children *may be* ready for academic achievement when they enter the first grade, quite a few will not.

There are a wide variety of reasons why a child may not be ready academically; perhaps one of the major reasons may be related to limited intellectual abilities. Other possible reasons may be physical disabilities (blindness, deafness, etc.), language and speech disorders, emotional disorders (schizophrenia, autism) and severe behavioral problems (extreme noncompliance, severe hyperactivity, or highly deviant behavior). There is also one other category of problems which is believed to seriously affect school performance in the early years and that involves those children classified as having minimal brain dysfunction. (Eaves, Kendall and Chrichton, 1972), a frequently poorly defined concept, but believed to be the result of uneven maturation within the central nervous system itself. Another problem related to preacademic screening has to do with the generalization of screening procedures originally developed to identify physical disabilities (medical disease model) being carried over to the identification of potential learning disorders, many of which may be unrelated to physical (medical) disabilities. This problem has been beautifully summarized in an article by Keogh and Becker (1973).

> When we seek to identify preschool or kindergarten children whom we fear may become learning failures, we are, in fact, *hypothesizing* (italics added) rather than confirming. That is the conditions which we view as atypical, namely, learning disability and failure in school, have not yet developed. Our concerns are that these conditions *will develop*. Yet, children who have not been exposed to a reading program cannot really be said to have reading problems; and children who have not participated in a first grade program cannot be classified as first grade failures.

In other words, one of the major differences between the early identification of physical disabilities as compared with learning disorders is that for those learning disorders for which there is no physiological basis, such as limited visual acuity, severe hearing impairment, we are actually making a prediction that cannot be confirmed by referral to a diagnostic specialist; the confirmation of the disability can only occur *after* the child has actually participated in a series of school experiences. It is with these kinds of problems in mind that one should consider the discussion that follows.

Prevalence rates for children with educational problems appear to vary substantially depending on the age-group studied, the socioeconomic and ethnic status of the sample population and the criterion measures used. Some of the criteria for evaluation may include teacher ratings and judgements based on observations in kindergarten and grade one, while others may include standardized tests of reading, arithmetic and writing, and still others may involve pediatric, neurological, psychiatric and psychological assessment and diagnosis. For example, the incidence of reading problems on a sample of inner-city kindergarten children assessed at the end of the second grade may be as high as 35 percent (Jansky and deHirsch, 1972), as low as 5 percent for a sample of white middle-class children from a semi-rural population (Barnes, 1978), or, for other samples of children, somewhere in between (Askoff, Otto and Smith, 1972; Satz and Friel, 1974; Satz, Friel and Rudegeair, 1976). Similarly, teachers' ratings of academic nonreadiness for children entering the first or second grade may vary from 25 percent for children entering private schools in the first grade (Banham, 1959), to 14 percent for children entering the second grade in public schools (Pate and Webb, 1969).

Although, like many other areas of screening, the identification of children with potential educational problems is geared to diagnostic and early intervention programs, the task is not always as clear-cut as for other areas. For example, diagnostic and early intervention services for preschool children who have serious intellectual, visual and hearing disorders or disorders of speech and language are based on well-established procedures and training programs; however, diagnosis for reading disorder, emotional and social disorders, minimal brain dysfunction and something as poorly defined as maturational lag or academic underachievement, is frequently based on professional opinions and societal, educational and ethnic expectations, rather than on well-established empirical evidence and standardized clinical procedures. Furthermore, the intervention and training programs to deal with such conditions vary enormously so that their level of effectiveness is often hard to evaluate, and, in the case of minimal brain dysfunction or maturational lag, the success of a particular intervention procedure may have nothing to do with the program itself, but rather with physiological-maturational changes in the child himself. For example, it is well known that the incidence of reading disabilities is extremely low in the Scandinavian countries, a situation that is believed to exist simply because children there do not begin their formal schooling until they are at least seven years old (Downing, 1977). Furthermore, children may perform poorly on school readiness tests not because of their actual educational abilities, but because of fearfulness in the screening situation, because they are fatigued, uncooperative, lacking in motivation or simply because the testing situation is too distracting. Another difficulty, as pointed out by Goldstein (1975), may be related to the cultural and ethnic background of the child. The screening of bilingual children or children from non-English speaking backgrounds must be very carefully evaluated because very few preschool screening tests provide norms for children from such backgrounds.

Another major problem affecting the predictive validity of many preacademic screening tests has to do with the fact that many of the items are not reflective of actual behaviors required in a classroom setting. Adelman and Feshbach (1971) and Feshbach, Adelman and Fuller (1977) have reported at some length on this problem, particularly as it pertains to the prediction of reading failure. In essence, they have demonstrated that rating scales devised to evaluate actual student behavior in kindergarten classes are equal to standardized psychometric measures (WPPSI, Jansky Screening Index, Bender Gestalt Test) in predicting reading ability in the first, second and third grades of elementary school. In a somewhat parallel study Keogh and Smith (1970) showed a remarkably high level of teacher success in predicting school achievement at grade five from student rating scales administered in kindergarten, when compared with Bender-Gestalt Test scores also administered in the kindergarten year. In a similar vein, Forness, Guthrie and Hall (1976) reported on the effectiveness of actual time-sampling techniques for observing specific child behaviors in kindergarten and the prediction of school learning problems at the end of the first grade. These authors found that children observed as at-risk in kindergarten were still shown by teacher ratings to be achieving poorly at the end of the first grade.

These findings are important in that they illustrate the potential contribution that may be made by including the assessment of situational and behavioral factors in the early identification of children who are at-risk for later learning disorders. Indeed, Conrad and Tobiessen (1967) were able to distinguish a wide variety of behavioral dimensions useful in kindergarten screening, including such behaviors as clarity of speech, waiting and sharing, use of materials and the level of organization of play behavior. Finally, some comments should be made about the actual predictive usefulness of administering preacademic screening tests to children before entering kindergarten. The initial thrust for the use of such measures has come from the general consensus that the earlier the child is screened the earlier an identified at-risk child's preacademic problems can be diagnosed and remediated. However, there is now a considerable body of evidence to suggest that in the area of predicting children at-risk for later learning difficulties, kindergarten teachers' observations and ratings may be *more predictively valid* than many screening measures administered at the same time or at an earlier age (Keogh and Smith, 1970; Tobiessen, Duckworth and Conrad, 1971; Keogh and Tchir, 1972; Cowgill, Friedland and Shapiro, 1973; Schaer and Crump, 1976; Feshbach, Adelman and Fuller, 1977), although Stevenson, Parker, Wilkinson, Hegion and Fish (1976a; 1976b) have indicated that such ratings are not necessarily as predictive as *multiple correlations* of specific psychometric measures. Still, in terms of time and economy, kindergarten teachers' identification of children at-risk for later school problems may be preferable to the administration of a battery of psychometric tests.

The following review of selected screening measures for academic readiness is in two parts; the first deals with general functioning measures for children up to kindergarten age, while the second part deals with tests designed to measure specific areas of preacademic functioning. The reader may find the author's selection of some of the general functioning measures under the category of academic readiness, as compared with general development, somewhat arbitrary; however, the general principle of selection followed has been to categorize each measure according to the objectives of the test developers. Thus, if a developer states that his major goal in developing the test was to screen for academic readiness, then his measure has been reviewed in that category.

Developmental Indicators for the Assessment of Learning (DIAL)

This test was designed by Mardell and Goldenberg (1975) to measure four major areas of functioning; Gross Motor (seven tasks), Fine Motor (seven tasks), Concepts (seven tasks) and Communications (seven tasks). In addition, the examiners look for twelve specific social/emotional behaviors over the course of the assessment. In total, the child is assessed on 118 items and the average length of testing is around twenty-five to thirty minutes.

One of the unique aspects of DIAL is that it is structurally and administratively quite different from other screening measures. Structurally it requires the use of a large room where four activity stations can be located together with a registration-play area, an area where the child may be photographed and a parent observation area. The administration of the test requires four examiners (one for each station) plus volunteers for manning the registration desk, the play area and for taking photographs.

The major goal of the developers was to design a measure that would screen preschool children into three major categories: OK, or where the child functions below age level in just one area (except Communications); REDIAL, or where the child performs at below age level in two areas (other than Communications); or FOLLOW-UP, where the child functions below age level in three areas or in Communications. Basically, children falling in the OK category are considered normal in their current functioning, while children in the REDIAL category are requested to come in at another time to take the screening measure again; children in the FOLLOW-UP category are referred for full diagnostic evaluation.

The construction of DIAL was done with considerable care and was pilot tested on two different groups of children (one group was in a day-care setting, while the other group was in an early childhood development program) prior to the initial standardization procedure. The standardization sample consisted of 4,356 children ranging in age from thirty to sixty-six months selected from a volunteer sample stratified by sex, race, socioeconomic status and demographic characteristics for the state of Illinois. Because the original sample was skewed toward the upper age range, the original norms had to be reconstituted, so from the original 4,356 children, one hundred children were randomly selected for each month of age from thirty to sixty-six months and also controlled for sex. This sample of children then made up the norms for males and females.

The reliability of DIAL has been looked at in three ways; inter-rater reliability was evaluated by having sixteen examiners score videotapes of eight children being screened by DIAL and the percent agreement ranged from .81 to .99 (Mardell and Goldenberg, 1978). Wick, Anderson and Major (1973) looked at the reliability of DIAL by randomly selecting 520 children who were initially screened in 1972 and then retesting them one year later.

These 520 children were split into two groups of 260; one group was selected from the upper 90 percent of their 1972 DIAL scores, while the other group was selected from the lower 10 percent. The authors report that these two groups of children were still very distinctive when retested one year later. If one looks at the actual test-retest coefficients for these two groups, broken down by activity area, one finds that the correlations tend to run between .43 and .67; given the fact that many of the test items are measuring developmental function susceptible to changes with chronological age, this finding is quite respectable.

The validity of DIAL has been evaluated by Woodcock (reported in Mardell and Goldenberg, 1978) and Hall, Mardell, Wick and Goldenberg (1976). Woodcock compared the relationships between scores on several preschool screening measures and performance on the Stanford Binet and the Peabody Picture Vocabulary Test (PPVT) on a sample of forty four-year olds attending a day care centre in Minneapolis. This correlation coefficient between DIAL and PPVT was .60, while DIAL scores correlated .74 with the Stanford Binet. The Hall et al. (1976) study on 249 children tested on DIAL in 1972 used as external criteria the Metropolitan Reading Readiness Test (MRRT) plus the Iowa Test of Basic Skills (ITBS), the Metropolitan Achievement Test (MAT), the Stanford Achievement Test (SAT) and a teacher rating scale of social-affective behaviors. The multiple correlations between DIAL scores and these test criterion measures ranged from .47 to .60, all of which were statistically significant.

Concurrent validity was evaluated by Mardell and Goldenberg (1976) in a study of twelve children assessed on DIAL and reassessed by a diagnostic team of psychologists, social workers, nurses and elementary education counselors; the correlation coefficient between these two assessment techniques was .92.

DIAL is limited in the areas of norms and predictive validity. Although the developers have done a rather comprehensive job in sample selection for the state of Illinois, the norms for DIAL are restrictive in the sense that all the subjects in the standardization sample were volunteers and no samples of children were assessed from other geographic areas of North America; thus, the degree to which the norms published in the manual are applicable to the rest of the general population is at present hard to determine. Perhaps the greatest drawback of using DIAL, however, is related to the fact that the measure's actual ability to predict later learning problems in the school situation is virtually unknown. It is more than likely that this latter drawback will be remedied when the developers report further on their longitudinal studies of DIAL. In the meantime, if the measure is to be used for mass screening, local norms should be collected and children falling into the FOLLOW-UP category should be subjected to careful diagnostic evaluation, as maintained by the test authors, before any conclusions are drawn about a child's later school performance.

Minnesota Preschool Inventory
(MPI)

The MPI is a screening measure based on parental report which was derived from the Minnesota Child Development Inventory (MCDI). It consists of 150 descriptive statements of child behavior, eighty-seven of which describe developmental characteristics and sixty-three of which describe adjustment problems and symptoms. The major purpose of the MPI as stated by the test's developers (Ireton and Thwing, 1979) is to "identify children whose development and/or adjustment pose a high risk for failure in kindergarten."

The MPI was standardized on 360 white children from the Bloomington, Minnesota region. The children ranged in age from fifty-six to sixty-seven months and came from families who were well educated and of above average socioeconomic status. In total, the MPI purports to measure seven areas of development (self help, fine motor, expressive language, comprehension, memory, letter recognition and number comprehension); four areas of adjustment (immaturity, hyperactivity, behavior problems and emotional problems) and four categories of symptoms (motor, language, somatic and sensory).

Split-half reliability coefficients for the developmental and adjustment scales range from .29 to .81 with a median of .62. The intercorrelations between the seven developmental subscales range from a low of .19 to a high of .84; with one or two exceptions the subscale intercorrelations are relatively high indicating that most of the developmental areas measured are not uniquely independent of each other, i.e. each subscale is measuring a common behavioral dimension. The developers provide no evidence in the manual on test-retest reliability, nor have any studies been published elsewhere on this topic. There is also no indication given of how long this screening inventory takes to complete or what the inter-rater reliability may be between a child's mother and father.

The inventory's predictive validity has been evaluated in only one study to date (Ireton and Thwing, 1979). In this study, 287 preschoolers were assessed on the MPI prior to their kindergarten year; at the end of kindergarten they were assessed by their teachers and placed into one of two categories of performance, adequate or poor. The data from this study is summarized in Table XVI. The Inventory's sensitivity for poor school performance for this sample of children was 60.00 percent, while the specificity rate was 89.51 percent; the false-positive rate was 10.49 percent and the false-negative rate was 40.00 percent. The false-positive rate is not excessively high for a preschool screening measure, but the false-negative rate is and may be an indication of potential parental bias in filling in the MPI by failing to report areas of development where their children may be somewhat delayed. To date, there have been no published studies on the concurrent or content validity of the MPI. One thing of note that the test authors point out in the manual is that the "self-help, fine motor and expressive language scales have little or no predictive power." However, letter recognition, number comprehension, comprehension and memory "are relatively powerful predictors of poor kindergarten performance."

In general, many of the concerns expressed about the MCDI are also legitimate for the MPI. The standardization sample is not representative of the general population and there is no evidence to date on the stability of the parents' observations over time. Most of the subscale intercorrelations are of high magnitude, which suggests that many of the eleven subscales are not independent of each other, thereby indicating relatively high internal inconsistency but with a corresponding low level of prediction from individual subscales. This observation is supported by the test authors' own research. Although the one reported study on predictive validity shows a good normal hit-rate (specificity) for later kindergarten performance, the actual hit-rate for poor school performance (sensitivity) is only 60.00 percent. Although the false-positive rate is very acceptable, the false-negative rate is very substantial and there is no evidence so far on whether the MPI can actually predict to *specific areas* of later learning deficit.

Table XVI

**PREDICTIVE VALIDITY OF MPI SCORES
WITH TEACHER RATINGS AT THE END OF KINDERGARTEN**

PREDICTIVE MEASURE

MPI

Outcome Measure Teacher Ratings	*Normal*	*At-Risk*	
Normal	239	28	267
At-Risk	8	12	20
			287

Specificity $= \dfrac{239}{267} = 89.51\%$

Sensitivity $= \dfrac{12}{20} = 60.00\%$

False-Positive Rate $= \dfrac{28}{267} = 10.49\%$

False-Negative Rate $= \dfrac{8}{20} = 40.00\%$

Source: Ireton & Thwing, 1979.

On the positive side and to give the test developers their due, they have been rightfully cautious about the use of this inventory without the use of adequate local norms and their manual is very explicit about the way the measure was constructed and how the test results should be interpreted. Again, like their earlier MCDI, the MPI is a very promising screening inventory and may have much to offer in the future providing its early potential is supported by solid empirical evidence.

Minneapolis Preschool Screening Instrument (MPSI)

The MPSI is a very recent revision of Search/Screen, a screening measure developed for the Minneapolis public school by Lichtenstein, Clark and Cronin (1978). It is a fifty-item test which consists of eleven subtests (building, copying shapes, information, matching, sentence completion, hopping and balancing, naming colors, counting, prepositions, identifying body parts and repeating sentences). The whole test can be given in about twelve to fifteen minutes and may be administered by paraprofessionals and trained volunteers.

The MPSI was designed to be used as the initial step in a decision-making sequence of preschool child assessment. The major objectives of the developer were "to design an instrument that: required relatively little time to administer, yielded reliable results, assessed a broad range of functioning, predicted to a child's performance in school and provided a non-diagnostic outcome of pass or refer." Lichtenstein (1980).

The MPSI was standardized on 1,320 children between the ages of forty-three and sixty-four months, all of whom lived in the Minneapolis area. This sample population was recruited on the basis of an extensive mailing and media campaign directed at parents of preschool children to participate with their children in a health and development screening program. Hence, although this sample contained children from different racial backgrounds, it cannot be considered a stratified random sample of preschoolers from the Minneapolis region of Minnesota.

An item analysis was carried out as a check of both item validity and item difficulty. Validity was measured by item correlations with MPSI total score and with MPSI decision (pass or refer). All item correlations were found to be positive and ranged between .33 and .69 for total scores and between .24 and .63 for MPSI decision scores; the median correlations were .53 and .46 respectively. Apart from two or three exceptions (primarily in the counting subscale) each item in each subscale is progressively more difficult than the one before it. No evidence is provided in the draft manual on subscale intercorrelations, so one has no way of knowing how independent from each other or how homogeneous the various subscales may be; i.e. one cannot tell precisely whether the test meets the objective of assessing a broad range of functioning or not.

Test-retest reliability was determined by assessing fifty-one preschool children six to nine days apart. The correlation coefficient for the total group was .92; for seventeen children fifty-two months and younger it was .90; and for thirty-four children fifty-three months and older it was .92. Inter-rater reliability on individual items for forty-five children ranged from .94 to 1.00; for total test scores it was .97. Internal consistency was determined for 728 children using the Kuder Richardson (20) Formula and the coefficient was .95.

Test validity was evaluated by both concurrent and predictive studies, all of which are reported on in the draft manual. Concurrent validity between MPSI and DIAL total scores for 420 children between ages of forty-four and sixty-one months was .90. The correlations between MPSI total scores and mental age scores on the Stanford Binet Intelligence Scale and the Preschool Language Scale on a sample of fifty-four Minneapolis children were .71 and .62 respectively, while similar coefficients between MPSI and the Learning Accomplishment Profile and the Peabody Picture Vocabulary Test were as follows: with LAP fine motor .52; cognitive .69; language .57; gross motor .29 and with the PPVT .54.

Predictive validity was determined by looking at the MPSI scores and teacher ratings of kindergarten performance for 432 children in nine areas of functioning (learning habits, reading readiness, speech, gross motor, social emotional development, preacademic skills, language development, fine motor/perceptual

Table XVII

PREDICTIVE VALIDITY OF MPSI SCORES
WITH TEACHER RATINGS OF KINDERGARTEN PERFORMANCE

PREDICTIVE MEASURE

MPSI

Outcome Measure Teacher Ratings	*Normal*	*At-Risk*	
Normal	341	25	366
At-Risk	24	42	66
			432

$$\text{Specificity} = \frac{341}{366} = 93.17\%$$

$$\text{Sensitivity} = \frac{42}{66} = 63.64\%$$

$$\text{False-Positive Rate} = \frac{25}{366} = 6.83\%$$

$$\text{False-Negative Rate} = \frac{24}{66} = 36.36\%$$

Source: Lichtenstein, 1980.

motor and readiness for first grade). The above 2 X 2 contingency table (Table XVII) summarizes the data for the overall teacher ratings.*

The sensitivity for school problems was 63.64 percent, while the specificity rate was 93.17 percent; the false positive rate was

*For purposes of classification into the 2 X 2 table, children rated as having severe, moderate and mild problems have been grouped together.

a low 6.83 percent and the false negative rate was a high 36.36 percent. However, if one drops from the sample those thirty-six children classified as having mild problems, the predictive validity of the MPSI changes, with the sensitivity rate for school problems increasing to 86.67 percent, specificity and false-positive rates that remain the same at 93.17 percent and 6.83 percent respectively and a false-negative rate that drops to a low 13.33 percent. In terms of correlations between MPSI total scores and overall teacher ratings, the coefficient was .71. An almost identical relationship ($r = .70$) is reported between MPSI scores and Metropolitan Readiness Test raw scores for a sample of 296 children enrolled in the first grade.

The construction of the MPSI has been very carefully carried out and appears to be a fine revision of the Search/Screen instrument. However, like so many of the previous measures reviewed, the norms developed may not be generalizable to the general population simply because they do not constitute a stratified sample and also because they were not selected at random, but were essentially based on volunteer subjects. On the other hand, at least for the one sample of children studied, the MPSI does appear to be a good predictor of kindergarten functioning, at least as evaluated by kindergarten teachers. In fact, when one excludes those children classified as having mild problems, the MPSI has one of the best sensitivity rates and false-positive/false-negative rates of any preacademic screening measure currently reviewed. The most important and unanswered research question here is whether these results can be replicated in other parts of North America on different samples of preschool children. The other major unanswered question is whether the MPSI is capable of predicting at an equally high level actual classroom functioning in grade one. Despite these unanswered questions, the test's author has made a fine start in developing this preacademic screening measure and seems to have met, at least on a preliminary level, most of his objectives.

Sprigle School Readiness Screening Test (SSRST)

The SSRST was designed to screen out those preschool children who might not be ready for school entrance. Originally, it was planned that the test be administered by physicians and nurses; however, as neither of these professional groups have any formal training in psychometrics, both Brian (1975) and Egeland (1975) believe the measure can effectively be used by paraprofessionals and trained volunteers.

The test purports to measure nine different areas of preschool functioning (verbal comprehension, awareness of size relationships, reasoning ability, understanding numbers, visual discrimination, comprehension of analogies, information background, spatial relationships and vocabulary); unfortunately, the manual (Sprigle and Lanier, 1965) provides no information on item selection or other aspects of test construction. For purposes of scoring, children are grouped into one of four age-groups (4.6 to 4.11, 5.0 to 5.5, 5.6 to 5.11 and 6.0 to 6.9 years) and are classified, according to their total scores, into one of three categories, below average, average to above-average, and superior. In general the test takes between fifteen and twenty minutes to administer and score.

The SSRST was standardized on 475 preschoolers randomly selected from a variety of preschool settings in four cities in the eastern, midwestern and southern areas of the United States. Although the sample consisted of children from lower, lower middle and middle class families, it is restricted to those children who were actually attending kindergarten and day care nursery classes.

Only one reliability study has so far been reported and that was on a sample of thirty randomly selected children tested and then retested one week apart (Sprigle and Lanier, 1967). The test-retest correlation was .96; a very substantial coefficient, although based on a very small sample.

The validity of the measure was concurrently validated on the original standardization sample on three separate measures; the Stanford Binet (r - .95 to .96) the Metropolitan Readiness Test (r - .86 to .90) and the Gates Primary Reading Test (r - .78 to .92), with these latter two measures being used on children from the three highest age-groups (i.e. over five years of age). A later concurrent validity study on 100 preschool and kindergarten children (Seda and Michael, 1971) reported a correlation coefficient of .73 between SSRST total scores and scores on the MRT and a correlation of .61 between the same scores and scores on the PPVT. There are no reported studies so far on the SSRST's ability to predict actual school performance; similarly, there are no cross-validational studies reported for either the test's reliability or its validity. The lack of predictive studies is a serious oversight for it prevents any kind of evaluation of the test's utility; in addition, one would certainly like to see some replication of the test's reliability on larger and more geographically varied samples of preschool children.

All in all, despite the lack of data on item selection and sampling and the fact that the norms are based on a sample of less than 600 children, the SSRST appears to have considerable potential as a screening measure, although at the moment one can make no judgements about the test's overall predictive utility. Perhaps the most surprising finding is that this measure has received so little attention from the psychometric research community, for its promise certainly seems to warrant more extensive evaluation.

Jansky Screening Index
(JSI)

The JSI is a five subtest screening measure designed to select out those kindergarten-age children at-risk for reading disabilities by the end of the second grade. The five subtests (Letter Naming, Picture Naming, Word Matching, Bender Motor Gestalt and Binet Sentence Memory) were selected as the best predictors of later reading performance taken from a pool of nineteen kindergarten tests, many of which had been clinically evaluated in an earlier study (de Hirsch, Jansky and Langford, 1966). This five-test predictive battery was then administered to 402 kindergarten children who constituted the standardization sample. This sample of preschoolers consisted of all children who spoke and understood conversational English and who attended six public schools and two Catholic schools in two school districts in New York City. Hence, the children were neither randomly selected nor occupationally stratified. The JSI takes approximately twenty minutes to administer and may be given by paraprofessionals or trained volunteers; the test itself is relatively inexpensive;

however, there is no separate test manual; [the manual is part of another publication by Jansky and de Hirsch (1972)].

In terms of reliability, Jansky and de Hirsch (1972) report test-retest correlations for two of the subtests (Bender Gestalt and Word Matching) of .23 and .52 respectively. Split half correlations based on the Kuder-Richardson (20) Formula are given for sentence memory, picture naming and letter naming; these coefficients were .40, .86 and .89 respectively. No reliability coefficients are reported for the total score. In terms of determining whether a child is at-risk for later reading disability, the test developers recommend the establishment of cut-off scores based on local norms. This is a very important recommendation in view of the fact that the normative data presented by the test authors is extremely restricted; i.e. to children living in a specific area of New York City.

Although the rationale behind the JSI was based on years of developmental research on reading disability by the test developers and their colleagues, the Index itself still requires additional research. For example, there is no reliability data whatsoever on the total scores of the JSI; furthermore, with the exception of the subtests Picture Naming and Letter Naming, the reliability coefficients for the subtests are unacceptably low. In fact, it is possible that reducing the index to just picture naming and letter naming subtests would be just as predictive of reading disability as the use of all five subtests. Another problem which is related to the use of the JSI for mass screening purposes is the necessity for collecting local norms in order to accurately determine appropriate cut-off scores. This is a crucial procedure because the selection of the cut-off scores specifically affects not only the Index's false-positive and false-negative rates but also its overall utility in predicting reading disability.[1]

The JSI shows considerable promise as a screening measure for later reading disability; however, until the reliability issue has been resolved and more studies have been completed on its predictive validity on large samples across the country, the use of the Index should be restricted to research and experimental studies only.

---

[1] Although Trimble (1970) and Zaeske (1970) studied the predictive validity of the early form of the JSI, only Jansky and de Hirsch (1972) and Barnes (1978) have studied the predictive validity of the current form of the JSI. (See Tables IV and V for predictive hit rates.)

Peabody Picture Vocabulary Test
(PPVT)

The PPVT (Dunn, 1959; 1965) is a measure designed to assess a person's verbal intelligence between the ages of two years six months and eighteen years. As the PPVT has been extensively reviewed over the past few years (Lyman, 1965; Piers, 1966; Datta, 1975; Hunt, 1975) and has been subjected to over 500 research studies, the present review will be brief and restricted to its use with preschool age children.

The test items consist of a series of pictures used in conjunction with a list of increasingly difficult words and the child is requested to identify the one picture out of four on each page of the test book which illustrates the word spoken by the examiner.

The PPVT consists of two parallel forms (A and B) which were administered to a standardization sample of 545 preschool white children from the Nashville, Tennessee area, who were divided into six-month age-groups and who ranged in age from two years six months to four years six months. The basal level is met when eight consecutive correct responses are made, while the ceiling level is reached when the subject makes six errors in his last eight responses. The alternate-form reliability coefficients for the standardization sample range from .72 to .81 depending on age-group; no other data on reliability are reported on in the manual. Only one study on concurrent validity is reported on in the manual for children between the ages of 2.8 and 13.8 years and this showed a correlation between PPVT MA scores of .82 with Stanford Binet MA scores and .50 with Vineland SA scores. However, not only was the sample extremely small ($N = 37$) but it was also selected from a clinical population. In a more extensive study (Di Lorenzo and Brady, 1968), on a sample of 563 children between the ages of 3.5 and 4.5 years, the concurrent validity coefficient between PPVT I.Q. scores and scores on the Stanford Binet was .79. There are no predictive validity studies reported in the manual for preschool-age children.

Although the PPVT is a screening measure that has been around for a long time, it should be used with considerable caution for screening preschool-age children. Despite all the research, there has been no comprehensive attempt to standardize the test on stratified random samples across the country and the number of cross-validational studies on normal subjects is exceedingly small. Furthermore, data on the test's predictive validity is badly needed for children of preschool age.

Probably one of the most useful functions of the PPVT is in screening children for language comprehension who may have speech problems, be shy or verbally reticent. It should *not* be employed as a measure of overall intelligence or cognitive ability, and until there are more representative norms and more data on its predictive validity, it should not be used (except for experimental research purposes) as a measure of reading readiness for prekindergarten children. For those readers requiring an in-depth look at the more recent research on the PPVT, the following selected references will be of interest: Durret and Henman (1972), Lessler and Bridges (1973), Pascale (1973), Armistead and Crawford (1974), Taylor (1975), Covin (1976), Telegdy (1976) and Goh and Lund (1977).

Chapter 10

MEASURES AT THE
EXPERIMENTAL–RESEARCH STAGE

A S WE enter the final chapter of this book on preschool screening, what can be said about the present state of the art, particularly as that state may relate to the development of screening measures for the future?

It is apparent that many of the screening measures reviewed have not met some of the basic criteria for the construction of high quality test instruments. Probably, in most cases, this finding can be traced to a lack of significant funding or of funding running out before the construction phase was finally completed. Still, even when this fact is taken into account, many of the screening measures currently available fail to meet certain standards of evaluation which would not necessarily create additional costs. For example, the function of screening measures is to classify individuals into one of two possible categories, normal or at-risk. Yet, despite this fact, very few of the currently available measures have included in their manuals information on indexes of reliability or validity where the data is presented in 2 X 2 contingency tables. In other words, most screening test manuals only report reliability and validity data in correlational coefficients, which is the usual procedure for tests where a person's exact score is to be compared with the total distribution of scores for the standardization sample. However, in the primary use of screening measures one is not usually interested in that type of comparison but rather whether an individual's score will reliably and validly place him in the same normal or at-risk category each time he is assessed. Thus, the inclusion of such reliability and validity indexes would be very useful to a person attempting to select a screening measure of maximum efficiency. This issue of a standardized method for the evaluation of screening procedures has been beautifully discussed in a paper by Lichtenstein (1979), who has just recently developed (Lichtenstein, 1980) an Index of Comparison, in an attempt to incorporate into a single measure the false-positive and false-negative error rates of any given screening test. In addition, this Index has two other distinct advantages; first, it allows for a test of significance to determine if the relationship between the screening measure and the outcome measure is greater than expected by chance and, secondly, for a person trying to select the best screening measure available in a specific area, it provides an easy and quick reference guide in that the higher the index, the more predictively efficient a measure has been found to be.

One of the most persistent and distressing factors surrounding the development and construction of preschool screening measures has been the lack of national, randomized, stratified samples used in the standardization process. In so many instances the test constructor simply standardized his screening measure on whatever populations seemed to be available locally and, even when the test appeared to have high potential for large-scale screening programs, made little or no attempt to standardize his measure on samples of children from across the country. This situation is particularly serious in regards to screening tests because very few of the measures currently available have been subjected to cross-validational studies.

Another difficulty related to the development of predictively useful screening tests, especially in the selecting out of at-risk children for significant developmental delay and preacademic readiness, is the issue of performance *now* as compared to performance *later*. Essentially, all screening tests evaluate a child's functioning at the moment of testing, but the usefulness of the measure is evaluated on the basis of how well that child's current level of performance predicts to some later level of functioning in an entirely different situation. In the screening of children for serious visual problems or auditory dysfunction, this type of generalization is based on pretty solid ground in that a child whose current level of visual functioning is seriously impaired will have at least the same basic level of impairment (if left uncorrected) in other situations later on. However, as has previously been discussed, when a child's current functioning level is found to be *delayed* or *academically not ready,* the degree to which one can generalize such a finding may vary substantially, depending on not only the types of assessment items used and the situation that the test was given in, but also the particular environment the child lives in, the socioeconomic status of his parents and the type of situation that the child will be required to function in at some later date.

Coupled with this problem area is the *adequacy of sampling* of specific child behaviors and task performance. One of the major dilemmas faced by the developer of any particular screening test is to obtain an adequate sample of child behaviors at the same time keeping the length of the test as short as possible. This latter factor is important because the longer a test takes to administer, the more it costs, the fewer the number of children it can be given to in a given block of time and the harder it is to give to younger children, due to their relatively short attention spans. Although most test constructors try to achieve some kind of compromise, very few of the screening measures developed have been subjected to the kind of internal analysis in which the length of the test has been determined on the basis of relating number of items to maximum predictive utility.

A final area of concern, both now and for the development of future screening tests, is the serious lack of any built-in follow-up studies both as a check on the long-term predictive efficiency of a measure and as a way of evaluating whether different samples of children continue to respond to the test items in a consistent way over a substantial period of time. Any significant deviation of responses to specific test items or subscales would indicate that the test is probably ready for a major revision. Certainly it was distressing to find, in the current review of preschool screening measures, so many promising instruments that have been around for ten to fifteen years and still have not been subjected to adequate follow-up studies.

However, even if all these concerns were to be rectified, it would continue to be very difficult to completely predict those children who will experience serious difficulties from those who will not. As McCall (1980) recently reported, there are at least two separate factors that govern the developmental function; one of these is related to the stability or instability of individual differences, while the other is related to the continuity or discontinuity of the developmental process. He reports further that this difficulty in developmental prediction is particularly apparent when screening children under the age of two years because there appear to be quite powerful self-righting tendencies up until the age of two. The difficulties in developmental prediction for children older than two, on the other hand, seem to be related to the increasingly influential power of both environmental and genetic factors.

One recent model that has been proposed for increasing our predictive screening capabilities (Lewis, 1980) has been an interactional one that combines the biological model of development with the environmental one. This interactional model postulates that if we look at the biological state of the organism at one point in time *in conjunction with* its environmental state at the same point in time, our accuracy of prediction for later developmental function will always be greater than if we look at both of these states separately. Lewis makes two other very important points; one is that when we include in our screening an evaluation of the child's environment it is not enough to simply look at the mother's involvement, but we must extend our assessment to other family members and the overall richness of that environment. The other is that every screening measure needs some index of its *ecological validity;* i.e. the impact on the screening outcome of the interaction between the screening examiner and the examinee during the screening procedure.

If preschool screening measures will never be more than 75 percent to 80 percent predictively accurate (and the present evidence clearly supports such a statement), what, if anything, can be done to improve the screening process and are there any alternatives to the use of screening tests? One obvious solution might be to develop screening measures with greater care so that they meet all the essential criteria of *A.P.A. Standards for Educational and Psychological Tests;* however, because of environmental factors, individual differences and the continuity/discontinuity of individual human development, even this approach will not produce screening measures with 100 percent predictive accuracy. One approach which may improve our ability to predict at-risk children is to use a more comprehensive battery of screening measures and to replicate this procedure several times before the child is five years old. Although such an approach would not increase the predictive power of any single screening test, it might increase our *overall ability* to predict which children are at-risk simply because it would include parental observations together with samples of not only the child's behavior, but also his home environment, his physical development and his readiness for later academic learning.

An alternative to preschool screening, particularly for younger preschoolers, has been recently proposed by Ireton and Thwing (1980a). Their recent development of the Minnesota Infant Development Inventory (1980b) was designed principally to review the development of infants in the first fifteen months of life. This *developmental review* is provided by the mother in the form of a summary of her observations and concerns regarding her baby's current development. At the same time, a professional health worker makes his own observations of the infant's development, which he incorporates with data from a parental interview to round out the overall assessment (review). Although the reliability and predictive validity of such a procedure is currently unknown, it is an approach to screening that warrants further consideration.

As space is limited, this chapter does not contain an exhaustive examination of all screening measures at the experimental stage, but instead selection is based on those principles of measurement discussed in Chapters 2, 3, 4 and 5. It is possible that some measures have also been excluded not because they do not meet such principles but simply because they were missed or not identified in the computer searches of the measurement literature.

Matching Symbol Test
(frequently referred to as the HOTV test)

This screening test, developed by Lippman (undated), has many characteristics of the STYCAR Single Letter Test except it only uses four Sloan letters rather than seven. These four letters are opto-types (which fit the Snellen 25 squares) and are presented either at a ten- or twenty-foot distance from the child. The child's task is to match the letter presented with one of the four letters on his response panel. The examiner progresses down to the smallest size symbols the child says he can see; if the child correctly identifies four out of six test symbols on one test line, that line represents his visual acuity level.

There appear to be no published reports on the standardization procedure for this test nor anything on the samples of children selected. There is no published manual, but a one-page set of directions is available from the Good-Lite Company (undated). Lippmann (1974) reports that "comparative studies of the reliability and validity rank the test as better than the Snellen E Test." However, he does not cite any references for such studies, so the actual empirical bases for such a statement are unknown; hence, the actual hit-rates and false-positive/false-negative rates remain unreported.

Some of the more obvious advantages of the HOTV test include its simplicity of administration, the shortness of the administration time and the fact that, for three- and four-year-olds, it does not require the development of a highly accurate sense of direction. However, because it shares many similarities with the STYCAR, from which it was originally modified (Lippmann, 1980), it has been placed in the experimental edition category pending the results of published research findings on its use with large samples of preschool children.

Preschool Preposition Test
(PPT)

The PPT (Aaronson, undated) is a receptive language screening test designed to identify children between the ages of three and five years who have difficulty in comprehending verbal directions. The test consists of twenty-three items each of which contains a preposition or prepositional phrase, i.e. "put the ball *into* the boy's hands, or put the ball *in back of* the car." The items may be administered by a nonprofessionally-trained or volunteer examiner and for normal children the test takes approximately five to ten minutes to administer and score. The child earns one point for each correct response made, with the highest obtainable score being twenty-three. The test is not suitable for children whose native language is other than English and because the measure has a distinct ceiling effect by sixty-five months of age, it is of limited usefulness for screening normal children older than five years of age.

The PPT was standardized on 985 preschoolers between the ages of twenty-four and seventy-one months, all of whom came from *normal settings*. Three hundred and twenty-eight children came from urban settings, 145 from suburban settings and 294 from a very rural setting. Four hundred and fifty-two were Caucasian, fifty-five were black and 478 were racially mixed. Three hundred and ninety-two came from lower SES families, 158 from upper middle class families and 435 from mixed SES families. These samples came from a variety of geographical areas, including the states of Maine, Maryland, New York, Washington, D.C., Kansas, Michigan, North Carolina and Utah.

The test's manual provides a comprehensive table which lists the means and standard deviations by age-group for the entire sample. The author recommends that any child who scores above the mean requires no further evaluation. A child whose score is between the mean and one standard deviation below the mean requires no additional evaluation unless the PPT score is coupled with serious behavioral problems. However, all children whose scores fall one standard deviation below the mean should be referred for further evaluation. The manual also provides data on item difficulty level (measured by percent passing), correlations of PPT items with PPVT raw scores, PPVT I.Q.s and M.A.s as well as an analysis of skewness and kurtosis by age-groups. However, there is no data reported in the manual for reliability or validity coefficients; instead this information is available in another publication (Aaronson and Phillips, 1977).

In regards to the test's reliability, Aaronson and Phillips (1977) report that an item analysis of all twenty-three items revealed that each item correlated significantly ($P < .005$) with the total test score. The average correlation coefficient of all items with total test score (with the exception of items twelve, fifteen and twenty-two) was .55, and for ten of these items it exceeded .60. The Kuder-Richardson 20 correlation coefficient was also computed and had a value of .86. The authors report no data for the test-retest reliability or for inter-rater agreement.

The authors report a concurrent validity coefficient for total PPT scores of .72 with PPVT total raw scores on a sample of 122 preschoolers. For another small sample of subjects ($N = 29$) the correlation between PPT total scores and Stanford Binet I.Q. scores was .60. A third sample ($N = 27$(who were also administered the ABC Inventory (Adair and Blesch, 1965) had a correlation coefficient for total scores between the two measures of .63. The correlation of PPT total scores and the teacher ratings on the Classroom Behavior Category (Aaronson and Schaeffer, 1971) was reported by Aaronson, Phillips and Bertolucci (1978) for a sample of 122 children to be .57 for cognitive behavior and .41 for overall adjustment. In the area of predictive validity, these same authors report on the correlation between total PPT scores and scores five years later on the Cognitive Abilities Test (Thorndike and Hagen, 1971) and the Iowa Test of Basic Skills (Hieronymus and Linquist, 1971), for a sample of forty-three and forty subjects respectively. The coefficients for the CAT in the areas of quantitative and nonverbal were .38, while the correlation for the composite score on the ITBS was .41. These correlations, although statistically significant, are not very substantial, and unfortunately the authors do not report their data in such a way that hit-rates and false-positive/false-negative rates can be computed.

One other study of interest just recently reported (Aaronson, Phillips, Bertolucci and Aaronson, 1979) provides some preliminary validity evidence on a small sample ($N = 28$) to suggest that scores on the PPT may be inversely related to a child's level of hostile and belligerent behavior ($r = -.53$ and $-.46$ respectively) as well as such negative maternal behaviors as punitiveness ($-.60$), withdrawal of relationship ($-.55$), use of fear to control ($-.50$), punishment ($-.47$), and irritability ($-.46$).

The PPT has been now used experimentally for twelve years on a wide variety of preschoolers in normal and Head Start settings. The care and amount of time devoted by the authors to evaluate this test is highly commendable. Although the actual selection of the standardization sample is not reported on, the

developers have certainly tried to assess as many children as possible from a variety of SES levels and from many geographic areas
in the United States. The two major areas that require further research study are reliability (test–retest and inter–rater agreement)
and predictive validity, particularly using larger samples of subjects and reporting hit-rates and false-positive/false-negative error
rates. When this research is completed, the PPT may prove to be
the best test of receptive language currently available for the
screening of preschool-age children.

Developmental Screening Inventory
(DSI)

Although the DSI was constructed almost fifteen years ago
(Knobloch, Pasamanick and Sherard, 1966), it remains an experimental-research test because much of the basic research required
for its widespread use has yet to be reported on. Basically, the
DSI consists of selected items from the Gesell Developmental
Schedules (Gesell and Amatruda, 1954) which cover five areas
of development; adaptive, gross motor, fine motor, language and
personal-social behavior. The Inventory is applicable to children
between the ages of four weeks and eighteen months and requires
approximately thirty minutes to administer.

The DSI was not subject to the usual standardization process
but was simply administered to a group of patients admitted to
hospital who were between the ages of 3.5 and eighteen months.
The examiners were medical students and the results of their
DSI assessments were compared with developmental examinations
performed by two members of the hospital's medical staff. The
total number of infants screened was fifty-eight; no information
is available on their SES or their respective ages.

There is no data yet reported on test-retest reliability and although one finding is mentioned on inter-rater reliability, it is
not given in statistical terms. Concurrent validity of the DSI with
scores on the Gesell Developmental Schedules ranged from .94 to
.98; however, as the items on the DSI come directly from the
GDS, such high correlations are not too surprising. In comparing
DSI scores on the original fifty-eight subjects with diagnostic
categories assigned by members of the hospital's medical staff,

if one excludes those children falling into the questionable category, the sensitivity rate for developmental disability was 90 percent, the false-positive rate was 10.34 percent and the false-negative rate was 10.00 percent. Considering that the children screened on the DSI were less than nineteen months old, this is an impressive finding, although one must remember that the infants were all patients in a hospital and in that respect constituted a biased sample. Still, if such a finding was replicated on other samples of infants, the DSI could prove to be a very useful screening tool for early developmental assessment.

HOME Screening Questionnaire
(HSQ)

The HSQ, a screening measure developed by Coons, Frankenburg, Garrett, Headley and Fandal (1978) and currently being revised (Coons, Frankenburg, Gay, Fandal, Lefly and Ker, 1980), was designed to be used for the mass screening of a child's home environment based on parental report.

The items on the HSQ were taken directly from the HOME Inventory and the zero-to-three year form consists of thirty-two questions, while the three-to-six year form has thirty-six questions. The correlations between these two measures, HOME and HSQ, range from the low .70s to the high .80s. The rate of agreement between HOME and HSQ for the correct identification of at-risk families was .84.

To date, the HSQ has only been standardized on samples of children from low social class families because the authors report there is very little variability in HOME scale scores across children when used on samples of middle to upper-class populations. So far there are no published reports on the questionnaire's test-retest reliability nor on inter-rater agreement. Data on concurrent validity between HSQ and scores on the Bayley Scales of Infant Development and the Stanford Binet Intelligence Scale reveal a correlation of .30 which, although significant, indicates that the HSQ is obviously measuring something other than environmental factors related to intelligence.

Although the predictive validity of the HSQ as its scores relate to actual school performance is yet to be evaluated, some preliminary data (Coons et al., 1980) indicate that in looking at the school records of 191 siblings of children in the standardization samples, 55 percent are currently experiencing academic or behaviorally related school problems.

In view of what has been said earlier on the importance of evaluating a child's home environment, the HSQ could fill a real gap in the area of screening a child's home background. However, at present it does have two major drawbacks; it is applicable only to children from low social class families and it requires further evaluation from cross-validational studies before being used across the country.

Child Behavior Checklist and Profile
(CBCP)

The CBCP is a 138-item behavioral questionnaire which is completed by one of the child's parents or principal caregiver. One hundred and eighteen of the items are on behavioral problems, while the other twenty are on social competence. The major goal of the CBCP is to identify those children between the ages of four and sixteen years who are in need of Mental Health services. The checklist takes approximately twenty-minutes to complete, with the parent responding to each item by checking one of three categories; not true, somewhat or sometimes true and very or often true. To date, three sets of profiles have been developed for age-groups four to five, six to eleven and twelve to sixteen years (Edelbrock, 1980). For preschool-age children (four to five years) eight reliable behavior problem factors have been identified; social withdrawal, somatic complaints, depressed, immature, sex problems, schizoid, aggressive and delinquent. Several kinds of information can be obtained from the CBCP, including profile scores for the eight problem areas, three social competence scores, a global index of maladjustment and a global index of social competence.

The standardization sample for the four- to five-year-old group consisted of fifty boys and fifty girls in each of the two groups who had been referred to Mental Health services to one of thirty East Coast Mental Health facilities together with a matched sample of the same number of randomly selected normal children who had not been referred to Mental Health services. This matched sample of normal children was selected from households in Washington, D. C., Northern Virginia and Southern Maryland and constituted the normative group. The children from these two samples were matched on both race and socioeconomic status.

The reliability data for children aged six through sixteen has been reported in some considerable detail (Achenbach, 1978; Achenbach and Edelbrock, 1979). When subjects were tested and then retested one week later, the reliability coefficients for normal children ranged from .72 to .97, while inter-parent reliability ranged from .58 to .87. An internal analysis revealed, further, very significant differences between referred and nonreferred (normal) children in all of the behavioral problem and social competence areas. However, as yet no data have been reported for the four- to five-year-old age-group.

In order to determine the CBCP's screening efficiency and predictive utility, the test developer has selected cutting scores based on the incidence rate of psychopathological disorders among children. For the total behavior problem score, the cut-off point selected was above the ninetieth percentile for normal children, while for the total social competence score, the cut-off score selected was below the tenth percentile for the normal sample of children. However, as Edelbrock (1980) does not report the number of true positives and true negatives for the four- to five-year-old group, it is not possible to evaluate the hit-rates and false-positive/false-negative rates for the referred sample of children.

As the CBCP has only just been recently developed, a considerable amount of research on its effectiveness still needs to be carried out, particularly in regards to utilizing the measure on larger samples of young children. For example, now that the test is available for experimental-research use, it will be of substantial value to: (a) cross-validate the CBCP on other normal (nonreferred) samples of children in other parts of the country to see if the norms of the original matched control sample are valid for the rest of North America; and (b) routinely use the CBCP in randomly selected preschool screening programs and follow the children assessed longitudinally to see how many ultimately are referred for Mental Health services. As the number of measures available for screening preschool children for emotional disabilities is extremely small, the CBCP could be an important addition to the overall screening process. Furthermore, the idea of using referral to Mental Health Services as the major criterion for validating screening measures of emotional/social difficulties may well prove to be a considerable improvement over psychiatric diagnosis, as the inter-rater reliability across psychiatrists is a very low .50 (Achenbach and Edelbrock, 1980).

The two potentially troublesome aspects of the CBCP have to do with the fact that: (1) a child's mental stability is based solely on parental report with all of the biases that may entail; and (2) all of the items in the entire checklist are negative descriptions of child behavior, an orientation that may contribute to substantial false negative error rates, i.e. by being faced with 138 negative items concerning child behavior, parents may consciously or subconsciously check fewer items as very or often true in order to reduce the probability of being considered negative or nonsupportive parents.

Basic School Skills Inventory
(BSSI)

This Inventory was designed by its authors (Goodman and Hammill, 1975) to screen or identify those children who, by the first grade, may experience learning and behavioral difficulties. Since the BSSI is both a norm-referenced and criterion-referenced measure, the examiner may compare a child's performance with that of his age-related peers, as well as assess his performance in specific behavioral areas. Because of the way it has been constructed, the Inventory can only be administered by the child's preschool teacher or day-care instructor, and it is not suitable for children under four years of age.

The BSSI evaluates the child's mastery of certain behaviors by the teacher rating his performance on eighty-four operationally defined items divided into seven subtests (basic information, reading readiness, number readiness, self-help, handwriting, oral communication and classroom behavior). Each item is scored pass or fail and is based on the authors' instructions that "a passing score for this item is given to the child whose need for assistance is equal to or less than that of most of the other children who comprise the class." This evaluation is usually based on a period of observation, by the teacher, of approximately three to four weeks.

The standardization sample consisted of 459 preschool children from fourteen different states. Although no attempt was made to select a stratified random sample, the authors did include a percentage of black (22 percent) and Mexican-American (8 percent) children. Test norms are given for the following age-groups: 4.0 to 4.5, 4.6 to 4.11, 5.0 to 5.5, 5.6 to 5.11, 6.0 to 6.5, 6.6 to 6.11 years and the total number of items passed is converted to a standard score, which is called a skill quotient.

Internal consistency coefficients reported by the authors range from .50 to .94 for the seven subtests; the median reliability for four-year-olds is .88, for five-year-olds .85, and for six-year-olds .79. Total score reliability coefficients range from .93 to .97 but no information is reported on inter-observer reliability. Test-retest reliability was evaluated by Hawthorne and Larsen (1977) in a study of fifteen low SES preschoolers over a seven-to-fourteen day time period. The coefficients ranged from .87 to .98, with a mean of .96.

In the area of validity, Goodman and Hammill (1975) report concurrent validity coefficients of .65 between total BSSI and total MRT scores, and of .71 between BSSI total scores and teacher ratings. Hawthorne and Larsen (1977) report on the predictive validity of the BSSI by comparing BSSI total scores acquired in kindergarten with total Teacher Rating Scores (White, 1973) acquired in grade one. The overall correlation was .74; however, as the authors do not report their data in a 2 X 2 contingency table format, it is not possible to compute hit-rates and false-positive/false-negative error rates. In a concurrent validity study using the First Grade Screening Test (FGST), Gacka (1978) assessed 159 kindergarten-age children and reported a correlation coefficient of —.76 for total BSSI scores, with a range between —.45 and —.83 across subtests.

As with most of the measures reviewed in this chapter, the BSSI requires a great deal more supportive evidence before it can be seriously considered for mass screening programs. Some of the more essential research still required is studies on larger representative samples, as well as more extensive data on the BSSI's reliability and validity, particularly with samples of children from higher SES backgrounds. On the positive side, the test's authors have made a really serious attempt to meet the critical evaluations of preacademic screening tests made by Adelman and Feshbach (1971) and Keogh and Becker (1973), namely, that such screening measures should closely sample the actual types of skill behaviors that will be required in the classroom setting.

Cooperative Preschool Inventory
(CPI)

The CPI is a sixty-four item screening achievement measure broken down into four subtests. These subtests cover four areas of functioning; personal-social responsiveness, associative vocabulary, concept activation-numerical, and concept activation-sensory. The inventory was developed by Caldwell (1967; 1970) to provide a screening measure for achievement in areas she regarded as necessary for success in school. It was designed initially for assessing Head Start children with two major objectives in mind: (a) to delineate the degree of disadvantage a child from an economically and educationally deprived background may have at the time of entering school; and (b) to have an instrument available that was sensitive enough to a child's experiences that it could be used as a measure of change related to educational intervention.

The Inventory was standardized on over 1500 children in 150 Head Start classes throughout various regions of the United States. The manual (Caldwell, 1970) provides national norms for five age-groups covering a range of from three to 6.5 years. The Inventory takes approximately fifteen minutes to administer and score and may be given by paraprofessionals and trained volunteers; it is inexpensive to purchase and appears to have a high interest level for even three-year-old children.

The reliability of the CPI has been evaluated by both split-half (Caldwell, 1970) and test-retest (Miller and Dyer, 1970) coefficients. The split-half correlations range from .84 to .93 depending on age-groups, while the coefficient for the total sample was .92. The test-retest correlation for a six-month time period was .79, which is a very creditable relationship considering the number of learning experiences preschoolers may be exposed to over that length of time.

The validity data on the CPI so far reported has looked at the relationships between CPI total scores and scores on the Stanford Binet (Caldwell, 1970; Miller and Dyer, 1970), the Boehm Test of Basic Concepts, the Graham Ernhart Copy Forms Test and the PPVT (Ernhart, Spaner and Jordan, 1977). In general, the correlations with Stanford Binet scores range from .39 to .65. For a sample of three- and four-year-old white children the correlation between the CPI and the Boehm Test was .68, for the Graham Ernhart .63 and for the PPVT .52. Although these reported relationships are relatively high and positive, they do not really tell us much about how well the CPI predicts to actual later kindergarten and school performance. In fact, to date the author has found only one published study on the predictive validity of the CPI; this study, by Bridgeman and Shipman (1975), reported on the relationships between CPI scores at ages four to five and scores on the mathematics and reading subtests of the Cooperative Primary Test (CPT) at the end of the third grade. The correlation coefficients for the mathematics scores ranged from .08 to .45, while for the reading scores the correlations were from .29 to .42. Although all but one of these coefficients are significant, they do not tell us very precisely how predictively accurate CPI scores are in classifying children who are at-risk for later underachievement in reading or mathematics. Thus, the actual predictive utility of the CPI is still not known.

Although earlier reviews of the CPI have reported very positively on its potential for providing information to preschool teachers and as a screening measure of cognitive ability (Ernhart, 1975; Hunt, 1975), there is very little empirical evidence to support such viewpoints. In fact, the initial construction of the CPI was rather hurried to say the least in that the original edition was put together in approximately a two-week period (Caldwell, 1967). It is true that the 1970 revision was much more carefully constructed and standardized; however, even for the revision, the children assessed were restricted to those enrolled in Head Start classes. In a way, this is the CPI's greatest strength and also one of its major weaknesses. The fact that it was standardized on Head

Start children makes it ideal for screening such disadvantaged pre-schoolers, but highly restrictive for use as a mass screening instrument. Another problem has to do with what the Inventory is supposed to screen for. The basic objectives of the developer were to design a measure that would determine the degree of disadvantage and would be sensitive to experience. Although the Inventory is considered to be a screening measure, Caldwell (1967) also makes the following statement:

> It was decided to concentrate on specific achievements represent-ing what the child brought with him to the educational experi-ence rather than on broad areas of cognitive functioning that might predict how well he might do in the future.

On the basis of this statement it would appear that although the measure is supposed to determine various degrees of disadvantage, the level at which the child is currently functioning is not seen to predict later school performance. However, it is hard to imagine a situation where particular degrees of disadvantage and especially serious disadvantage do not adverseley affect cognitive function-ing and thereby strongly influence later school performance. In other words, if the CPI can successfully select out preschool chil-dren at different levels of disadvantage, then it should be capable of predicting later school functioning at least in the sense that the greater the disadvantage the more poorly the child will perform and the greater the need the child will have for remediation, ed-ucational intervention, enrichment or whatever.

At the present time, despite substantial promise, it would ap-pear that the CPI requires further empirical support in the area of predictive classification before moving out of the experimental-research category.

Preschool Behavior Rating Scale
(PBRS)

The PBRS is a Guttman-type rating scale which was developed from the Preschool Rating Scale (Barker, 1978). It was designed to meet the following two major objectives (Barker and Doeff, 1980):

> (1) to permit preschool personnel . . . to identify chil-dren who show incipient or manifest developmental problems; and

(2) to permit preschool personnel to monitor progress in preschool behavioral skill development over time.

Inherent in its development is the basic assumption that those people who deal with children on a daily basis over extended periods of time are in the best position to "make valid observations of preschool behavioral skill development." (Barker and Doeff, 1980).

The scale covers three factorially determined behavioral areas; psychomotor, cognitive (language) and social. There are twenty items altogether, with each item requiring one of five behavioral skill levels to be checked off. As the behavioral skills evaluated progress from lower to higher levels of functional development, each item carries a numerical rating score of one to five. Thus, a child rated at the lowest behavioral skill level on each item would have a total score of twenty, while a child rated at the highest level would receive a total score of 100.

The PBRS is designed to be used for children between the ages of thirty-six and seventy-one months who spend most of their waking hours in either Head Start, day care or other types of nursery settings. The person designated to perform the rating on the child is that person who works with the child in an educational or day care setting on a day-to-day basis. (Barker and Doeff, 1980.)

As the scale is so new, there is as yet no examiner's manual available; thus it is not known how the items were selected or how long a child has to be in the preschool before being evaluated or rated by the teacher; there is also no information on how long the scale takes to administer and score. Furthermore, although there is published data on the normative sample (Barker and Doeff, 1980), there is nothing so far reported on the standardization process, including the selection of the sample or from which parts of the United States the preschool children came.

Data so far reported by the Scale's authors indicate that the median inter-rater reliability coefficients, based on nine pairs of teachers assessing eighty-five children, were .89 for PBRS total, .79 for the language factor, .86 for the social factor and .90 for the psychomotor factor. Median split-half coefficients, based on 124 teachers rating 1,367 children were .94 (PBRS total), .92 (language), .87 (social) and .89 (psychomotor). There are no data reported on test-retest reliability, so the stability of the scale over time is unknown.

The Scale's authors report one study on concurrent validity in which they assessed the ability of the PBRS to distinguish between *typical* children and those children previously diagnosed as having a problem *(atypical)*. They give no information on who carried out the diagnosis but do mention that all the children were from families of low socioeconomic status. Through the use of discriminant function analysis, they found that when all item scores are used, the overall hit-rate was 92.00 percent for a total sample of 579 children; however, the hit-rate for *atypical* behavior was only 56.00 percent, while the false-positive rate was a very acceptable 2.00 percent, and the false-negative rate was a very substantial 44.00 percent. It is possible, of course, that these hit and error rates might be changed significantly by changing the cut-off scores on the PBRS; however, even using that procedure would not provide validity data on children from higher SES families.

Obviously, the PBRS still requires a great deal more research before being considered a highly efficient screening measure. Data must be provided on the standardization sample, and the Scale's ability to predict later developmental and/or preacademic behavior, particularly for higher SES children, must be researched before it can be used for any kind of mass screening program. In addition, the use of the scale is seriously restricted to those children between the ages of three and six years who are currently enrolled in some form of preschool setting. Although the actual number of such children is increasing, they in no way make up the vast majority of the preschool population; whether the scale could be used by the parents of children not in preschool settings is a question that can only be answered by further research. Furthermore, the PBRS must be cross-validated on other samples of children across the country as well as subjected to careful analysis as to how long a child must be in a preschool setting before being rated.

However, despite this need for further research, the PBRS has some unique properties that endow it with considerable potential. For example, the items do provide preschool teaching personnel with some rather objective means of observing behavior and perhaps assist them in being more perceptive in identifying specific areas of development. Further, because the scale may be used after several weeks of observation, it allows for day-to-day fluctuations in skill behaviors to be taken into account; it also allows for gradations in skill performance, so that a child's progress in a given skill area can be monitored over time. The scale could also be used to evaluate intervention procedures introduced in a child's daily routine to improve particular behavioral skills that are known to be below par for his particular age-group. Although much more work needs to be done on the development of the PBRS, it is a measure worthy of further investigation.

Satz Screening Battery
(SSB)

The SSB is the outcome of over ten years of research by neuropsychologist Paul Satz and his colleagues at the University of Florida at Gainesville into the developmental and predictive precursors of reading disability. Although the original standardization sample was assessed on a battery consisting of sixteen variables, the SSB has now been abbreviated to a measure of five variables (Satz, Taylor, Friel and Fletcher, 1979) consisting of the Finger Location Test (FL), the Recognition-Discrimination Test (RD), the Beery Visual-Motor Integration Test (VMI), the Alphabet Recitation Test (AR) and the Peabody Picture Vocabulary Test (PPVT).

The battery was designed to screen preschool children of kindergarten age who were to be subjects in a longitudinal research study on reading disabilities. The theory that Satz et al. (1979) wanted to test was one that conceptualized reading disabilities as a multidimensional phenomenon. The authors explain reading disorders as "delays in those crucial early sensory-perceptual and later conceptual-linguistic skills that are intrinsic to the acquisition of reading. Underlying these delays is a lag in the maturation of the cerebral cortex." Thus, the SSB was constructed not only to try and detect children at-risk for reading disability, but to test whether the relationship between early sensory-perceptual delay and reading disorder really stands up under careful empirical scrutiny.

The original SSB was standardized on 497 white male children from Alachua County, Florida. These boys were tested at the beginning of their kindergarten year and represented virtually the *entire* population of white children available in the school district.

With the exception of the R-D test, the reliabilities of the tests have been described elsewhere (Lindgren, 1975), but in general range from the low .70s to the high .90s. However, there have been no published reports so far on the reliability of the SSB as a whole.

Most of the research on validity has been of the predictive type (Satz et al., 1979). For example, the original sample's reading skills were assessed at the end of their grade two year by a combination of both teacher ratings of reading level and the IOTA Word Recognition Test. When children are then categorized as normal (average plus superior) and at-risk (mild to severe reading problems) readers, the hit-rate for reading disability is 79.17 percent, while the false-positive/false-negative rates are 23.08 percent and 20.83 percent respectively. When the same analysis is done for the standardization sample at the end of their grade five year, the hit-rate for reading disability is 72.28 percent, while the false-positive/false-negative rates are 27.63 percent and 27.72 percent respectively. The predictive accuracy of the SSB over a six-year period is indeed impressive and shows remarkable stability between the follow-up years of grades two and five.

In view of the preliminary success of the SSB, Satz, Friel and Rudegair (1976) carried out a cross-validational study on a completely independent sample of 175 white boys of kindergarten age using the same criterion measures (teacher ratings; IOTA scores) for assessing reading skills at the end of their grade two year. The results of this study revealed a hit-rate for reading disability of 58.14 percent, while the false-positive/false-negative rates were 23.48 percent and 41.86 percent respectively. In a second cross-validational study (Satz and Friel, 1979) on 114 kindergarten age children, using the same criterion measures, but for the end of the grade one year, the hit-rate for reading disability was 85.71 percent, while the false-positive/false-negative rates were 11.83 percent and 14.29 percent respectively.

The empirical evidence so far reported on the SSB is impressive to say the least; however, despite the comprehensive research carried out by Satz and his coworkers, there are still some gaps which must be filled in before the SSB can be considered for full-scale mass screening. Perhaps the most obvious gap is the fact that there is no evidence on the effectiveness of the battery for girls. A second gap has to do with the fact that although the SSB has been subjected to cross-validational studies, all the subjects have resided in the state of Florida and are not, therefore, necessarily representative of the population as a whole. Thirdly, there is no evidence yet to suggest that the battery can be used as effectively with trained non-professional examiners as it has been with professionally trained examiners. Finally, two other major drawbacks to the expanded use of the battery are the lack of an examiner's manual and the fact that even the abbreviated version takes close to an hour to administer, plus additional time for scoring.

In spite of these shortcomings, the SSB is probably the most powerful predictor of later reading difficulties currently available, and the diligence and comprehensiveness of Satz' research over such a long period of time is highly commendable.

BIBLIOGRAPHY

1. Aaronson, M.: *The Preschool Preposition Test* (manual). Rockville, National Institute of Mental Health, DHEW, undated.
2. Aaronson, M., and Phillips, J.: *The Preschool Preposition Test: A Preliminary Report.* Paper presented at the Annual Meeting of the American Educational Research Association. New York, 1977.
3. Aaronson, M., Phillips, J., and Bertolucci, D.: *The Preschool Preposition Test: Developmental Screening for Head-Start.* Paper presented at the Annual Meeting of the American Education Research Association. Toronto, 1978.
4. Aaronson, M., Phillips, J., Bertolucci, D., and Aaronson, D.: *Preschool Preposition Test Linkage With Maternal Behavior.* Paper presented at the Annual Meeting of the American Education Research Association. San Francisco, 1979.
5. Aaronson, M., and Shaeffer, E. S.: *Classroom Behavior Description,* unpublished manuscript. National Institute of Mental Health, DHEW, 1971.
6. Achenbach, T. M.: The Child Behavior Profile: I. Boys aged 6-11. *Journal of Consulting and Clinical Psychology, 46:*478-488, 1978.
7. Achenbach, T. M., and Edelbrock, C. S.: The Child Behavior Profile: II. Boys aged 12-16 and girls aged 6-11 and 12-16. *Journal of Consulting and Clinical Psychology, 47:*223-233, 1979.
8. Achenbach, T. M., and Edelbrock, C. S.: Behavioral problems and competences reported by parents of normal and disturbed children aged 4 through 16. *Monographs of the Society for Research in Child Development,* 1980, In Press.
9. Acheson, R. M.: Thoughts on a service for the presymptomatic diagnosis of disease. *Public Health, 77:*261-273, 1963.
10. Adair, N., and Blesch, G.: *The ABC Inventory,* Muskegan, Educational Studies and Development, 1965.
11. Adelman, N. S., and Feshbach, S.: Predicting reading failure: beyond the readiness model. *Exceptional Children, 37:*349-354, 1971.
12. Alberman, E.: The early prediction of learning disorders. *Developmental Medicine and Child Neurology, 15:*202-204, 1973.

13. Allen, H. F.: A new picture series for preschool vision testing. *American Journal of Ophthalmology, 44:*38-41, 1957.
14. Allen, H. F.: Testing of visual acuity in preschool children. *Pediatrics, 19:*1093-1097, 1957.
15. American Psychological Association: *Standards for Educational and Psychological Tests,* 1974 revision. Washington, American Psychological Association, 1974.
16. Anastasi, A.: *Psychological Testing.* New York, Macmillan, 1954.
17. Anderson, U. M.: The incidence and significance of high-frequency deafness in children. *American Journal of Diseases in Children, 113:*560-565, 1967.
18. Angoff, W. H., and Anderson, S. B.: The standardization of Educational Psychological Tests. In D. A. Payne and R. F. McMorris (Eds.), *Educational and Psychological Measurement.* Waltham, Blaisdell, 1967.
19. Anthony, R. J.: The behavior disorders in childhood. In P. H. Mussen (Ed.), *Carmichael's Manual of Child Psychology.* New York, Wiley, 1970, Vol. II.
20. Armistead, L. M., and Crawford, E. E.: An easy developmental screening test for public health use. *American Journal of Public Health, 64:* 241-244, 1974.
21. Arndt, W. B.: A psychometric evaluation of the North-Western Syntax Screening Test. *Journal of Speech and Hearing Disorders, 42:*316-319, 1977.
22. Arnott, E. J., and Calcutt, M.: Early surgery for strabismus. *Trans Ophthalmological Society of the United Kingdom, 90:*959-964, 1970.
23. Askov, W., Otto, W., and Smith, R.: Assessment of the de Hirsch Predictive Index Tests of reading failure. In R. C. Aakerman (Ed.), *Some Persistent Questions on Beginning Reading.* Newark, International Reading Association, 1972.
24. Banham, K.: *Maturity Level for School Entrance and Reading Readiness Manual.* Circle Pines, American Guidance Service, 1959.
25. Barker, W. F.: *Teacher Rating Versus Developmental Testing for Screening Preschool Children.* Paper presented at the meeting of the Eastern Educational Research Association, Williamsburg, 1978.
26. Barker, J., and Barmatz, H. E.: Eye function. In W. K. Frankenburg and B. W. Camp (Eds.), *Pediatric Screening Tests.* Springfield, Thomas, 1975.
27. Barker, W. F., and Doeff, A.: *Preschool Children's Psychomotor, Language and Social Skill Level Assessment Using Teacher Ratings.* Paper presented at the National Council on Measurement in Education, Boston, 1980.
28. Barnes, K. E.: Preschool Play Norms: A Replication. *Developmental Psychology, 5:*99-103, 1971.

29. Barnes, K. E.: The Jansky Predictive Index: A cross-validational study. In W. K. Frankenburg (Ed.), *Proceedings of the Second International Conference on Developmental Screening.* Denver, University of Colorado, 1978.

30. Barnes, K. E.: *The Jansky Screening Index: A Cross-Validational Four Year Follow-up Study.* Manuscript in preparation, 1980.

31. Barnes, K. E., and Stark, A.: The Denver Developmental Screening Test: a normative study. *American Journal of Public Health, 65:*363-369, 1975.

32. Barrett, T. C.: The relationship between measures of pre-reading visual discrimination and first grade reading achievement: a review of the literature. *Reading Research Quarterly, 1:*51-87, 1965.

33. Bates, E.: Language and Context: *The Acquisition of Pragmatics.* New York, Academic Press, 1976.

34. Battin, R. R.: Templin-Darley Tests of Articulation. In W. F. Frankenburg and B. W. Camp (Eds.), *Pediatric Screening Tests,* Springfield, Thomas, 1975.

35. Bentzen, F.: Sex ratios in learning and behavior disorders. *American Journal of Orthopsychiatry, 33:*529-531, 1963.

36. Berens, C.: Kindergarten visual acuity chart. *American Journal of Ophthalmology, 21:*667-668, 1938.

37. Bergstrom, L., Hemenway, W. G., and Downs, M. P.: A high-risk registry to find congenital deafness. *Otolaryngologic Clinics of North America, 4:*No. 2., 1971.

38. Bernard, M. E., Thelen, M. O., and Garber, H. L.: *The Use of Gross Feature Tabulation for the Analysis of Early Language Development.* Madison, University of Wisconsin, undated.

39. Bijou, S. W., and Peterson, R. F.: The psychological assessment of children: a functional analysis. In P. Reynolds (Ed.), *Advances in Psychological Assessment,* New York, Academic Press, 1974, Vol. II.

40. Bloom, L., and Lahey, M.: *Language Development and Language Disorders.* New York, John Wiley & Sons, 1978.

41. Borg, G., and Sundmark, E.: A comparative study of visual acuity tests for children. *Acta Ophthalmology, 45:*105-113, 1967.

42. Bower, T. G. R.: *Development in Infancy.* San Francisco, W. H. Freeman, 1974.

43. Bower, T. G. R. : *The Perceptual World of the Child.* San Francisco, W. H. Freeman, 1977.

44. Bowlby, J.: *Attachment and Loss: Attachment.* New York, Basic Books, 1969, Vol. I.

45. Bradley, R. H.: *The HOME Inventory: A Review of the First Fifteen Years.* Paper presented at the Third International Conference on Early Identification of Children who are Developmentally "At-Risk." Teton Village, 1980.

46. Bradley, R. H., and Caldwell, B. M.: Early home environment and changes in mental test performance in children from 6 to 36 months. *Journal of Developmental Psychology, 12:*93-97, 1976.
47. Bradley, R. H., and Caldwell, B. M.: The relation of infants' home environments to mental test performance at fifty-four months: a follow-up study. *Child Development, 47:*1172-1174, 1976.
48. Bradley, R. H., and Caldwell, B. M.: Home observation for measurement of the environment: a validation study of screening efficiency. *American Journal of Mental Deficiency, 81:*417-420, 1977.
49. Bradley, R. H., and Caldwell, B. M.: Home environment, learning processes and I.Q. In W. K. Frankenburg (Ed.), *Proceedings of the Second International Conference on Developmental Screening,* Denver, University of Colorado, 1978.
50. Bradley, R. H., and Caldwell, B. M.: Screening the environment. *American Journal of Orthopsychiatry, 48:*114-130, 1978.
51. Bradley, R. H., and Caldwell, B. M.: Home observation for measurement of the environment: a revision of the preschool scale. *American Journal of Mental Deficiency, 84:*235-244, 1979.
52. Bradley, R. H., Caldwell, B. M. and Elardo, R.: Home environment, social status and mental test performance. *Journal of Educational Psychology, 69:*697-701, 1977.
53. Bradley, R. H., Caldwell, B. M., and Elardo, R.: Home environment and cognitive development in the first 2 years: a cross-lagged panel analysis. *Developmental Psychology, 15:*246-250, 1979.
54. Brian, M. M.: The Sprigle School Readiness Screening Test. In W. K. Frankenburg and B. M. Camp (Eds.), *Pediatric Screening Tests.* Springfield, Thomas, 1975.
55. Bridgeman, B., and Shipman, V. C.: Predictive value of measures of self-esteem and achievement motivation in four-to-nine-year-old low-income children. In *Disadvantaged Children and Their First School Experiences. ETS-Head Start Longitudinal Study.* Princeton, Educational Testing Service, 1975.
56. Brooks, D.: The use of the electro-acoustic impedance bridge in the assessment of middle ear function. *International Audiology, 8:* 563-569, 1969.
57. Brooks, D.: Electroacoustic impedance bridge studies on normal ears of children. *Journal of Speech and Hearing Research, 14:*247-253, 1971.
58. Byrne, M. C.: A clinician looks at the Northwestern Syntax Screening Test. *Journal of Speech and Hearing Disorders, 42:*320-322, 1977.
59. Caldwell, B. M.: *The Preschool Inventory* (Technical Report). Princeton, Educational Testing Service, 1967.
60. Caldwell, B. M.: *The Preschool Inventory* (Revised Edition). Princeton, Educational Testing Service, 1970.

61. Caldwell, B. M., and Bradley, R. H.: *Home Observation for Measurement of the Environment: Administration Manual.* Little Rock, University of Arkansas at Little Rock, undated.

62. Caldwell, B. M., and Drachman, R. H.: Comparability of three methods of assessing the developmental level of young infants. *Pediatrics, 34:* 51-57, 1964.

63. Camp, B. W., van Doorninck, W. J., Frankenburg, W. K. and Lampe, J. M.: Preschool developmental testing in prediction of school problems. *Clinical Pediatrics, 16:*257-263, 1977.

64. Campbell, D. T., and Fiske, D. W.: Convergent and discriminant validation by the multitrait-multimethod matrix. *Psychological Bulletin, 56:*81-105, 1959.

65. Campbell, W. D., and Camp, B. W.: Developmental Screening. In W. K. Frankenburg & B. W. Camp (Eds.), *Pediatric Screening Tests,* Springfield, Thomas, 1975.

66. Capute, A. J., and Biehl, R. F.: Functional developmental evaluation. *Pediatric Clinics of North America, 20:*3-26, 1973.

67. Cohen, M. A., and Gross, P. J.: *The Developmental Resource: Behavioral Sequences for Assessment and Program Planning.* New York, Grune & Stratton, 1979, Vol. I.

68. Cohen, M. A., and Gross, P. J.: *The Developmental Resource: Behavioral Sequences for Assessment and Program Planning.* New York, Grune & Stratton, 1979, Vol. II.

69. Colligan, R. C.: Predictions of kindergarten reading success from preschool report of parents. *Psychology in the Schools, 13:*304-308, 1976.

70. Conrad, W. G., and Tobiessen, J.: The development of kindergarten behavior rating scales for the prediction of learning behavior disorders. *Psychology in the Schools, 4:*359-363, 1967.

71. Cools, T., and Hermanns, J.: Early detection. In W. K. Frankenburg (Ed.), *Proceedings of the Second International Conference on Developmental Screening.* Denver, University of Colorado, 1978.

72. Coons, C. E., Frankenburg, W. K., Garrett, C. J., Headley, R., and Fandal, A. W.: Home Screening Questionnaire (HSQ). In W. K. Frankenburg (Ed.), *Proceedings of the Second International Conference on Developmental Screening.* Denver, University of Colorado, 1978.

73. Coons, C. E., Frankenburg, W. K., Gay, E. C., Fandal, A. W., Lefly, D., and Ker, C. Y.: *Preliminary Results of a Combined Developmental/ Environmental Screening Procedure.* Paper presented at the Third International Conference on Early Identification of Children Who are Developmentally At-Risk. Teton Village, 1980.

74. Couch, A., and Kenistan, K.: Yeasayers and naysayers: agreeing response set as a personality variable. *Journal of Abnormal and Social Psychology, 60:*151-174, 1960.

75. Covin, T. M.: Alternate form reliability of the Peabody Picture Vocabulary Test. *Psychological Reports, 39:*1286, 1976.

76. Cowgill, M. D., Friedland, S., and Shapiro, R.: Predicting learning disabilities from kindergarten reports. *Journal of Learning Disabilities, 6:*577-582, 1973.

77. Cromer, R.: The cognitive hypothesis of language acquisition and its implications for child language deficiency. In D. Morehead & A. Morehead (Eds.), *Normal and Deficient Child Language.* Baltimore, University Park Press, 1976.

78. Cronbach, L. J.: Test Validation. In R. L. Thorndike (Ed.), *Educational Measurement,* 2nd Ed. Washington, American Council on Education, 1971.

79. Cronbach, L. J., and Gleser, G. C.: *Psychological Tests and Personnel Decisions,* 2nd Ed. Urbana, University of Illinois Press, 1965.

80. Cronbach, L. J., Gleser, G. C., Nanda, H., and Rajaratnam, N.: *The Dependability of Behavioral Measurements: Multifacet Studies of Generalizability.* New York, John Wiley & Sons, 1971.

81. Cronbach, L. J., and Meehl, P. E.: Construct validity in psychological tests. *Psychological Bulletin, 52:*281-302, 1955.

82. Cross, L.: Case finding. In L. Cross and K. W. Goin (Eds.), *Identifying Handicapped Children.* New York, Walker and Company, 1977.

83. Darwin, C.: A biographical sketch of an infant. *Mind, 2:*285, 1877.

84. Datta, L. E.: The Peabody Picture Vocabulary Test. In W. K. Frankenburg and B. W. Camp (Eds.), *Pediatric Screening Tests.* Springfield, Thomas, 1975.

85. de Hirsch, K., Jansky, J. J., and Langford, W. S.: *Predicting Reading Failure.* New York, Harper & Row, 1966.

86. De Lorenzo, L. T., and Brady, J. J.: Use of the Peabody Picture Vocabulary Test with Preschool Children. *Psychological Reports, 22:* 247-251, 1968.

87. Doster, M. E.: Vision screening in schools - why, what, how and when? *Clinical Pediatrics, 10:*662-665, 1971.

88. Downing, A. H.: Ocular defects in sixty thousand selectees. *Archives of Ophthalmology, 33:*137-140, 1945.

89. Downing, J.: *Social Factors in Reading Disability.* Paper presented at the Twelfth Annual Neuropsychology Workshop. Victoria, 1977.

90. Downs, M. P., and Silver, H. K.: The A.B.C.D.'s to H.E.A.R.: Early identification in nursery, office and clinic of the infant who is deaf. *Clinical Pediatrics, 11:*563-566, 1972.

91. Drumwright, A. F.: Speech and language. In W. K. Frankenburg and B. W. Camp (Eds.), *Pediatric Screening Tests.* Springfield, Thomas, 1975.

92. Drumwright, A., Van Natta, P., Camp, B., Frankenburg, W., and Drexler, H.: The Denver Articulation Screening Exam. *Journal of Speech & Hearing Disorders, 38:*3-14, 1973.

93. Duke-Elder, W. S.: *System of Ophthalmology, Volume 6: Motility and Strabismus.* London, Henry Kimpton, 1973.

94. Dunn, L. M.: *The Peabody Picture Vocabulary Test* (expanded manual). Circle Pines, American Guidance Association, 1965.
95. Durkin, D.: *Children Who Read Early*. New York, Teacher College Press, 1966.
96. Durkin, D.: Children who read before grade one: a second study. *Elementary School Journal, 64:*143-148, 1963.
97. Durrell, D. D.: *Improving Reading Instruction*. New York, World Book Company, 1956.
98. Durrell, D. D. and Sullivan, H. B.: *Reading Capacity and Achievement Tests*. Yonkers, World Book Company, 1937.
99. Durrett, M. E., and Henman, J.: Concurrent validity of the Peabody Picture Vocabulary Test, Draw-a-Man and Children's Embedded Figures Test with four-year old children. *Educational & Psychological Measurement, 32:*1089-1093, 1972.
100. Eaves, L. C., Kendall, D. C., and Crichton, J. U.: The early detection of minimal brain dysfunction. *Journal of Learning Disabilities, 5:* 5-13, 1972.
101. Ebel, R. L.: Evaluating content validity. In D. A. Payne and R. F. McMorris (Eds.), *Educational and Psychological Measurement*. Waltham, Blaisdell, 1967.
102. Edelbrock, C. S.: *The Child Behavior Checklist and Profile: A Comparison of Strategies for Identifying Children in Need of Mental Health Services*. Paper presented at the Third International Conference on the Early Identification of Children Who Are Developmentally At-Risk. Teton Village, 1980.
103. Edwards, A.L.: *The Social Desirability Variable in Personality Research*. New York, Dryden, 1957.
104. Edwards, A. L.: Social desirability and personality test construction. In B. M. Bass and I. A. Berg (Eds.), *Objective Approaches to Personality Assessment*. Princeton, Van Nostrand, 1959.
105. Egan, D., Illingworth, R. S., and MacKeith, R. C.: Developmental Screening, 0-5 years. *Clinics in Developmental Medicine*, No. 30. London, The Spastics International Medical Publications in association with William Heinemann Medical Books, Ltd., 1969.
106. Egeland, B.: The Sprigle School Readiness Screening Test. In W. K. Frankenburg, and B. W. Camp (Eds.), *Pediatric Screening Tests*. Springfield, Thomas, 1975.
107. Elardo, R., Bradley, R. H., and Caldwell, B. M.: The relation of infants' home environments to mental test performance from six to thirty-six months: a longitudinal analysis. *Child Development, 46:*71-76, 1975.
108. Erickson, M. L.: *Assessment and Management of Developmental Changes in Children*. St. Louis, Mosby, 1976.
109. Ernhart, C. B., Spaner, S. D., and Jordan, T. E.: Validity of selected preschool screening tests. *Contemporary Educational Psychology, 2:* 78-89, 1977.

110. Ernhart, C.B.: The Cooperative Preschool Inventory. In W. K. Frankenburg and B. W. Camp (Eds.), *Pediatric Screening Tests*, Springfield, Thomas, 1975.

111. Feinmesser, M., and Tell, L.: Neonatal screening for detection of deafness. *Archives of Otolaryngology, 102:*297-299, 1976.

112. Feshbach, S., Adelman, H. S., and Fuller, W.: Prediction of reading and related academic problems. *Journal of Educational Psychology, 69:*299-308, 1977.

113. Flavell, J. H.: *Cognitive Development.* Englewood Cliffs, Prentice-Hall, Inc., 1977.

114. Fleeson, W. P., and Wenk, R. E.: Pitfalls of mass chemical screening. *Post Graduate Medicine, 48:*59-63, 1970.

115. Fontana, M. C.: The Northwestern Syntax Screening Test. In O. K. Buros (Ed.), *The Eighth Mental Measurements Yearbook.* Highland Park, Gryphon Press, 1978.

116. Foote, F. M.: An evaluation of vision screening of exceptional children. *Exceptional Children, 20:*153-158, 1954.

117. Forness, S. R., Guthrie, D., and Hall, R.: Follow-up of high-risk children identified in kindergarten through direct classroom observation. *Psychology in the Schools, 13:*45-49, 1976.

118. Francois, J.: *Heredity in Ophthalmology.* St.Louis, Mosby, 1961.

119. Frankenburg, W. K.: Evaluation and screening procedures. In A. Oglesby and H. Sterling (Eds.), *Proceedings, Bi-Regional Institute on Earlier Recognition of Handicapping Conditions.* Berkeley, University of California School of Public Health, 1970.

120. Frankenburg, W. K.: *Proceedings of the Second International Conference on Developmental Screening.* Santa Fe, 1978.

121. Frankenburg, W. K., and Camp, B. W.: *Pediatric Screening Tests.* Springfield, Thomas, 1975.

122. Frankenburg, W. K., Camp, B. W., and Van Natta, P. A.: Validity of the Denver Developmental Screening Test. *Child Development, 42:*475-485, 1971.

123. Frankenburg, W. K., Camp, B. W., Van Natta, P. A., Demersseman, J. A., and Voorhees, S. F.: Reliability and stability of the Denver Developmental Screening Test. *Child Development, 42:*1315-1325, 1971.

124. Frankenburg, W. K., Dick, N. P., and Carland, J.: Development of preschool-aged children of different social and ethnic groups: Implications for developmental screening. *Journal of Pediatrics, 87:*125-132, 1975.

125. Frankenburg, W. K., and Dodds, J. B.: The Denver Developmental Screening Test. *Journal of Pediatrics, 71:*181-191, 1967.

126. Frankenburg, W. K., Dodds, J. B., and Fandal, A. *The Revised Denver Developmental Screening Test Manual.* Denver, University of Colorado Press, 1970.

127. Frankenburg, W. K., Goldstein, A., and Camp, B. W.: The revised Denver Developmental Screening Test: its accuracy as a screening instrument. *Journal of Pediatrics, 79:*988-995, 1971.

128. Frankenburg, W. K., Goldstein, A., Chabot, A., Camp, B. W., and Fitch, M.: Training the indigenous non-professional: The screening technician. *Journal of Pediatrics, 77:*564-470, 1970.

129. Fraser, C., Bellugi, U., and Brown, R.: Control of grammar in imitation, comprehension and production. *Journal of Verbal Learning and Verbal Behavior, 2:*121-135, 1963.

130. Friedlander, B. Z.: Automated evaluation of selective listening in language impaired and normal infants and young children. *Maternal and Child Health Exchange, 1:*9-12, 1971.

131. Funk and Wagnall: *Standard Dictionary.* Britannica World Language Edition, Chicago, Encyclopaedia Britannica, Inc., 1965, Vol. II.

132. Furuno, S., and Connor, A.: *Use of Non-Professional Personnel for Health Screening of Head-Start Children.* Paper presented at the 47th Annual Meeting of the American Orthopsychiatric Association, San Francisco, 1970.

133. Gacka, R. C.: The Basic School Skills Inventory as a preschool screening instrument. *Journal of Learning Disabilities, 11:*593-595, 1978.

134. Gallagher, J. J., and Bradley, R. H.: Early identification of developmental difficulties. In I. J. Gordon (Ed.), *Early Childhood Education,* Chicago, University of Chicago Press, 1972, Vol. 71, No. 2.

135. Garmezy, N.: Vulnerable and invulnerable children: theory research and intervention. Manuscript #1337, *Selected Documents in Psychology,* American Psychological Association, Washington, *6(4):* 96, 1976.

136. Gavel, S. R.: June reading achievements of first grade children. *Journal of Education, 140:*37-48, 1958.

137. Gay, E. C., Coons, C. E., and Frankenburg, W. K.: The application of decision analysis in selecting screening cut-off scores. In W. K. Frankenburg (Ed.), *Proceedings of the Second International Conference on Developmental Screening.* Denver, University of Colorado, 1978.

138. Gesell, A. L.: *The First Five Years of Life: A Guide to the Study of the Preschool Child.* New York, Harper, 1940.

139. Gesell, A. L., and Amatruda, C. S.: *Developmental Diagnosis.* New York, Paul B. Hoeber, 1941.

140. Gesell, A. L., and Armatruda, C. S.: *Developmental Diagnosis,* 2nd Ed., New York, Paul B. Hoeber, 1954.

141. Gibson, J. J., and Levin, H.: *The Psychology of Reading.* Cambridge, The MIT Press, 1975.

142. Gibson, J. J., and Yonas, P.: A new theory of scribbling and drawing in children. In *The Analysis of Reading Skill.* Final Report, Project No. 5-1213, Cornell University and U. S. Office of Education, December, 1968.

143. Goh, D., and Lund, J. M.: Verbal reinforcement, socioeconomic status and intelligence test performance of preschool children. *Perceptual and Motor Skills, 44:*1011-1014, 1977.

144. Goldstein, A. D.: School readiness and achievement. In W. K. Frankenburg and B. M. Camp (Eds.), *Pediatric Screening Tests.* Springfield, Thomas, 1975.

145. Goldstein, A. D. and Camp, B. W.: A procedure for the selection of non-professional workers. *HSMHA Health Reports, 86:*533, 1971.

146. Goodman, L., and Hammill, D.: *Basic School Skills Inventory.* Chicago, Follett, 1975.

147. Goodwin, W. L.: The Minnesota Child Development Inventory. In O. K. Buros (Ed.), *The Eighth Mental Measurements Yearbook.* Highland Park, Gryphon Press, 1978.

148. Gordon, D. A., Zeidner, J., Zagorski, H. J., and Uhlaner, J. E.: A psychometric evaluation of Ortho-Rater and Wall-Chart tests. *American Journal of Ophthalmology, 37:*699-705, 1954.

149. Griffing, T. S., Simonton, K. M., and Hedgecock, L. D.: Verbal auditory screening for preschool children. *Trans American Academy of Ophthalmology and Otolaryngology, 71:*105-110, 1967.

150. Grimes, J. W., and Allinsmith, W.: Compulsivity, anxiety, and school achievement. *Merrill-Palmer Quarterly, 7:*247-271, 1961.

151. Gunderson, T.: Early diagnosis and treatment of strabismus. *Sight Saving Review, 40:*129-133, 1970.

152. Hall, J., Mardell, C., Wick, J., and Goldenberg, D.: Further development and refinement of DIAL. *Resources in Education,* May, 1976.

153. Harbin, G.: Educational assessment. In L. Cross and K. Goin (Eds.), *Identifying Handicapped Children.* New York, Walker and Company, 1977.

154. Hardy, J. B.: The young deaf child: identification and management. *ACTA Otolaryngologica,* Supplementum No. 206, 1965.

155. Harlap, S., and Davies, A. M.: Infant admissions to hospital and maternal smoking. *Lancet, 1:*529-532, 1974.

156. Hatfield, E. M.: Progress in preschool vision screening. *Sight Saving Review, 37:*194-201, 1967.

157. Hatfield, E. M.: Methods and standards for screening preschool children. *Sight Saving Review,* Summer:71-84, 1979.

158. Hatfield, E. M., Barrett, G. D., and Nudell, R. J.: Detroit project 20/20. *Sight Saving Review, 37:*202-205, 1967.

159. Hawthorne, L. W., and Larsen, S. C.: The predictive validity of the Basic School Skills Inventory. *Journal of Learning Disabilities, 10:*44-50, 1977.

160. Heber, R., and Garber, H. L.: *Rehabilitation of Families At-Risk of Mental Retardation: A Progress Report.* Madison, University of Wisconsin, 1971.

161. Hejna, R.: *Developmental Articulation Test.* Madison, College Print and Typing, 1959.

162. Hermanns, J., and Cools, T.: Developmental screening: a longitudinal study with the Denver Ontwikkeling Screening Test (DOS). In W. K. Frankenburg (Ed.), *Proceedings of the Second International Conference on Developmental Screening.* Denver, University of Colorado, 1978.
163. Hieronymus, A. N., and Lindquist, E. F.: *Iowa Tests of Basic Skills.* Boston, Houghton-Mifflin, 1971.
164. Hoyt, C.: Test reliability obtained by analysis of variance. *Psychometrika, 6:*153-160, 1941.
165. Hunt, J. V.: The Peabody Picture Vocabulary Test. In W. K. Frankenburg and B. M. Camp (Eds.), *Pediatric Screening Tests.* Springfield, Thomas, 1975.
166. Ireton, H., and Thwing, E.: *The Minnesota Child Development Inventory Manual.* Minneapolis, Behavior Science Systems, 1974.
167. Ireton, H., and Thwing, E.: Minnesota Child Development Inventory: Identification of children with developmental disorders. *Journal of Pediatric Psychology, 2:*18-22, 1974.
168. Ireton, H., and Thwing, E.: *Minnesota Preschool Inventory* (Manual). Minneapolis, Behavior Science Systems, Incorporated, 1979.
169. Ireton, H. R., and Thwing, E. J.: *Early Identification of Developmentally Delayed Children by Maternal Report.* Paper presented at the Third International Conference on Early Identification of Children who are Developmentally At-Risk, Teton Village, 1980a.
170. Ireton, H. R., and Thwing, E. J.: *The Minnesota Infant Development Inventory.* Minneapolis, Behavior Science Systems, 1980b.
171. Jackson, D. N., and Messick, S.: *Problems in Human Assessment.* New York, McGraw-Hill, 1967.
172. Jansky, J., and de Hirsch, K.: *Preventing Reading Failure: Prediction, Diagnosis, Intervention.* New York, Harper & Row, 1972.
173. Jerger, J.: Clinical experience with impedance audiometry. *Archives of Otolaryngology, 92:*311-324, 1970.
174. Jerger, S., Jerger, J., Mauldin, S., and Segal, P.: Studies in impedance audiometry: II. Children less than six years old. *Archives Otolaryngology, 99:*1-9, 1974.
175. Keith, R.: Impedance audiometry with neonates. *Archives of Otolaryngology, 97:*465-467, 1973.
176. Keith, C. G., Diamond, Z., and Stansfield, A.: Visual acuity testing in young children. *British Journal of Ophthalmology, 56:*827-832, 1972.
177. Kelley, T. L.: The selection of upper and lower groups for the validation of test items. *Journal of Educational Psychology, 30:*17-24, 1939.
178. Keogh, B. K., and Becker, L. D.: Early detection of learning problems: Questions, cautions and guidelines. *Exceptional Children, 39:*5-11, 1973.

179. Keogh, B. K., and Tchir, C.: *Teachers' Perceptions of Educationally High-Risk Children.* Technical Report. Los Angeles, University of California, 1972.
180. Keogh, B. K., and Smith, C. E.: Early identification of educationally high potential and high risk children. *Journal of School Psychology, 8:*285-290, 1970.
181. Knobloch, H., Pasamanick, B., and Sherard, E. S.: A developmental screening inventory for infants. *Pediatrics, 38:*1095-1108, 1966.
182. Knobloch, H., Stevens, F., Malone, A., Ellison, P., and Risemberg, H.: The validity of parental reporting of infant development. *Pediatrics, 63:*872-878, 1979.
183. Larson, G. W., and Summers, P. A.: Response patterns of preschool-age children to the Northwestern Syntax Screening test. *Journal of Speech and Hearing Disorders, 41:*486-497, 1976.
184. Lee, L.: A screening test for syntax development. *Journal of Speech and Hearing Disorders, 35:*103-112, 1970.
185. Lee, L.: *The Northwestern Syntax Screening Test.* Evanston, Northwestern University Press, 1971.
186. Lee, L. L.: Reply to Arndt and Byrne. *Journal of Speech and Hearing Disorders, 42:*323-337, 1977.
187. Lessler, K., and Bridges, J. S.: The prediction of learning problems in rural settings: can we improve on readiness tests? *Journal of Learning Disabilities, 6:*90-94, 1973.
188. Lewis, M.: *Developmental Models and Assessment Issues.* Invited address presented at the Third International Conference on Early Identification of Children Who Are Developmentally At-Risk. Teton Village, 1980.
189. Lichtenstein, R., Clark, C. R., and Cronin, J. P.: *Search Screen: A Pre-Kindergarten Developmental Screening Instrument.* Minneapolis, Minneapolis Public Schools, 1978.
190. Lichtenstein, R.: *Classificational Methods for the Psychometric Evaluation of Screening Procedures.* Paper presented at the Bi-Annual Meeting of the Society for Research in Child Development, San Francisco, 1979.
191. Lichtenstein, R.: *The Minneapolis Preschool Screening Instrument* (draft manual). Minneapolis, Minneapolis Public Schools, 1980.
192. Lichtenstein, R.: *Early Identification of Psychoeducational Problems: Assessing the Limits of Prediction.* Paper presented at the Third International Conference on Early Identification of Children Who Are Developmentally At-Risk. Teton Village, 1980.
193. Lillie, D. L.: Screening. In L. Cross and K. W. Goin (Eds.), *Identifying Handicapped Children.* New York, Walker and Company, 1977.
194. Lillywhite, H.: Doctor's manual of speech disorders. *Journal of the American Medical Association, 167:*850-857, 1958.
195. Lin Fu, J. S.: *Vision Screening of Children.* Washington, U. S. Department of Health, Education and Welfare, Maternal and Child Health Service, 1971.

196. Lindgren, S. D.: *The Early Identification of Children at Risk for Reading Disabilities.* Unpublished M.A. Thesis, Iowa City, University of Iowa, 1975.

197. Lippmann, O.: Choice of preschool vision test. *Eye, Ear, Nose and Throat,* 195-199, May, 1974.

198. Lippman, O.: Vision of young children. *Archives of Ophthalmology, 81:*763-775, 1969.

199. Lippman, O.: Vision screening of young children. *American Journal of Public Health, 61:*1586-1601, 1971.

200. Lippman, O.: *Directions for Use of the HOTV Test.* Forest Park, Good-Lite Company, undated.

201. Lippman, O.: *Personal Communication,* December, 1980.

202. Logue, R. D.: The Northwestern Syntax Screening Test. In O. K. Buros (Ed.), *The Eighth Mental Measurements Yearbook.* Highland Park, Gryphon Press, 1978.

203. Lord, F. M., and Novick, M. R.: *Statistical Theories of Mental Test Scores.* Reading, Addison-Wesley, 1968.

204. Lowell, K., and Dixon, E. M.: The growth of the control of grammar in imitation, comprehension and production. *Journal of Child Psychology and Psychiatry, 8:*31-39, 1967.

205. Lyman, H B.: The Peabody Picture Vocabulary Test. In O. K. Buros (Ed.), *The Sixth Mental Measurements Yearbook.* Highland Park, Gryphon Press, 1965.

206. Mardell, C. D., and Goldenberg, D. S.: *Developmental Indicators for the Assessment of Learning* (manual). Highland Park, DIAL, Incorporated, 1975.

207. Mardell, C. D., and Goldenberg, D. S.: The predictive validation of a pre-kindergarten screening test. *Resources in Education,* August, 1976.

208. Mardell, C. D., and Goldenberg, D. S.: DIAL as a screening tool. In W. K. Frankenburg (Ed.), *Second International Conference on Developmental Screening.* Denver, University of Colorado, 1978.

209. Meehl, P. E., and Rosen, A.: Antecedent probability and the efficiency of psychometric signs, patterns or cutting scores. *Psychological Bulletin, 52:*194-216, 1955.

210. Meier, J.: *Screening and Assessment of Young Children at Developmental Risk.* Washington, Department of Health, Education and Welfare Publication No. (OS) 73-90, 1973.

211. Melnick, W., Eagles, E. L., and Levine, H. S.: Evaluation of a recommended program of identification audiometry with school-age children. *Journal of Hearing Disorders, 29:*3-13, 1964.

212. Mencher, G. T., and McCullogh, B. F.: Auditory screening of kindergarten children using the VASC. *Journal of Speech and Hearing Disorders, 35:*241-247, 1970.

213. Menyuk, P.: A preliminary evaluation of grammatical capacity in children. *Journal of Verbal Learning and Verbal Behavior. 2:*429-439, 1963.

214. Milisen, R.: The incidence of speech disorders. In L. Travis (Ed.), *Handbook of Speech Pathology*, New York, Appleton-Century-Crofts, 1957.

215. Miller, L. B., and Dyer, J. L.: *Experimental Variation of Head-Start Curricula: A Comparison of Current Approaches*. Eric, No. ED 045 196, 1970.

216. Moghadam, H. K., Robinson, G. C., and Cambon, K. G.: A comparison of two audiometers in screening the hearing of school children. *Canadian Medical Association Journal, 99:*618-620, 1968.

217. Moore, M. G.: Program evaluation. In L. Cross and K. Goin (Eds.), *Identifying Handicapped Children*. New York, Walker and Company, 1977.

218. McCall, R. C.: *The Process of Early Mental Development: Implications for Prediction and Intervention*. Paper presented at the Third International Conference on Early Identification of Children Who Are Developmentally At-Risk, Teton Village, 1980.

219. Neal, W. R.: Verbal auditory screening with the educable mentally retarded. *Training School Bulletin, 71:*62-66, 1974.

220. Nelson, K.: Structure and strategy in learning to talk. *Monographs of the Society for Research in Child Development, 38:*1-2, Serial No. 149, 1973.

221. Nicholson, A.: Background abilities related to reading success in first grade. *Journal of Education, 140:*7-21, 1958.

222. Norman-Taylor, W., and Dickinson, V. A.: Dangers for children in smoking families. *Community Medicine, 128:*32-33, 1972.

223. Northern, J. L.: Auditory screening. In W. K. Frankenburg and B. W. Camp (Eds.), *Pediatric Screening Tests*. Springfield, Thomas, 1975.

224. Northern, J. L., and Downs, M. P.: *Hearing in Children*. Baltimore, Williams & Wilkins, 1974.

225. Oliver, M., and Nawratzki, I.: Screening of preschool children for ocular anomalies I. Screening methods and their practicability at different ages. *British Journal of Ophthalmology, 55:*462-466, 1971.

226. Oliver, M., and Nawratzki, I.: Screening of preschool children for ocular anomalies II. Amblyopia. Prevalence and therapeutic results at different ages. *Brit. J. Opth., 55:*467-471, 1971.

227. Oppe, T. E.: Risk registers for babies. *Developmental Medicine and Child Neurology, 9:*13. 1967.

228. Orne, M. T.: On the social psychology of the psychological experiment: with particular reference to demand characteristics and their implications. *American Psychologist, 17:*776-783, 1962.

229. Osborn, C.: *Air-borne Gap Measurement in Identification Audiometry*. Maico Audiological Library Series, Report No. 2, IX, 1970.

230. Parten, M. B.: Social participation among preschool children. *Journal of Abnormal and Social Psychology, 27:*243-269, 1932.

231. Pascale, P. J.: Validity concerns of preschool testing. *Educational and Psychological Measurement, 33:*977-978, 1973.

232. Pate, J. E., and Webb, W. W.: *First Grade Screening Test Manual.* Circle Pines, American Guidance Service, 1969.

233. Payne, D. A., and McMorris, R. F.: *Educational and Psychological Measurement: Contributions to Theory and Practice.* Waltham, Blaisdell, 1967.

234. Perkins, W. H.: *Speech Pathology: An Applied Behavioral Science.* St. Louis, C.V. Mosby, 1971.

235. Peterson, H. A.: The Denver Articulation Screening Exam. In O. K. Buros (Ed.), *The Eighth Mental Measurements Yearbook.* Highland Park, Gryphon Press, 1978.

236. Piers, E. V.: The Peabody Picture Vocabulary Test. In O. K. Buros (Ed.), *The Sixth Mental Measurements Yearbook.* Highland Park, Gryphon Press, 1965.

237. Popham, W. J. and Husek, T. R.: Implications of criterion-referenced measures. *Journal of Educational Measurement, 6:*1-9, 1969.

238. Pratt-Johnson, J. A., Lunn, G. T., Pop, A. E., and Wee, H. I.: The significance and characteristics of ametropic amblyopia. *Trans Pacific Coast Oto-Ophthalmological Society, 49:*231-235, 1968.

239. Press, E., and Austin, C.: Screening of preschool children for amblyopia. *Journal of the American Medical Association, 204:*767-770, 1968.

240. Prutting, C. A., Gallagher, T. M., and Mulac, A.: The expressive portion of the NSST compared to a spontaneous language sample. *Journal of Speech and Hearing Disorders, 40:*59-68, 1975.

241. Ramey, C., Mills, R., Campbell, F., and O'Brien, C.: Infants' home environments: A comparison of high-risk families and families from the general population. *American Journal of Mental Deficiency, 80:* 40-42, 1975.

242. Ratusnik, D. L., and Koenigsknecht, R. A.: Internal consistency of the Northwestern Syntax Screening Test. *Journal of Speech and Hearing Disorders, 40:*59-68, 1975.

243. Reid, J. B.: Reliability assessment of observation data: A possible methodological problem. *Child Development, 41:*1143-1148, 1970.

244. Reinke, W. A.: Decisions about screening programs: Can we develop a rational basis? *Archives of Environmental Health, 19:*403-411, 1969.

245. Richmond, J. B.: *Program Implications of New Knowledge Regarding the Physical, Intellectual and Environmental Growth and Development of the Unmet Needs of Children and Youths.* Conference on Health Services for Children and Youths, American Public Health Association, 1969.

246. Ritchie, B. C., and Merklein, R. A.: An evaluation of the efficiency of the Verbal Auditory Screening for Children (VASC). *Journal of Speech and Hearing Research, 15:*280-286, 1972.

247. Robertson, E. O., Peterson, J. C., and Lamb, L. E.: Relative impedance measurements in young children. *Archives of Otolaryngology, 88:* 162-168, 1968.

248. Robinson, H.: Perceptual training - does it result in reading improvement? In R. Aukerman (Ed.), *Some Persistent Questions on Beginning Reading*. Newark, International Reading Associaton, 1972.

249. Rogers, M. G. H.: The early recognition of handicapping disorders in childhood. *Developmental Medicine and Child Neurology, 13:* 88-101, 1971.

250. Rosenthal, A. R., and Von Noorden, G. K.: Clinical findings and therapy in unilateral high myopia associated with amblyopia. *American Journal of Ophthalmology, 71:*873-878, 1971.

251. Sameroff, A. J.: *Infant Risk Factors in Developmental Deviancy.* Paper presented at the International Association for Child Psychiatry and Allied Professions, Philadelphia, 1974.

252. Sandler, L., Van Campen, J., Ratner, G., Stafford, C., and Weismar, R.: Responses of urban preschool children to a developmental screening test. *Journal of Pediatrics, 77:*775-781, 1970.

253. Satz, P.: *Learning Disorders and Remediation of Learning Disorders.* Research Task Force, National Institute of Mental Health, Section on Child Mental Illness and Behavior Disorders, 1975.

254. Satz, P., Fennell, E., and Reilly, C.: The predictive validity of six neurodiagnostic tests: A decision theory analysis. *Journal of Consulting and Clinical Psychology, 34:*375-381, 1970.

255. Satz, P., and Fletcher, J. M.: Early screening tests: Some uses and abuses. *Journal of Learning Disabilities, 12:*65-69, 1979.

256. Satz, P., and Friel, J.: Some predictive antecedents of specific reading disability: A preliminary two-year follow-up. *Journal of Learning Disabilities, 17:*437-444, 1974.

257. Satz, P., and Friel, J.: The predictive validity of an abbreviated screening battery: A three-year cross-validational follow-up. *Journal of Learning Disabilities,* In Press, 1979.

258. Satz, P., Friel, J., and Rudegeair, F.: Some predictive antecedents of specific reading disability: A two- three- and four-year follow-up. In J. T. Guthrie (Ed.), *Aspects of Reading Acquisition.* Baltimore, John Harper Press, 1976.

259. Satz, P., Taylor, H. G., Friel, J., and Fletcher, J. M.: Some developmental and predictive precursors of reading disabilities: A six-year follow-up. In D. Pearl and A. Benton (Eds.), *Dyslexia: A Critical Appraisal of Current Theory.* Oxford, Oxford University Press, 1979.

260. Savitz, R. A., Reed, R. B., and Valadian, I.: *Vision Screening of the Preschool Child.* U. S. Department of Health, Education and Welfare, Children's Bureau, Washington, D. C., 1964.

261. Savitz, R. A., Valadian, I., and Reed, R. B.: Vision screening of preschool children at home. *American Journal of Public Health, 55:* 1555-1562, 1965.

262. Sax, G.: *Principles of Educational Measurement and Evaluation.* Belmont, Wadsworth, 1974.

263. Schaer, H. F., and Crump, W. D.: Teacher involvement and early identification of children with learning disabilities. *Journal of Learning
Disabilities, 9:*91-95, 1976.

264. Seda, M. S., and Michael, J. J.: The concurrent validity of the Sprigle
School Screening Readiness Test for a sample of preschool and
kindergarten children. *Educational and Psychological Measurement, 31:*995-997, 1971.

265. Shaycoft, M. F.: *Handbook of Criterion Referenced Testing.* New
York, Garland STPM Press, 1979.

266. Sheridan, M. D.: *Manual for the STYCAR Vision and Hearing Tests.*
Slough, National Foundation for Educational Research, 1969.

267. Sjogren, H.: New series of test cards for determining visual acuity in
children. *Acta Ophthalmology, 17:*67-68, 1939.

268. Sloane, A. E., Dunphy, E. B., Emmons, W. V., and Gallagher, J. R.:
A comparison of refraction results on the same individuals. *American Journal of Ophthalmology, 37:*696-699, 1954.

269. Slobin, D.: Cognitive prerequisites for the development of grammar.
In C. Ferguson and D. Slobin (Eds.), *Studies of Child Language Development.* New York, Holt, Rinehart & Winston, 1973.

270. Smith, M. E.: An investigation of the development of the sentence
and the extent of vocabulary in young children. In B. Baldwin
(Ed.), *University of Iowa Studies in Child Welfare,* Iowa City, University of Iowa Press, 1926.

271. Smith, A. C., Flick, G. L., Farris, G. S., and Sellmann, A. H.: Prediction of developmental outcome at seven years from prenatal, perinatal and postnatal events. *Child Development, 43:*495-507, 1972.

272. Smith, P. A., and Marx, R. W.: Some cautions on the use of the Frostig
Test. *Journal of Learning Disabilities, 5:*357-362, 1972.

273. Spreen, O.: Prediction of school achievement from kindergarten to
grade five: Review and report of a follow-up study. *Research Mono-
graph No. 33.* Department of Psychology, University of Victoria,
1979.

274. Sprigle, H. A., and Lanier, M. D.: *The Sprigle School Readiness Screening Test* (manual). Jacksonville, Learning to Learn School, Inc.,
1965.

275. Sprigle, H. A., and Lanier, J.: Validation and standardization of a
school readiness screening test. *Journal of Pediatrics, 70:*602-607,
1967.

276. Stanley, J. C.: Reliability. In R. L. Thorndike (Ed.), *Educational Measurement,* 2nd Ed. Washington, American Council on Education,
1971.

277. Stevenson, J., Parker, T., Wilkinson, A., Hegion, A., and Fish, E.:
Predictive value of teachers' ratings on young children. *Journal of
Educational Psychology, 68:*507-517 (6), 1976.

278. Stevenson, J., Parker, T., Wilkinson, A., Hegion, A., and Fish, E.: A longitudinal study of individual differences in cognitive development and scholastic achievement. *Journal of Educational Psychology, 68:*337-400 (a), 1976.

279. Stinchfield, S. M., and Young, E. H.: *Children with Delayed or Defective Speech.* Palo Alto, Stanford University Press, 1938.

280. Strong, E. K., and Campbell, D. P.: *The Strong-Campbell Interest Interest* Inventory (manual). Stanford, Stanford University Press, 1977.

281. Tager, I. B., Weiss, S. T., Rosner, B., and Speizer, F. E.: Effect of parental cigarette smoking on the pulmonary function of children. *American Journal of Epidemiology 110:*15-26, 1979.

282. Taubenhaus, L. J., and Jackson, A. A.: *Vision Screening of Preschool Children.* Springfield, Thomas, 1969.

283. Taylor, L. J.: The Peabody Picture Vocabulary Test: What does it measure? *Perceptual and Motor Skills, 41:*777-778, 1975.

284. Telegdy, G. A.: The validity of I.Q. scores derived from readiness screening tests. *Psychology in the Schools, 13:*394-396, 1976.

285. Templin, M. C., and Steer, M.: Studies of growth of speech in preschool children. *Journal of Speech Disorders, 4:*71-77, 1939.

286. Templin, M. C.: Spontaneous initiated verbalization in testing articulation in preschool children. *Journal of Speech Disorders, 12:*293-300, 1947.

287. Templin, M. C.: Norms on a screening test of articulation for ages three through eight. *Journal of Speech and Hearing Disorders, 18:*323-331, 1953.

288. Thorndike, E. L., and Lorge, I.: *The Teacher's Word Book of 30,000 Words.* New York, Columbia University, 1944.

289. Thorndike, R. L.: Reliability. In D. N. Jackson and S. Messick (Eds.), *Problems in Human Assessment.* New York, McGraw-Hill, 1967.

290. Thorndike, R. L.: The analysis and selection of test items. In D. N. Jackson and S. Messick (Eds.), *Problems in Human Assessment.* New York, McGraw-Hill, 1967.

291. Thorndike, R. L.: *Educational Measurement,* 2nd Ed. Washington, American Council on Education, 1971.

292. Thorndike, R. L., and Hagen, E. P.: *Cognitive Abilities Test.* Boston, Houghton-Mifflin, 1971.

293. Thorndike, R. L., and Hagen, E. P.: *Measurement and Evaluation in Psychology and Education,* 4th Ed. New York, J. Wiley, 1977.

294. Thorpe, H. S., and Werner, E. E.: Developmental screening of preschool children: A critical review of inventories used in health and educational programs. *Pediatrics, 53:*362-370, 1974.

295. Tobiessen, J., Duckworth, B., and Conrad, G.: Relationships between the Schenectady Kindergarten Rating Scales and first grade achievement and adjustment. *Psychology in the Schools, 3:*29-36, 1971.

296. Trimble, A. C.: Can remedial reading be eliminated? *Academic Therapy, 5:*207-213, 1970.

297. Ueda, R.: The standardization of the DDST for Japanese children. In W. K. Frankenburg (Ed.), *Proceedings of the Second International Conference on Developmental Screening.* Denver, University of Colorado, 1978.

298. Ueda, R.: *Child Development in Iwate Compared with Tokyo and Okinawa and Its Implications for Developmental Screening.* Paper presented at the Third International Conference on Early Identification of Children Who Are Developmentally At-Risk. Teton Village, 1980.

299. Ullman, D., and Kausch, D.: Early identification of developmental strengths and weaknesses in preschool children. *Exceptional Children,* 8-13, 1979.

300. van Doorninck, W. J.: Predictions of school performance from infant and preschool developmental screening. In W. K. Frankenburg (Ed.), *Proceedings of the Second International Conference on Developmental Screening.* Denver, University of Colorado, 1978.

301. van Doorninck, W. J., Dick, N. P., Frankenburg, W. K., Liddell, T. N., and Lampe, J. M.: *Infant and Preschool Developmental Screening and Later School Performance.* Paper presented at the Society for Pediatric Research, St. Louis, 1976.

302. Walker, R. G.: An assessment of the current status of the at-risk register. *Scottish Health Services Study,* No. 4. Edinburgh, Scottish Home and Health Department, 1967.

303. Weaver, W. W., and Kingston, A. J.: Modeling the effects of oral language upon reading literature. In A. J. Kingston (Ed.), *Toward a Psychology of Reading and Language: Selected Writings of Wedell W. Weaver.* Athens, University of Georgia Press, 1977.

304. Weber, H. J., McGovern, F. J., and Zink, D.: An evaluation of 1,000 children with hearing loss. *Journal of Speech and Hearing Disorders, 32:*343-348, 1967.

305. Werner, E. E., Bierman, J. M., and French, R. E.: *The Children of Kauai.* Honolulu, University of Hawaii Press, 1971.

306. Werner, E. E., and Smith, R. S.: *Kauai's Children Come of Age.* Honolulu, The University Press of Hawaii, 1977.

307. Wick, J., Anderson, C., and Major, S.: *Validation and Normative Study of the DIAL Battery.* Evanston, Northwestern University, 1973.

308. Williams, P. D.: *The Metro-Manila Developmental Screening Test (MMDST):* A Normative Study. Paper presented at the Third International Conference on Early Identification of Children Who Are Developmentally At-Risk. Teton Village, 1980.

309. Wingert, R. C.: Evaluation of a readiness training program. *The Reading Teacher, 22:*325-328, 1969.

310. Woodruff, M. E.: Observations on the visual acuity of children during the first five years of life. *American Journal of Optometry, 49:* 205-215, 1972.

311. Yarrow, M. R., Campbell, J. D., and Burton, R. V.: Recollections of childhood: A study of the retrospective method. *Monographs of the Society for Research in Child Development,* 35, No. 138, 1970.

312. Young, N. B.: Auditory screening. In W. K. Frankenburg and B. W. Camp (Eds.), *Pediatric Screening Tests.* Springfield, Thomas, 1975.

313. Zaeske, A.: The validity of predictive index tests in predicting reading failure at the end of grade one. In W. K. Durr (Ed.), *Reading Difficulties: Diagnosis, Correction and Remediation.* Newark, International Reading Association, 1970.

314. Zeitlin, S.: *Kindergarten Screening: Early Identification of Potential High Risk Learners.* Springfield, Thomas, 1976.

PUBLISHER'S DIRECTORY
OF SELECTED SCREENING MEASURES

Allen Picture Card Test

1. American Association of Ophthalmology
   1100 17th Street North West
   Washington, D.C. 20036

2. LADOCA Foundation
   East 51st Avenue and Lincoln Street
   Denver, Colorado 80216

3. House of Vision
   137 North Wabash Avenue
   Chicago, Illinois 60602

Basic School Skills Inventory (BSSI)

Follett Publishing Company
Chicago, Illinois 60607

Child Behavior Checklist and Profile (CBCP)

Unpublished. Write to: Craig Edelbroch, Ph.D.
Boys Town Center
Boys Town, Nebraska 68010

Cooperative Preschool Inventory (CPI)

Addison-Wesley Publishing Company
Menlo Park, California 94025

Denver Articulation Screening Exam (DASE)

Unpublished. Write to: Amelia F. Drumwright
Department of Pediatrics
University of Colorado School of Medicine
Denver, Colorado 80220

Denver Developmental Screening Test (DDST)

LADOCA Foundation
East 51st Avenue and Lincoln Street
Denver, Colorado 80216

Developmental Indicators for the Assessment of Learning (DIAL)

DIAL Inc.
Box 911
Highland Park, Illinois 60035

Developmental Screening Inventory (DSI)

Unpublished. Write to: Hilda Knobloch, M.D.
Department of Pediatrics
The Albany Medical College of Union University
Albany, New York 12208

Home Observation for Measurement of the Environment (HOME)

Bettye M. Caldwell and Robert H. Bradley
University of Arkansas at Little Rock
Little Rock, Arkansas 72204

Home Screening Questionnaire (HSQ)

Unpublished. Write to: Cecilia E. Coons, John F. Kennedy
Child Development Center
University of Colorado Medical Center
Denver, Colorado 80220

Illiterate E Test

The Good-Lite Company
7426 West Madison Street
Forest Park, Illinois 60130

Jansky Screening Index (JSI)

Unpublished. Write to: Jeanette J. Jansky
120 East 89th Street
New York, New York 10028

Matching Symbol Test (HOTV)

The Good-Lite Company
7426 West Madison Street
Forest Park, Illinois 60130

Minneapolis Preschool Screening Instrument (MPSI)

Minneapolis Public Schools
Minneapolis, Minnesota 55440

Minnesota Child Development Inventory (MCDI)

Behavior Science Systems Inc.
Box 1108
Minneapolis, Minnesota 55440

Minnesota Preschool Inventory (MPI)

Behavior Science Systems Inc.
Box 1108
Minneapolis, Minnesota 55440

Northwestern Syntax Screening Test (NSST)

Northwestern University Press
Evanston, Illinois 60201

Peabody Picture Vocabulary Test (PPVT)

American Guidance Service Inc.
720 Washington Avenue S.E.
Minneapolis, Minnesota 55414

Preschool Behavior Rating Scale (PBRS)

Unpublished. Write to: William F. Barker
122 Webster Avenue
Chittenham, Pennsylvania 19095

Preschool Preposition Test (PPT)

Unpublished. Write to: May Aaronson, Ph.D.
National Institute of Mental Health
Rockville, Maryland 20857

Satz Screening Battery (SSB)

Unpublished. Write to: Paul Satz, Ph.D.
Director of Research in Neuropsychology
Camarillo State Hospital
Camarillo, Callifornia 93010

Screening Tests for Young Children and Retardates (STYCAR)

1. The Good-Lite Company
   7426 West Madison Street
   Forest Park, Illinois 60130

2. Institute of Psychological Research
   34 Quest, rue Fleury Street West
   Montreal 357, Quebec

Sjogren Hand Test

1. The Good-Lite Company
   135-137 North Wabash Avenue
   Chicago, Illinois 60130

Sprigle School Readiness Screening Test (SSRST)

Unpublished. Write to: Herbert A. Sprigle, Ph.D.
Psychological Clinic and Research Center
Jacksonville, Florida 32204

Verbal Auditory Screening for Children (VASC)

Auditory Instruments Division
Zenith Hearing Aid Sales Corporation
6501 West Grand Avenue
Chicago, Illinois 60635

AUTHOR INDEX

247

SUBJECT INDEX

251